Verse by Verse Commentary on

PSALMS 1-40

Enduring Word Commentary Series
By David Guzik

The grass withers, the flower fades,
but the word of our God stands forever.
Isaiah 40:8

Commentary on Psalms 1-40

Copyright ©2019 by David Guzik

Printed in the United States of America
or in the United Kingdom

Print Edition ISBN: 978-1-939466-49-5

Enduring Word

5662 Calle Real #184

Goleta, CA 93117

Electronic Mail: ewm@enduringword.com

Internet Home Page: www.enduringword.com

Scripture references, unless noted, are from the New King James Version of the Bible, copyright ©1979, 1980, 1982, Thomas Nelson, Inc., Publisher.

Contents

Psalm 1 – The Ways of the Righteous and the Ungodly 7

Psalm 2 – The Reign of the LORD's Anointed 13

Psalm 3 – Peace in the Midst of the Storm 18

Psalm 4 – Talking to God and Men 22

Psalm 5 – A Morning Prayer 27

Psalm 6 – A Confident Answer to an Agonized Plea 32

Psalm 7 – Confidence in God's Deliverance 37

Psalm 8 – The Glory of God in Creation 44

Psalm 9 – God Remembers, Man Forgets 52

Psalm 10 – From Times of Trouble to Calm Confidence 62

Psalm 11 – The Answer of Faith to the Advice of Fear 69

Psalm 12 – The Words of Man and the Word of God 74

Psalm 13 – Enlighten My Eyes 79

Psalm 14 – Fallen Man and a Faithful God 86

Psalm 15 – The Character of the One God Receives 93

Psalm 16 – The Benefits of a Life-Commitment to God 99

Psalm 17 – Shelter Under the Shadow of His Wings 107

Psalm 18 – Great Praise from a Place of Great Victory 117

Psalm 19 – The Heavens, the Word, and the Glory of God 135

Psalm 20 – The LORD Saves His Anointed 146

Psalm 21 – The Joyful King 153

Psalm 22 – God's Servant Forsaken, Rescued, & Triumphant 160

Psalm 23 – The LORD Is My Shepherd and My Host 177

Psalm 24 – The Great and Sovereign God 186

Psalm 25 – A Plea for Help from the Humble & Reverent 194

Psalm 26 – Standing in an Even Place 203

Psalm 27 – The Seeking, Waiting Life Rewarded 209

Psalm 28 – Praise from Prayer Heard and Answered................217

Psalm 29 – The Voice of the LORD in the Storm................223

Psalm 30 – Remembering the Greatness of God................229

Psalm 31 – Shelter in the Secret Place of God's Presence................237

Psalm 32 –Blessings of Forgiveness, Protection, & Guidance................249

Psalm 33 – The Great and Awesome God................257

Psalm 34 – Praise from the Cave................265

Psalm 35 – "Awake to My Vindication"................275

Psalm 36 – Mercy to the Heavens................284

Psalm 37 – Wisdom Over Worry................292

Psalm 38 – The Sick Sinner's Only Hope................307

Psalm 39 – Wisdom to Speak Under God's Correction................314

Psalm 40 – The Servant Comes to Do God's Will................321

Bibliography - 333

Remarks from the Author - 335

Psalm 1 – The Way of the Righteous and the Way of the Ungodly

Verse six presents a key to understanding Psalm 1: "For the LORD knows the way of the righteous, but the way of the ungodly shall perish." In this psalm, the way of the righteous and the way of the ungodly are contrasted.

A. The way of the righteous.

1. (1) What the righteous man does not do.

Blessed *is* the man
Who walks not in the counsel of the ungodly,
Nor stands in the path of sinners,
Nor sits in the seat of the scornful;

> a. **Blessed is the man**: The Hebrew word *esher* is here translated **blessed**, which has the idea of happiness or contentment. *Esher* is a form of the Hebrew word *ashar*, which in its root means "to be straight" or "to be right." **Blessed is the man** speaks of the happiness, the blessedness, the contentment in the life of the man or woman who is right or "straight" with God. The righteous man will be a **blessed** man, a happy man.

> > i. "*Blessed* means supremely happy or fulfilled. In fact, in Hebrew the word is actually a plural, which denotes either a multiplicity of blessings or an intensification of them." (Boice)

> > ii. "It is not 'Blessed is the king, blessed is the scholar, blessed is the rich,' but, 'Blessed is the man.' This blessedness is as attainable by the poor, the forgotten and the obscure, as by those whose names figure in history, and are trumpeted by fame." (Spurgeon)

> b. **Walks not...nor stands...nor sits**: The blessed man does *not* do certain things. There is a way he will *not* walk, a path he will *not* stand in, and a seat he will *not* sit in.

7

i. We can say these speak of *thinking, behaving,* and *belonging.* The righteous man and the ungodly man are different in how they *think,* how they *behave,* and to whom they *belong.*

ii. Others have also seen in this a progression of sin. "The great lesson to be learned from the whole is, sin is *progressive*; one evil propensity or act leads to another. He who acts by *bad counsel* may soon do *evil deeds*; and he who abandons himself to *evil doings* may end his life in *total apostasy* from God." (Clarke)

c. **Walks not in the counsel of the ungodly**: The ungodly have **counsel**, and the righteous man will not walk in it. With all the advice that comes to us, from so many different sources, the righteous man knows how to stay away from the **counsel of the ungodly**.

i. First, it means the righteous man knows how to *discern* the **counsel of the ungodly**. Many fail at this point. They do not even consider if **counsel** is godly or **ungodly**. They hear advice, or theories about their problems, and they find themselves agreeing or disagreeing without considering, "Is this godly or ungodly counsel?"

ii. The righteous man is also discerning enough to know the **counsel of the ungodly** can come from one's own self. Our own conscience, our own mind, our own heart, can give us ungodly counsel.

iii. The righteous man knows where to find completely godly counsel: *Your testimonies also are my delight and my counselors* (Psalm 119:24). God's word is always the best counselor, and godly counselors will always bring the truth of God's word to help someone who wants counseling.

d. **Nor stands in the path of sinners**: Sinners have a **path** where they stand, and the righteous man knows he does not belong on that path. **Path** speaks of a way, a road, a direction – and the righteous man is not traveling in the same direction as sinners.

i. The righteous man is not afraid to take a less-traveled road, because he knows it leads to blessing, happiness, and eternal life. *Enter by the narrow gate; for wide is the gate and broad is the way that leads to destruction, and there are many who go in by it* (Matthew 7:13).

ii. The righteous can have the confidence of Psalm 16:11: *You will show me the path of life; in Your presence is fullness of joy; at Your right hand are pleasures forevermore.* God has a path, and it is a good road to take.

e. **Nor sits in the seat of the scornful**: The scornful love to sit and criticize the people of God and the things of God. The righteous man will not sit in that **seat**!

i. When others are putting down Christians, it is easy to sit with them and criticize them. It is easy because there are many things to criticize about Christians. But it is wrong, because we are then sitting **in the seat of the scornful**.

ii. Instead, we should be proud to follow Jesus Christ. "Be out-and-out for him; unfurl your colours, never hide them, but nail them to the mast, and say to all who ridicule the saints, 'If you have any ill words for the followers of Christ, pour them out upon me...but know this – ye shall hear it whether you like it or not – 'I love Christ.'" (Spurgeon)

2. (2) What the righteous man *does*.

But his delight *is* in the law of the LORD,
And in His law he meditates day and night.

a. **His delight is in the law of the LORD**: Throughout Psalms, the phrase **law of the LORD** is used to describe God's entire word, not only the "law" portion of the first five books of the Bible. The righteous man is delighted with the word of God!

i. What makes you happy? What gets you excited? This is a good way to see what is important to you. If personal pleasure is the only thing that makes you happy, then you are a selfish, self-centered person. If being with your family or friends delights you, that can be better, but it still falls short. The righteous man finds **his delight...in the law of the LORD**.

ii. Martin Luther said that he could not live in paradise *without* the word of God, but he could live well enough in hell *with* it.

iii. "Man must have some delight, some supreme pleasure. His heart was never meant to be a vacuum. If not filled with the best things, it will be filled with the unworthy and disappointing." (Spurgeon)

iv. If a person delights in something, you don't have to beg him to do it or to like it. He will do it all by himself. You can measure your **delight** for the word of God by how much you hunger for it.

b. **In His law he meditates day and night**: The righteous man *ponders* the word of God. He does not just hear it and forget it; he *thinks* about it. Christians should meditate on God's word!

i. In eastern meditation, the goal is to *empty* the mind. This is dangerous, because an empty mind may present an open invitation to deception or a demonic spirit. But in Christian meditation, the goal is to *fill* your mind with the word of God. This can be done by carefully thinking about each word and phrase, applying it to one's self, and praying it back to the Lord.

ii. "Meditation chews the cud, and gets the sweetness and nutritive virtue of the Word into the heart and life: this is the way the godly bring forth much fruit." (Ashwood, cited by Spurgeon)

iii. Many lack because they only *read* and do not *meditate*. "It is not only reading that does us good; but the soul inwardly feeding on it, and digesting it. A preacher once told me that he had read the Bible through twenty times on his knees and had never found the doctrine of election there. Very likely not. It is a most uncomfortable position in which to read. If he had sat in an easy chair he would have been better able to understand it." (Spurgeon)

iv. The righteous man only has God's word on his mind two times a day: **day and night**. That about covers it all!

3. (3) How the righteous man is blessed.

He shall be like a tree
Planted by the rivers of water,
That brings forth its fruit in its season,
Whose leaf also shall not wither;
And whatever he does shall prosper.

a. **He shall be like a tree planted by the rivers of water**: A tree by a river has a continual source of water. It will never wither away, because it is always getting what it needs. If we are constantly needy, it may be worth examining if we are **planted by the rivers of water** or not.

i. This would also be a **tree** that is strong and stable, sinking down deep roots. The life of the righteous man is marked by strength and stability.

b. **That brings forth its fruit in its season**: The righteous man bears fruit, such as the fruit of the Spirit (Galatians 5:22-23). The fruit comes naturally from this tree, because it is **planted by the rivers of water**. It is abiding in a life-source. As Jesus spoke of bearing fruit in John 15:5, as we abide in Him. Fruit also has a **season**. Some get discouraged when they begin to walk as righteous men, and fruit is not immediately evident. They need to wait until they bring forth **fruit in its season**.

i. "There are no barren trees in God's orchard, and yet they may have their fits of barrenness, as an apple tree sometimes hath; but they will reflourish with advantage." (Trapp)

c. **Whose leaf also shall not wither**: Brown, dead, withered leaves are signs of death and dryness. The righteous man does not have these signs of death and dryness; his "leaves" are green and alive.

d. **And whatever he does shall prosper**: It isn't that the righteous man has a "Midas Touch," and everything he does makes him rich and comfortable. But in the life of the righteous man, God brings forth something good and wonderful out of everything. Even tough circumstances bring forth something that **shall prosper**.

B. The way of the ungodly.

1. (4) The dangerous place of the ungodly.

The ungodly *are* not so,
But *are* like the chaff which the wind drives away.

a. **The ungodly are not so**: Everything true about the righteous man – stable as a tree, continual life and nourishment, fruitful, alive, and prosperous – is **not so** regarding the **ungodly**.

i. It may often seem like the **ungodly** have these things, and sometimes it seems they have them more than the righteous. But it is **not so**! Any of these things are fleeting in the life of the **ungodly**; it can be said that they don't really have them at all.

b. **Are like the chaff which the wind drives away**: **Chaff** is the light "shell" around a kernel of grain, which must be stripped away before the kernel of grain can be ground into flour. **Chaff** was light enough that it could be separated from the grain by throwing a scoopful into the wind and letting the wind drive away the **chaff**. This is how unstable, how lacking in substance, the ungodly are.

i. Spurgeon on **chaff**: "Intrinsically worthless, dead, unserviceable, without substance, and easily carried away." There is a huge difference between a tree and **chaff**.

2. (5) The dangerous future of the ungodly.

Therefore the ungodly shall not stand in the judgment,
Nor sinners in the congregation of the righteous.

a. **Therefore the ungodly shall not stand in the judgment**: Because the **ungodly** have no "weight," they will be found lacking on the day of judgment. As it was said of King Belshazzar in the book of Daniel, *You have been weighed in the balances, and found wanting* (Daniel 5:27).

b. **Nor sinners in the congregation of the righteous**: This is true in the future, because **sinners** will not share the same glorious future of the **righteous**. It is also true in the present, because **sinners** sense they do not belong **in the congregation of the righteous** if they insist on remaining **sinners**.

3. (6) Summary: The way of the righteous and the way of the ungodly.

For the LORD knows the way of the righteous,
But the way of the ungodly shall perish.

a. **The LORD knows the way of the righteous**: The righteous can have peace because a loving God in heaven knows their way, and will protect and preserve them.

i. "Or, as the Hebrew has it yet more fully, 'The Lord is *knowing* the way of the righteous.' He is constantly looking on their way, and though it may be often in mist and darkness, yet the Lord knoweth it." (Spurgeon)

b. **The way of the ungodly shall perish**: The way of the ungodly leads to destruction. They are on a broad path that may seem comfortable now and the path gives them lots of company, but in the end they **shall perish**.

c. At least four times in the Book of Acts, Christianity is called *the Way*. Certainly, it is the **way of the righteous**, not the **way of the ungodly**. Which way are you on?

Psalm 2 – The Reign of the LORD's Anointed

Like many psalms, the theme of Psalm 2 is emphasized in the final verse. We can defy God and perish, or we can surrender to Him and be blessed. The psalm itself does not identify its author, but Acts 4:25-26 clearly attributes it to David.

A. The rage of nations and the laugh of God.

1. (1-3) The nations rebel.

**Why do the nations rage,
And the people plot a vain thing?
The kings of the earth set themselves,
And the rulers take counsel together,
Against the LORD and against His Anointed,** *saying,*
**"Let us break Their bonds in pieces
And cast away Their cords from us."**

> a. **Why do the nations rage**: The psalmist seems genuinely mystified. The nations have no *reason* to rage against God, and they have no *benefit* in raging against Him. Their opposition against God is nothing but a **vain thing**.

> b. **The rulers take counsel together**: Since the time of Babel, men have continued to band themselves together against God. Their mistaken belief is that two or more men united against God have a better chance than one man set against God.

> c. **Against the LORD and against His Anointed**: They oppose both the LORD and His Anointed. **Anointed** speaks of the Christ, the Anointed One. Since Jesus is the perfect representation of the Father (John 10:30, 14:9), opposing God the Father, is to oppose Jesus. If you are against Jesus, you are against God the Father.

> d. **Let us break Their bonds in pieces**: Those who oppose the LORD and His Anointed think of God as a bondage-bringer. This attitude is evidence

13

of spiritual insanity, because God is a bondage-breaker, not a bondage-bringer.

i. "To a graceless neck the yoke of Christ is intolerable, but to the saved sinner it is easy and light.... We may judge ourselves by this, do we love that yoke, or do we wish to cast it from us?" (Spurgeon)

2. (4-6) The LORD's laugh from heaven.

He who sits in the heavens shall laugh;
The LORD shall hold them in derision.
Then He shall speak to them in His wrath,
And distress them in His deep displeasure:
"Yet I have set My King
On My holy hill of Zion."

a. **He who sits in the heavens shall laugh**: God looks at the way man plots against Him and He laughs. God isn't afraid or confused or depressed about the opposition of man. God laughs at it.

i. God laughs because He *sits* in the heavens. He sits as the Great King on a glorious throne. He isn't pacing back and forth in the throne room of heaven, wondering what He should do next. God **sits** in perfect peace and assurance.

ii. God laughs because He **sits in the *heavens***. It isn't an earthly throne He occupies; it is the throne of heaven with authority over all creation. What does heaven have to fear from earth?

iii. "God does not tremble. He does not hide behind a vast celestial rampart, counting the enemy and calculating whether or not he has sufficient force to counter this new challenge to his kingdom. He does not even rise from where he is sitting. He simply 'laughs' at these great imbeciles." (Boice)

iv. "This derisive laughter of God is the comfort of all those who love righteousness. It is the laughter of the might of holiness; it is the laughter of the strength of love. God does not exult over the sufferings of sinning men. He does hold in derision all the proud boastings and violence of such as seek to prevent His accomplishment of His will." (Morgan)

b. **The LORD shall hold them in derision**: Through the centuries, many have opposed God and His Kingdom in Jesus Christ. Each one of these opponents shall be frustrated and crushed.

i. A famous example of an opponent of Christianity was the Roman Emperor Diocletian (reigning A.D. 284-305). He was such a determined enemy of Christians that he persecuted the church mercilessly, and fancied that he had defeated Christianity. He ordered the making a medal with this inscription: "The name of Christianity being extinguished."

ii. Diocletian also set up two monuments on the frontier of his empire with these inscriptions:

Diocletian Jovian Maximian Herculeus Caesares Augusti for having extended the Roman Empire in the east and the west and for having extinguished the name of Christians who brought the Republic to ruin

Diocletian Jovian Maximian Herculeus Caesares Augusti for having everywhere abolished the superstition of Christ for having extended the worship of the gods

iii. Diocletian is dead and gone, a footnote on the pages of history. The fame and glory of Jesus Christ is spread over all the earth. **The LORD shall hold them in derision**.

c. **He shall speak to them in His wrath**: God laughs in heaven, but He doesn't remain inactive. He laughs, but He doesn't *only* laugh. Before He acts against defiant mankind, He first *speaks* to rebellious humanity.

i. This shows the great mercy of God. He has every reason and every right to simply *act* against defiant men. Love and mercy compel God to **speak** a word of warning before He acts.

d. **I have set My King on My holy hill of Zion**: God wants defiant mankind to know that He has established a **King**. The defiant men closest in view in the psalm are kings and rulers, and God especially wants them to know there is a **King** greater than they are. God's King is *established* (**set**), and established in Jerusalem (**Zion**).

B. God's decree to the nations.

1. (7-9) The decree of the Son.

"I will declare the decree:
The LORD has said to Me,
'You *are* My Son,
Today I have begotten You.
Ask of Me, and I will give *You*
The nations *for* Your inheritance,
And the ends of the earth *for* Your possession.
You shall break them with a rod of iron;
You shall dash them to pieces like a potter's vessel.'"

a. **I will declare the decree**: The following passage indicates that this is the Lord's Anointed Himself speaking. He will **declare the decree** that God the Father spoke to Him.

b. **You are My Son, today I have begotten You**: The Lord's Anointed recalls what God the Father spoke to Him, identifying Him as the Son of the Father and emphasizing His standing as **begotten** of the Father.

i. The writer to the Hebrews quotes this passage in Hebrews 1:5 as evidence of the deity of Jesus and superiority to all angels. He mentions the *more excellent name* Jesus received, greater than all the angels. This is the "name" **Son**. While angels are sometimes called the *sons of God* in a generic sense (Job 1:6), the Father never said "**My Son**" to any angel in a specific sense. That is reserved for God the Son, the Second Person of the Trinity.

ii. **Begotten** is also an important idea, as a contrast to *created*. Jesus was not created; rather He created everything that was created (Colossians 1:16-17). **Begotten** describes a relationship between two beings of the same essential nature and being, but we *create* things of a different essential being and nature than ourselves. A man *creates* a statue but *begets* a child.

c. **I will give You the nations for Your inheritance**: The Lord's Anointed holds the nations as His inheritance. He will rule over all nations and all judgment is committed to Him (John 5:22).

i. Revelation 11:15 describes an exciting consummation of this inheritance: *Then the seventh angel sounded: And there were loud voices in heaven, saying, "The kingdoms of this world have become the kingdoms of our Lord and of His Christ, and He shall reign forever and ever!"*

d. **You shall break them with a rod of iron**: The Lord's Anointed has such power over the nations that they are like clay pots that he can shatter with a blow from a **rod of iron**. This shows why it is so foolish for the nations to defy the Lord and His Anointed. There is no *reason* and no *benefit* to their defiant opposition.

2. (10-12) The decree to the nations about the Son.

Now therefore, be wise, O kings;
Be instructed, you judges of the earth.
Serve the Lord with fear,
And rejoice with trembling.
Kiss the Son, lest He be angry,
And you perish *in* the way,

When His wrath is kindled but a little.
Blessed *are* all those who put their trust in Him.

a. **Be wise, O kings**: After the words of warning from the LORD's Anointed, the psalmist counsels the **kings** of the earth to give up their foolish defiance of the LORD.

b. **Serve the LORD with fear, and rejoice with trembling**: The psalmist calls the kings of the earth to surrender to God, giving Him proper reverence. In this submitted, surrendered place they can **rejoice** – yet with appropriate **trembling**.

c. **Kiss the Son**: This primarily has in mind the kiss of submission, where a dignitary receives the humble kiss of an inferior. It also hints at the *affection* God wants in relationship to Him. God wants us to recognize our proper place before Him, but to also **rejoice** in Him and be affectionate in our relationship.

i. "Kissing was the token of *subjugation* and *friendship*." (Clarke)

ii. If the **kings** and **judges** of the earth are commanded to humble themselves before the LORD's Anointed, recognizing His total superiority, then what of the rest of us? Speaking to the **kings** and **judges** therefore includes all of humanity.

d. **Blessed are all those who put their trust in Him**: Those who defy God are *broken*, but those who depend on Him are *blessed*. The psalmist leaves the choice with everyone: broken or blessed?

Psalm 3 – Peace in the Midst of the Storm

This is the first psalm with a title: **A Psalm of David when he fled from Absalom his son**. *James Montgomery Boice points out that since these titles are in the canonical text of the Hebrew Bible, "They are to be taken with absolute seriousness throughout." The events are recorded in 2 Samuel 15-18, but the heart of David at that difficult time is recorded in this psalm.*

A. David's trouble and God's help.

1. (1-2) What those who troubled David did.

LORD, how they have increased who trouble me!
Many *are* they who rise up against me.
Many *are* they who say of me,
"*There is* no help for him in God." Selah

a. **How they have increased who trouble me**: At the writing of this psalm David was in a great deal of trouble. His own son led what seemed to be a successful rebellion against him. Many of his previous friends and associates forsook him and joined the ranks of those who troubled him (2 Samuel 15:13).

b. **There is no help for him in God**: David's situation was so bad that many felt he was beyond God's help. Those who said this probably didn't feel that God was *unable* to help David; they probably felt that God was *unwilling* to help him. They looked at David's past sin and figured, "This is all what he deserves from God. **There is no help for him in God.**"

i. Shimei was an example of someone who said that God was against David, and he was just getting what he deserved (2 Samuel 16:7-8). This thought was most painful of all for David – the thought that God might be *against him* and that **there is no help for him in God**.

ii. "If all the trials which come from heaven, all the temptations which ascend from hell, and all the crosses which arise from the earth, could be mixed and pressed together, they would not make a trial so terrible as that which is contained in this verse. It is the most bitter of all afflictions to be led to fear that there is no help for us in God." (Spurgeon)

c. **Selah**: The idea in the Hebrew for this word (occurring 74 times in the Old Testament) is for a *pause*. Most people think it speaks of a reflective pause, a pause to meditate on the words just spoken. It may also be a musical instruction, for a musical interlude of some kind.

2. (3-4) What God did for David in the midst of trouble.

But You, O Lord, *are* **a shield for me,**
My glory and the One who lifts up my head.
I cried to the Lord with my voice,
And He heard me from His holy hill. Selah

a. **You, O Lord, are a shield for me**: Though many said there was no help for him in God, David knew that God was his **shield**. Others – even many others – couldn't shake David's confidence in a God of love and help.

   i. Under attack from a cunning and ruthless enemy, David needed a **shield**. He knew that God *was* his shield. This wasn't a prayer asking God to fulfill this; this is a strong declaration of fact: **You, O Lord, are a shield for me**.

b. **My glory and the One who lifts my head**: God was more than David's protection. He also was the **One** who put David on higher ground, lifting his head and showing him glory. There was nothing glorious or head-lifting in David's circumstances, but there was in his God.

   i. Men find **glory** in all sorts of things – fame, power, prestige, or possessions. David found his **glory** in the Lord. "Oh, my soul, hast thou made God thy glory? Others boast in their wealth, beauty, position, achievements: dost thou find in God what they find in these?" (Meyer)

c. **I cried to the Lord with my voice**: "Surely, silent prayers are heard. Yes, but good men often find that, even in secret, they pray better aloud than they do when they utter no vocal sound." (Spurgeon)

d. **He heard me from His holy hill**: Others said that God wanted nothing to do with David, but he could gloriously say, "**He heard me**." Though Absalom took over Jerusalem and forced David out of the capitol, David knew that it wasn't Absalom enthroned on God's **holy hill**. The Lord Himself still held that ground and would hear and help David from **His holy hill**.

B. Blessing from God and to God.

1. (5-6) God blesses David.

I lay down and slept;
I awoke, for the LORD **sustained me.**
I will not be afraid of ten thousands of people
Who have set *themselves* **against me all around.**

> a. **I lay down and slept; I awoke**: David used both of these as evidence of God's blessing. *Sleep* was a blessing, because David was under such intense pressure from the circumstances of Absalom's rebellion that sleep might be impossible, but he **slept**. *Waking* was another blessing, because many wondered if David would live to see a new day.

> > i. "Truly it must have been a soft pillow indeed that could make him forget his danger, who then had such a disloyal army at his back hunting of him." (Gurnall, cited in Spurgeon)

> > ii. God sustains us in our sleep, but we take it for granted. Think of it: you are asleep, unconscious, dead to the world – yet you breathe, your heart pumps, your organs operate. The same God who sustains us in our sleep will sustain us in our difficulties.

> b. **I will not be afraid of ten thousands of people**: With God sustaining him, David could stand against any foe. Before it was written, David knew the truth of Romans 8:31: *If God is for us, who can be against us?*

2. (7-8) David blesses God.

Arise, O LORD**;**
Save me, O my God!
For You have struck all my enemies on the cheekbone;
You have broken the teeth of the ungodly.
Salvation *belongs* **to the L**ORD**.**
Your blessing *is* **upon Your people. Selah**

> a. **Arise, O L**ORD**.... For You have struck all my enemies**: David's mind was on both what he trusted God to do (**Save me, O my God**) and on what God had done (**struck all my enemies...broken the teeth of the ungodly**). Knowing what God *had* done gives David confidence in what the L**ORD** *would* do.

> b. **Arise, O L**ORD: This recalled the words of Numbers 10:35, where Moses used this phrase as the children of Israel broke camp in the wilderness. It was a *military* phrase, calling on God to go forth to both defend Israel and lead them to victory.

c. **Broken the teeth of the ungodly**: This vivid metaphor is also used in Psalm 58:6. It speaks of the total domination and defeat of the enemy. David looked for protection in this psalm, but more than protection – he looked for *victory*. It wasn't enough for David to survive the threat to the kingdom. He had to be victorious over the threat, and he would be with the blessing of God.

d. **Salvation belongs to the LORD**: David understood that **salvation** – both in the ultimate and immediate sense – was God's property. It isn't the property of any one nation or sect, but of the LORD God. To be saved, one must deal with the LORD Himself.

e. **Your blessing is upon Your people**: This showed David's heart in a time of *personal* calamity. He wasn't only concerned for God's hand upon himself, but upon all God's people. He didn't pray for preservation and victory in the trial with Absalom just for his own sake, but because it was best for the nation.

Psalm 4 – Talking to God and Men

This psalm is titled **To the Chief Musician. With stringed instruments. A Psalm of David**. *The title of the psalm indicates that it was directed towards* **the Chief Musician**, *whom some suppose to be the Lord* GOD *Himself, and others suppose to be a leader of choirs or musicians in David's time, such as Heman the singer or Asaph (1 Chronicles 6:33, 16:5-7, and 25:6). The title also tells us that the song was deliberately written to be accompanied* **with stringed instruments**. *In it David pours out his complaint against slanderous enemies and finds peace and refuge in God.*

A. David talks to God and to men.

1. (1) David talks to God.

Hear me when I call, O God of my righteousness!
You have relieved me in *my* distress;
Have mercy on me, and hear my prayer.

> a. **Hear me when I call**: There is *passion* in David's cry. He doesn't want to just cast up words towards heaven. He needs God's attention to his present problem.
>
> > i. Often *power* in prayer is lacking because there is little *passion* in prayer. It isn't that we persuade God by emotional displays, but God wants us to care deeply about the things He cares deeply about. The prophet Isaiah spoke with sorrow about the lack of this in Israel: *And there is no one who calls on Your name, who stirs himself up to take hold of You* (Isaiah 64:7). This is a good example of David stirring himself up to take hold of God.
>
> b. **O God of my righteousness**: David knew that his righteousness came from God, and not from himself. He calls upon the God who makes him righteous.

c. **You have relieved me...Have mercy on me**: In a familiar pattern, David uses past mercy as a ground for future help. "God, I know you haven't blessed me thus far to abandon me, so **have mercy on me**."

> i. "This is another instance of David's common habit of pleading past mercies as a ground for present favour." (Spurgeon)

2. (2-3) David talks to men.

How long, O you sons of men,
Will you turn **my glory to shame?**
How long **will you love worthlessness**
And **seek falsehood? Selah**
But know that the LORD has set apart for Himself him who is godly;
The LORD will hear when I call to Him.

a. **How long**: David asked a valid question. Just **how long** will the ungodly keep to their way? They can't keep to it forever, so they may as well abandon it *now* and be blessed.

> i. If we find ourselves on a compromising course, it is valid to ask, "**How long**? If I extend this course of action out to its logical and inevitable conclusion, where will I be? Knowing this, **how long** will I play around with this sin?"

b. **How long, O you sons of men, will you turn my glory to shame?** Many try to connect Psalm 3 with Psalm 4, thinking that this was also written in connection with Absalom's rebellion. This is probably incorrect, because the focus in this psalm isn't David's physical safety or kingdom but his reputation. Wicked men slandered David.

> i. "In this psalm the problem is one of malicious slander and lies. It is the psalmist's reputation rather than his person that is being attacked." (Boice)

> ii. **Turn my glory to shame**: Jesus experienced what David experienced. Wicked men tried to turn almost every glorious thing in His ministry into shame.

c. **The LORD has set apart for Himself him who is godly**: David knew that he and other godly people were set apart for God. There are many reasons why we set things apart.

- We set things apart for our own enjoyment.
- We set things apart for greater purity.
- We set things apart for special service.

> i. For all these reasons and more, God sets us apart unto Himself.

d. **The LORD will hear when I call to Him**: The ungodly have a disaster waiting for them, but the **godly** have a great reward in the LORD. This is why David knows **the LORD will hear when I call to Him**.

i. All Christians should have the same assurance. They should be confident that God will hear their prayers. When prayer seems ineffective, it is worth it to take a spiritual inventory to see if there is a reason for unanswered prayer. The Bible tells us there are many reasons why prayer may not be answered.

- Not abiding in Jesus (John 15:7).
- Unbelief (Matthew 17:20-21).
- Failure to fast (Matthew 17:21).
- A Bad marriage relationship (1 Peter 3:7).
- Unconfessed sin (James 5:16).
- Lying and deceitfulness (Psalm 17:1).
- Lack of Bible reading and Bible teaching (Proverbs 28:9).
- Trusting in the length or form of prayer (Matthew 6:7).

B. David talks to himself.

1. (4-5) David calms himself before the Lord.

Be angry, and do not sin.
Meditate within your heart on your bed, and be still. Selah
Offer the sacrifices of righteousness,
And put your trust in the LORD.

a. **Be angry, and do not sin**: With the ungodliness around him, David had reason to **be angry**, but he had no reason to **sin**. He reminds himself to not sin in his anger, and to find solace in meditation before the LORD.

b. **Meditate within your heart**: David speaks of the Christian practice of meditation, not the Eastern practice of meditation. In Christian meditation, we *fill* our heart and mind with God's word. In eastern meditation, the idea is to *empty* the heart and mind, leaving it open for deceiving spirits.

c. **Offer the sacrifices of righteousness, and put your trust in the LORD**: David knew the value of doing religious things (**offer the sacrifices**), yet he also knew that those could not replace **trust in the LORD**. When religious observance is coupled with true trust in God, we draw near to God and experience the benefits of drawing near.

2. (6-8) David receives blessing from God.

There are **many who say, "Who will show us *any* good?"**
LORD, **lift up the light of Your countenance upon us.**
You have put gladness in my heart,
More than in the season that their grain and wine increased.
I will both lie down in peace, and sleep;
For You alone, O LORD, **make me dwell in safety.**

a. **Who will show us any good?** The voice of the ungodly cynic echoes in David's ear. After continual disappointment from man, we begin to doubt if God **will show us any good**.

b. **L**ORD, **lift up the light of Your countenance upon us**: Despite what the cynics say or think, David trusts that the LORD will show him good.

i. He claims it upon the Aaronic promise of blessing in Numbers 6:24-26:

*The L*ORD *bless you and keep you;*
*The L*ORD *make His face shine upon you,*
And be gracious to you;
*The L*ORD *lift up His countenance upon you,*
And give you peace.

c. **You have put gladness in my heart**: When we know that the face of God shines favorably on us, it puts **gladness** in the heart. Though David was in distress, vexed by ungodly men all around, he could still have **gladness** in his heart because the LORD put it there.

d. **More than in the season that their grain and wine increased**: The ungodly can be happy when the money is coming in and everything is prosperous. David can be happy even in distressing times, because the LORD **put gladness in** his heart.

e. **I will both lie down in peace, and sleep**: David can sleep well at night, even in distressing times and surrounded by the ungodly. He sleeps well because his safety is from the LORD, not from circumstances or even feeling.

i. We can imagine a man lying down to sleep, tormented by all of what his enemies or pretend friends say about him. David could be that man, but he trusts in the LORD. He has a gladness that the world can't take away, even with all their slander and lies.

ii. In his proverbs from *Poor Richard's Almanac*, Ben Franklin had some good advice: "Since I cannot govern my own tongue, tho' within my own teeth, how can I hope to govern the tongues of others?"

f. **For You alone, O Lord, make me dwell in safety**: G. Campbell Morgan points out that the idea here is not that it is the Lord and none other. Instead, the idea is that David finds safety in solitude with God.

> i. "The thought of the word *alone* is '*in loneliness,*' or as Rotherham renders it '*in seclusion*'; and the word refers to the one going asleep. This is a glorious conception of sleep. Jehovah gathers the trusting soul into a place of safety by taking it away from all the things which trouble or harass...the tried and tired child of His love is pavilioned in His peace." (Morgan)

Psalm 5 – A Morning Prayer

This psalm is titled **To the Chief Musician. With flutes. A Psalm of David**. *The title of the psalm indicates that it was directed towards* **the Chief Musician**, *whom some suppose to be the Lord GOD Himself, and others suppose to be a leader of choirs or musicians in David's time, such as Heman the singer or Asaph (1 Chronicles 6:33, 16:5-7, and 25:6). The title also tells us that the song was deliberately written to be accompanied* **with flutes**. *It shows David coming to the LORD in the morning and receiving the strength and joy he needs to make it through the day against many adversaries.*

A. Approaching God in the morning.

1. (1-3) David approaches God.

Give ear to my words, O LORD,
Consider my meditation.
Give heed to the voice of my cry,
My King and my God,
For to You I will pray.
My voice You shall hear in the morning, O LORD;
In the morning I will direct *it* **to You,**
And I will look up.

> a. **Give ear...consider...give heed**: David longs for an audience with God. Using the Hebrew method of parallelism, he repeats the same idea three times: "LORD, please listen to me."

> b. **For to You I will pray**: David prayed to God. This may sound elementary, but it is an essential aspect of prayer. Often we come to prayer so full of our request or our feelings that we never consciously focus on God and sense His presence. David was a great man of prayer because his prayer time was focused on God.

i. "Very much of so-called prayer, both public and private, is not unto God. In order that a prayer should be really unto God, there must be a definite and conscious approach to God when we pray; we must have a definite and vivid realization that God is bending over us and listening as we pray." (Torrey)

c. **My voice You shall hear in the morning**: David made it a point to pray **in the morning**. He did this because he wanted to honor God at the beginning of his day, and set the tone for an entire day dedicated unto God.

i. Hudson Taylor, the famous missionary to China, had trouble finding time alone with God. He began to wake himself up at 2:00 in the morning and used those quiet hours when everyone else slept to commune with God.

ii. "What is a slothful sinner to think of himself, when he reads, concerning the holy name of Jesus, that 'in the morning, rising up a great while before the day, he went out and departed into a solitary place, and there prayed!'" (Horne)

iii. "This is the fittest time for intercourse with God. An hour in the morning is worth two in the evening. While the dew is on the grass, let grace drop upon the soul." (Spurgeon)

d. **In the morning I will direct it to You, and I will look up**: David gives us what to do *before* and *after* prayer. Before we pray, we should **direct** our prayer. After we pray, we **look up** with expectancy to heaven, really believing that God will answer.

i. The idea behind **direct** is not "to aim" but "to order, to arrange." "It is the word that is used for the laying in order of the wood and pieces of the victim upon the altar, and it is used also for the putting of the shewbread upon the table. It means just this: 'I will arrange my prayer before thee,' I will lay it out upon the altar in the morning, just as the priest lays out the morning sacrifice." (Spurgeon)

ii. "It is manifestly a mistake to pray at haphazard. There is too much random praying with us all. We do not return again and again to the same petition, pressing it home with all humility and reverence, and arguing the case, as Abraham did his for the cities of the plain." (Meyer)

iii. "Do we not miss very much of the sweetness and efficacy of prayer by a want of careful meditation before it, and of hopeful expectation after it? Let holy preparation link hands with patient expectation, and we shall have far larger answers to our prayers." (Spurgeon)

2. (4-8) A contrast between the wicked man and the godly man.

For You *are* not a God who takes pleasure in wickedness,
Nor shall evil dwell with You.
The boastful shall not stand in Your sight;
You hate all workers of iniquity.
You shall destroy those who speak falsehood;
The LORD abhors the bloodthirsty and deceitful man.

But as for me, I will come into Your house in the multitude of Your
mercy;
In fear of You I will worship toward Your holy temple.
Lead me, O LORD, in Your righteousness because of my enemies;
Make Your way straight before my face.

a. **You are not a God who takes pleasure in wickedness**: David meditates on the righteous character of God. Our actions matter before a God who hates **all workers of iniquity**.

i. As David drew closer to God, he became more aware of God's holiness and man's sinfulness. "This is a good way to measure how well you are praying and whether, as you pray, you are drawing close to God or are merely mouthing words. If you are drawing close to God, you will become increasingly sensitive to sin, which is inevitable since the God you are approaching is a holy God." (Boice)

b. **I will come into Your house in the multitude of Your mercy**: This is David's confidence. It isn't that he is righteous and all others are sinners; his ground of confidence is the **mercy** of God.

c. **In fear of You I will worship**: David's worship isn't based on *his* feelings, but on his reverence for a righteous, merciful God.

d. **Make Your way straight before my face**: This reflects David's constant reliance on God. He needs God to lead him and to make the way **straight**. David walked the right way but was humble about it. David knew it was only God's power and work in him that kept him from the way of the wicked.

B. Description and destiny.

1. (9-10) The description and destiny of the wicked.

For *there is* no faithfulness in their mouth;
Their inward part *is* destruction;
Their throat *is* an open tomb;
They flatter with their tongue.
Pronounce them guilty, O God!

Let them fall by their own counsels;
Cast them out in the multitude of their transgressions,
For they have rebelled against You.

a. **There is no faithfulness in their mouth**: David focuses on what the wicked *say* as evidence of their wickedness. David understood what Jesus said later in Matthew 12:34: *Out of the abundance of the heart the mouth speaks.* Our righteousness or wickedness will sooner or later show up in our speech.

i. David felt the sting of wicked words and lies against him. Yet this prayer shows that something good came out of the attacks from the enemy. "Thus a man's enemies, while they oblige him to pray more fervently, and to watch more narrowly over his conduct, oftentimes become his best friends." (Horne)

b. **They flatter with their tongue**: "Always beware of people who flatter you, and especially when they tell you that they do not flatter you, and that they know you cannot endure flattery, for you are then being most fulsomely flattered, so be on your guard against the tongue of the flatterer." (Spurgeon)

c. **Let them fall by their own counsels**: David prays that the wicked will come to their deserved end. As rebels against God, they deserve the "guilty" sentence.

2. (11-12) The description and destiny of the righteous.

But let all those rejoice who put their trust in You;
Let them ever shout for joy, because You defend them;
Let those also who love Your name
Be joyful in You.
For You, O LORD**, will bless the righteous;**
With favor You will surround him as *with* a shield.

a. **Let all those rejoice who put their trust in You**: The righteous aren't made righteous by their words. The righteous are those who **trust** the LORD and **love** His **name**. But their righteousness is *evident* in their words. They **rejoice**, they **shout for joy**, and they are **joyful in** the LORD.

i. "A touch of enthusiasm would be the salvation of many a man's religion. Some Christians are good enough people: they are like wax candles, but they are not lighted. Oh, for a touch of flame! Then would they scatter light, and thus become of service to their families. 'Let them shout for joy.' Why not? Let not orderly folks object. One said to me the other day, 'When I hear you preach I feel as if I must have a shout!' My friend, shout if you feel forced to do so. (Here a hearer cried, 'Glory!') Our brother cries, 'Glory!' and I say so too. 'Glory!' The shouting need not always be done in a public service, or it might hinder devout hearing; but there are times and places where a glorious outburst of enthusiastic joy would quicken life in all around. The ungodly are not half so restrained in their blasphemy as we are in our praise." (Spurgeon)

b. **But let all those rejoice who put their trust in You**: This is a *permit*, a *precept*, a *prayer*, and a *promise*.

i. You have *permission* for joy. "You have here a ticket to the banquets of joy. You may be as happy as ever you like. You have divine permission to shout for joy." (Spurgeon)

ii. You have a *precept*, a command for joy: "Come, ye mournful ones, be glad. Ye discontented grumblers, come out of that dog-hole! Enter the palace of the King! Quit your dunghills; ascend your thrones." (Spurgeon)

iii. You should *pray* for joy, both in yourself and others – especially servants of the LORD. "If you lose your joy in your religion, you will be a poor worker: you cannot bear strong testimony, you cannot bear stern trial, you cannot lead a powerful life. In proportion as you maintain your joy, you will be strong *in* the Lord, and *for* the Lord." (Spurgeon)

iv. You have a *promise* for joy: "God promises joy and gladness to believers. Light is sown for them: the Lord will turn their night into day." (Spurgeon)

c. **You, O LORD, will bless the righteous; with favor You will surround him**: This is the greatest blessing of all – the **favor** of God. Knowing that God looks on us with favor and pleasure is the greatest knowledge in the world. This is our standing in *grace*.

i. A **shield** does not protect any one area of the body. It is large and mobile enough to cover any and every area of the body. It is armor over armor. This is how fully the favor of God, our standing in grace, protects us.

ii. When Martin Luther was on his way to face a Cardinal of the Roman Catholic Church to answer for what the church said were his heretical teachings, one of the Cardinal's servants taunted him saying, "Where will you find shelter if your patron, the Elector of Saxony, should desert you?" Luther answered, "Under the shelter of heaven."

Psalm 6 – A Confident Answer to an Agonized Plea

Psalm 6 is known as the first of seven penitential psalms – songs of confession and humility before God. It was a custom in the early church to sing these psalms on Ash Wednesday, 40 days before Resurrection Sunday. The title of this psalm is **To the Chief Musician. With stringed instruments. On an eight-stringed harp. A Psalm of David.** *The title tells us the recipient of the psalm –* **the Chief Musician,** *whom some suppose to be the Lord God Himself, and others suppose to be a leader of choirs or musicians in David's time, such as Heman the singer or Asaph (1 Chronicles 6:33, 16:5-7, and 25:6). Not only was it written for* **stringed instruments,** *but specifically for the* **eight-stringed harp.**

A. The agonized plea.

1. (1) A plea to lighten the chastening hand.

O LORD, do not rebuke me in Your anger,
Nor chasten me in Your hot displeasure.

> a. **Do not rebuke me in Your anger**: We don't know what the occasion of sin was, but because of his sin David sensed he was under the **rebuke** of God. Therefore, he called out to God to lighten the chastisement.

> > i. There may be times when we *believe* we are chastened by God's hand when really, we suffer trouble brought upon ourselves. Nevertheless, there are certainly times when the LORD does **chasten** His children.

> b. **Nor chasten me in Your hot displeasure**: We know that God's chastening hand is not primarily a mark of His **displeasure**, but rather it is a mark of adoption. Hebrews 12:7 makes it clear that chastening is evidence of our adoption: *If you endure chastening, God deals with you as with sons; for what son is there whom a father does not chasten?* When God corrects us it doesn't feel pleasant, but it is good and for our good.

> > i. **Anger...hot displeasure**: Living before the finished work of Jesus, David had less certainty about his standing with God. On this side of

the cross, we know that all the **anger** God has towards us was poured out on Jesus at the cross. God chastens the believer out of correcting love and not out of **anger**.

2. (2-3) Two kinds of trouble.

Have mercy on me, O LORD, for I *am* weak;
O LORD, heal me, for my bones are troubled.
My soul also is greatly troubled;
But You, O LORD – how long?

a. **I am weak...my bones are troubled**: David knew the trial of physical weakness and pain. In the midst of this kind of chastisement, he cries out to God for **mercy**.

i. "So we may pray that the chastisements of our gracious God, if they may not be entirely removed, may at least be sweetened by the consciousness that they are 'not in anger, but in his dear covenant love.'" (Spurgeon)

b. **My soul also is greatly troubled**: David knew the trials of spiritual weakness and pain. The difficulty of these trials drove David to seek mercy from God.

i. These trials of body and soul were amplified by David's sense of God's anger against him. When we are not confident in God's love and assistance, even small trials feel unbearable.

c. **How long?** David sensed he was under the chastisement of God, but he still knew he should ask God to shorten the trial. There is a place for humble resignation to chastisement, but God wants us to yearn for higher ground and to use that yearning as a motivation to seek Him and get things right with Him.

i. David seems to smart under the *result* of his sin, more than the sin itself. Ideally, we are all terribly grieved by sin itself, but there is something to be said for confession and humility for the sake of the result of our sins.

3. (4-5) The urgency of David's plea.

Return, O LORD, deliver me!
Oh, save me for Your mercies' sake!
For in death *there is* no remembrance of You;
In the grave who will give You thanks?

a. **Return, O LORD, deliver me**: In his agony David pleads for deliverance – but on the ground of God's mercy, not his own righteousness. David knew that the LORD's chastisement was righteous, but he also knew that God is rich in mercy.

i. The plea "**return**" also shows that David felt *distant* from God. This was part of the agony of the trial. When we sense God is near us, we feel that we can face anything, but when we sense that He is distant from us, we are weak before the smallest trial.

b. **Save me for Your mercies' sake**: The note of confession of sin is not strong in this psalm of penitence, but it is not absent. The fact that David appeals to the mercy of God for deliverance is evidence that he is aware that he doesn't *deserve* it.

i. "David's conscience is uneasy, and he must appeal to grace to temper the discipline he deserves." (Kidner)

c. **In death there is no remembrance of You**: It would be wrong to take these agonized words of David as evidence that there is no life beyond this life. The Old Testament has a shadowy understanding of the world beyond. Sometimes it shows a clear confidence (Job 19:25), and sometimes it has the uncertainty David shows here.

i. "Churchyards are silent places; the vaults of the sepulcher echo not with songs. Damp earth covers dumb mouths." (Spurgeon)

ii. 2 Timothy 1:10 says that Jesus *brought life and immortality to light through the gospel*. The understanding of the after-life was murky at best in the Old Testament, but Jesus let us know more about heaven and hell than anyone else could. Jesus could do this, because He had first-hand knowledge of the world beyond.

iii. David's point isn't to present a comprehensive theology of the world beyond. He is in agony, fearing for his life, and he *knows* he can remember God and give Him thanks now. He doesn't have the same certainty about the world beyond, so he asks God to act according to his certainty.

iv. "At rare moments the Psalms have glimpses of rescue from Sheol, in terms that suggest resurrection, or a translation like that of Enoch or Elijah (*c.f.* 16:10; 17:15; 49:15; 73:24)." (Kidner)

B. The determined resolution.

1. (6-7) A vivid description of David's agony.

I am weary with my groaning;
All night I make my bed swim;
I drench my couch with my tears.

My eye wastes away because of grief;
It grows old because of all my enemies.

a. **I am weary with groaning**: God's chastising hand was heavy upon David. His life seemed to be nothing but tears and misery. David's trial has at least three components: He felt God was angry with him, he lacked a sense of God's presence, and he couldn't sleep.

b. **All night I make my bed swim**: This is a good example of poetic exaggeration. David didn't want us to believe that his bed actually floated on a pool of tears in his room. Because this is poetic literature, we understand it according to its literary context. This understands the Bible *literally* – according to its literary context.

c. **My eye wastes away**: David's eyes were red and sore from all the tears and lack of sleep. "As an old man's eye grows dim with years, so says David, my eye is grown red and feeble through weeping." (Spurgeon)

d. **Because of all my enemies**: David is brought so low that his enemies no longer spur him to seize victory. He seems depressed and discouraged.

2. (8-10) David's confident declaration.

Depart from me, all you workers of iniquity;
For the LORD has heard the voice of my weeping.
The LORD has heard my supplication;
The LORD will receive my prayer.
Let all my enemies be ashamed and greatly troubled;
Let them turn back *and* be ashamed suddenly.

a. **Depart from me, all you workers of iniquity**: It may be that the sin that led David into this chastisement was association with the ungodly. Here we see David acting consistently with his change of heart and telling all ungodly associates to **depart**.

i. It is important to separate from ungodly associations. J. Edwin Orr describes some of the work among new converts in Halifax during the Second Great Awakening in Britain: "Among them was a boxer who had just won a money-prize and a belt. A crowd of his erstwhile companions stood outside the hall in order to ridicule him, and they hailed the converted boxer with a shout: 'He's getting converted! What about the belt? He'll either have to fight for it or give it up!' The boxer retorted, 'I'll both give it up and you up! If you won't go with me to heaven, I won't go with you to hell!' He gave them the belt but persuaded some of them to accompany him to the services, where another was converted and set busily working."

b. **The LORD has heard the voice of my weeping**: David ends the psalm on a note of confidence. He made his agonized cry to God, and God heard him.

i. **Weeping** has a **voice** before God. It isn't that God is impressed by emotional displays, but a passionate heart impresses Him. David wasn't afraid to cry before the LORD, and God honored the **voice** of his **weeping**.

ii. "Is it not sweet to believe that our tears are understood even when words fail! Let us learn to think of tears as liquid prayers." (Spurgeon)

iii. Once Luther wrestled hard with God in prayer and came jumping out of his prayer closet crying out, "*Vicimus, vicimus*" – that is, "Victory, victory!" David has the same sense of prevailing with God at the end of this prayer.

c. **Let all my enemies be ashamed and greatly troubled**: David knows that when God receives his prayer, it will be trouble for his enemy. David now sees that his temporary agony and *trouble* give way to a *permanent* agony and trouble for his enemies.

Psalm 7 – Confidence in God's Deliverance

The Hebrew title to this psalm reads: **A Meditation of David, which he sang to the LORD concerning the words of Cush, a Benjamite.** *The New King James Version translates the Hebrew word "shiggaion" as* **meditation,** *though the word is difficult to translate and is used elsewhere only in Habakkuk 3:1. The specific occasion is not easily connected with an event recorded in the historical books of the Old Testament; it may be a veiled reference to either Shimei's accusations against David in 2 Samuel 16:5 or to Saul's slanders against David. More likely this* **Cush, a Benjamite,** *was simply another partisan of Saul against David. The psalm contains both David's cry of anguish and shout of confidence in God's deliverance.*

A. David pleads for deliverance.

1. (1-2) A trust-filled plea.

O LORD my God, in You I put my trust;
Save me from all those who persecute me;
And deliver me,
Lest they tear me like a lion,
Rending *me* **in pieces, while** *there is* **none to deliver.**

a. **In You I put my trust**: When David was under attack from Cush the Benjamite, all he could trust was God. Every other support was gone, but he needed no other support.

i. "Nothing is known of *Cush*; but from Absalom's rebellion it emerged that Benjamin, Saul's tribe, held some bitter enemies of David (2 Samuel 16:5ff; 20:1ff)." (Kidner)

ii. "It is easy to understand how the slander described in the psalm could have emerged from the smoldering hostility of this tribe." (Boice)

iii. Some believe that this **Cush** was really Saul or Shimei. "Cush has been supposed to be Shimei or Saul himself, and to have been so called because of his swarthy complexion (Cush meaning African) or as a jest, because of his personal beauty." (Maclaren)

b. **And deliver me**: Sometimes God's strength is evident in helping through a trial. Other times it is evident in delivering us from trials. David was persuaded that God wanted to deliver him from this trial.

i. To be slandered is a severe trial. "It appears probable that Cush the Benjamite had accused David to Saul of treasonable conspiracy against his royal authority. This the king would be ready enough to credit, both from his jealousy of David, and from the relation which most probably existed between himself, the son of Kish, and this Cush, or Kish, the Benjamite.... This may be called the Song of the Slandered Saint." (Spurgeon)

c. **Lest they tear me like a lion**: David believed there would be grave consequences if he were not delivered from these lion-like enemies.

i. This understanding gave David urgency in prayer. God sometimes allows difficult circumstances, so they will awaken this urgency in us.

ii. "It will be well for us here to remember that this is a description of the danger to which the Psalmist was exposed from slanderous tongues. Verily this is not an overdrawn picture, for the wounds of a sword will heal, but the wounds of the tongue cut deeper than the flesh, and are not soon cured." (Spurgeon)

iii. David also knew what it was like to overcome a lion. "The metaphor of the lion is common in the psalms attributed to David, and is, at all events, natural in the mouth of a shepherd king, who had taken a lion by the beard." (Maclaren)

2. (3-5) The plea of innocence.

O Lord my God, if I have done this:
If there is iniquity in my hands,
If I have repaid evil to him who was at peace with me,
Or have plundered my enemy without cause,
Let the enemy pursue me and overtake *me*;
Yes, let him trample my life to the earth,
And lay my honor in the dust. Selah

a. **If there is iniquity in my hands**: With these words, David did not claim sinless perfection. Instead, he simply rejected the idea of moral equivalence between himself and his enemies.

i. "Although David expresses himself as perhaps we would not, his words do not mean that he is perfect, only that he is innocent of the crime of which he was charged.... The question is not whether David was morally perfect but whether he was innocent of this particular slander." (Boice)

ii. "From the Psalm we learn the nature of the charges, which he made against David. They were: that he had appropriated spoils which rightly belonged to the king; that he had returned evil for good; and that he had taken toll for some generosity." (Morgan)

b. **Let the enemy pursue me and overtake me**: David knew that his enemies were thirsty for his defeat. He was so confident in his righteousness in comparison to his enemies that he was willing to be given over to their desire if they were in the right.

B. The righteous judgment of God.

1. (6-7) A plea for God's righteous intervention.

Arise, O Lord, in Your anger;
Lift Yourself up because of the rage of my enemies;
Rise up for me *to* the judgment You have commanded!
So the congregation of the peoples shall surround You;
For their sakes, therefore, return on high.

a. **Arise, O Lord, in Your anger**: David believed that God was a being of human-like passions such as anger. David also believed that the passions of God were on his behalf; he believed God was or would be angry for him instead of against him.

i. It is a mistake to believe that God is without passions. Because He is God, we can say that these passions are not exactly like their human counterparts; yet they are certainly somewhat like them. God is not cold, distant, and dispassionate.

ii. Yet it is also a mistake to assume that the passions of God are always with us or support our opinion. Many dangerous fanatics have been wrongly inspired by the mistaken assurance that God was for them when He was not.

b. **Lift Yourself up...rise up for me**: David believed that God was for him and his cause; yet he did not hold this belief passively. He actively prayed for the accomplishing of what he believed God's will to be.

c. **For their sakes, therefore, return on high**: David's prayer for protection and vindication was not fundamentally selfish. He knew that his fate was vitally connected to the welfare of God's people. It was in large measure for their sakes, the sake of the congregation.

2. (8-10) David's defense.

The L<small>ORD</small> shall judge the peoples;
Judge me, O L<small>ORD</small>, according to my righteousness,
And according to my integrity within me.
Oh, let the wickedness of the wicked come to an end,
But establish the just;
For the righteous God tests the hearts and minds.
My defense *is* of God,
Who saves the upright in heart.

a. **The L<small>ORD</small> shall judge the peoples; judge me, O L<small>ORD</small>**: This was the attitude that protected David from presumption. He honestly invited God's judgment and correction.

i. Therefore, David asked for God's blessing **according to my righteousness, and according to my integrity within me**. In effect he prayed, "Lord, to the extent that I am righteous before You, bless me and protect me from my enemies."

ii. When David longed for justice, it wasn't that He wanted ultimate and perfect judgment before God; he looked for justice on the earthly level, justice between him and his false accuser.

b. **Let the wickedness of the wicked come to an end, but establish the just**: This reveals more of the heart of David's prayer. More than anything, he prayed for God to be just. In this sense, David did not pray for special favoritism with God; he prayed for God to be just, and he searched his own heart to help put him right before God.

i. David seemed to pray here beyond his own personal needs. "There is a great breadth of vision here, revealing a concern for universal justice which was always the motive behind David's personal appeals for vindication." (Kidner)

c. **My defense is of God**: David knew he was at a significant disadvantage before his enemies and had to rely on the defense that is of God.

i. With his trust in God, David did "Throw off slanders, as Paul did the viper; yea, in a holy scorning… laughs at them." (Trapp)

3. (11-13) God, the just judge.

God *is* a just judge,
And God is angry *with the wicked* every day.
If he does not turn back,
He will sharpen His sword;
He bends His bow and makes it ready.
He also prepares for Himself instruments of death;
He makes His arrows into fiery shafts.

a. **God is a just judge**: David's prior appeal to God's testing of man (Psalm 7:9) made him think of the justice of God. He declared this fundamental principle: God is a just judge.

> i. This is a commonly and dangerously rejected truth about God. Many anticipate that they will one day stand before a God of great love, great mercy, great warmth, and great generosity. They never imagine they will stand before a God who is perfectly just and who cannot ignore the crime of sin.

> ii. We can say that sin is a crime – that it breaks the good and holy law of God. And while all sins are not equally sinful (some sins are worse than others and will receive a greater condemnation, Matthew 23:14), there are no small sins against a great God.

> iii. The justice of God is easy to understand if we simply compare it to what we expect from an earthly judge. We don't think it is right or good if a human judge excuses crime in the name of compassion; we expect judges to be just. Yet many are absolutely confident that God will be an unjust judge on the Day of Judgment. They are so confident of it that they mistakenly rely on this idea for their salvation. David knew the truth: God is a just judge.

b. **He is angry with the wicked every day**: Adam Clarke believed a more accurate translation of Psalm 7:11 is, "He is NOT angry every day." He writes: "The mass of evidence supports the latter reading. The *Chaldee* first corrupted the text by making the addition, *with the wicked*, which our translators have followed."

> i. If the original is taken as more correct, "The sense seems to be, that there are daily instances in the world of God's favour toward his people; as also of his displeasure against the ungodly, who are frequently visited by sore judgments, and taken away in their sins." (Horne)

c. **He will sharpen His sword; He bends His bow and makes it ready**: David here considered the readiness of God to judge the sinner. David saw the sword sharpened and the bow bent. With God so ready to judge, the sinner should never presume that God will delay His judgment.

> i. When God delays judgment out of mercy, many people make a fatal error. They think this mercy means that God is not concerned with justice.

> ii. Instead, one should ask: "Why does God hold back the immediate application of justice?" Is it because:

> • The sinner is not really guilty?

- The Law is not really clear?

- Mankind, in fact, really deserves such mercy?

- God is not really powerful enough to bring justice?

- God is not really just?

iii. None of these are true. Instead, the sword is sharpened and the bow is bent. The only thing that holds back the immediate judgment of God against the sinner is the undeserved mercy of God, giving the sinner an unknown period of time to repent. Such mercy should never be presumed upon. "Did I say, *he will do it?* Nay, *he hath* already done it; his sword is drawn, his bow is bent, and the arrows are prepared and ready to be shot." (Poole)

iv. The real reason for any apparent delay in God's judgment is found in the line, **if he does not turn back**. In His great mercy, God waits for the sinner to **turn back**, to repent. The apparent delay is an expression of God's love for the sinner.

d. **Instruments of death...arrows into fiery shafts**: This powerful poetic imagery communicates the severity of God's judgment, hopefully providing another incentive to repentance.

i. "The wrath of God may be slow, but it is always sure. In thoughtless security man wantons and whiles away the precious hours; he knows not that every transgression sets a fresh edge on the sword, which is thus continually whetting for his destruction." (Horne)

C. The resolution of the matter.

1. (14) The wickedness of the wicked.

Behold, *the wicked* brings forth iniquity;
Yes, he conceives trouble and brings forth falsehood.

a. **Behold, the wicked brings forth iniquity**: This seemingly obvious statement is important. It shows that a wicked heart will show itself in wicked deeds.

i. Those wicked deeds may have the cover of respectability but will nonetheless be filled with iniquity (as was the case with the Pharisees of Jesus' day).

b. **He conceives trouble and brings forth falsehood**: This shows the source of sin – from within the sinner. The sinner gives birth to sin as a mother gives birth to children – from within.

2. (15-16) God deals with the wicked.

He made a pit and dug it out,
And has fallen into the ditch *which* he made.
His trouble shall return upon his own head,
And his violent dealing shall come down on his own crown.

a. **Fallen into the ditch which he made**: This shows a common method of God's distribution of justice. He often brings the same calamity on the wicked that they had planned for the righteous.

i. "God is righteous. The way of wickedness cannot prosper. It creates its own destruction. The pit digged is the grave of the man who digs it." (Morgan)

ii. "This is but the highly metaphorical way of saying that a sinner never does what he means to do, but that at the end of all his plans is disappointment." (Maclaren)

b. **His violent dealing shall come down on his own crown**: Two examples among many in the Bible are the fate of Haman the enemy of Mordecai (Esther 7:7-10) and the Jews, and the enemies of Daniel in the lion's den (Daniel 6:24).

3. (17) The response of praise.

I will praise the LORD according to His righteousness,
And will sing praise to the name of the LORD Most High.

a. **I will praise the LORD according to His righteousness**: David was wise enough to praise God according to His righteousness and not his own.

i. Though David appealed to God in this psalm on the basis of his comparative goodness, this was not a self-righteous prayer. David knew the difference between his relative righteousness and God's praiseworthy, perfect righteousness.

b. **And will sing praise to the name of the LORD Most High**: David ended this psalm – which began in gloom – on a high note of praise. He could praise, because he took his cause to God and in faith left it there.

Psalm 8 – The Glory of God in Creation

The title of this psalm reads, **To the Chief Musician. On the instrument of Gath. A Psalm of David.** *It indicates the audience of the psalm (***the Chief Musician***), the author of the psalm (of* **David***) and the sound of the psalm (***the instrument of Gath***). In this psalm David speaks of the glory of God, and how the glory of man and his destiny reflect upon God.*

A. The plainly seen glory of creation.

1. (1) The glory of God in the earth and the heavens.

O Lord, our Lord,
How excellent is Your name in all the earth,
Who have set Your glory above the heavens!

> a. **O Lord, our Lord**: Here, David recognized both the covenant *name* of God (**Lord**) and the position of Yahweh to His people (**Lord**). It was a simple, straightforward, and common way to say that "Our God is our Master."

> > i. *"Yehovah Adoneynu; O Jehovah our Prop, our Stay, our Support….* The root *dan* signifies *to direct, rule, judge, support.* So *Adonai* is the Director, Ruler, Judge, Supporter of men." (Clarke)

> b. **How excellent is Your name in all the earth**: David also recognized that though the Lord was Israel's covenant God, He was also God of more than just Israel. His name is **excellent…in all the earth**.

> c. **Who have set Your glory above the heavens**: At the same time, the **earth** was not enough to measure the glory and excellence of God. His glory is **above the heavens**.

2. (2) The glory of God in His strength over His enemies.

Out of the mouth of babes and nursing infants
You have ordained strength,

Because of Your enemies,
That You may silence the enemy and the avenger.

a. **Out of the mouth of babes and nursing infants You have ordained strength**: In the first verse, David considered the greatness of God by His evident power and glory in creation, both across the earth and in the heavens. Now, he considers that the power and glory of God can be seen in small children – **babes and nursing infants** – as God's **strength** is evident in them.

i. David here touched on a familiar theme in the Bible: the idea that God uses otherwise weak things to display His glory and strength. 1 Corinthians 1:27 is an example of this idea: *But God has chosen the foolish things of the world to put to shame the wise, and God has chosen the weak things of the world to put to shame the things which are mighty.*

ii. It is hard to think of anything more weak and helpless than a baby; yet the same God who can ordain strength **out of the mouth of babes and nursing infants** can give strength and support to me in the midst of my weakness.

iii. "The word here rather means *a strength*...that, out of such frail material as children's speech, God builds a tower of strength, which, like some border castle, will bridle and still the restless enemy." (Maclaren)

iv. "The praises of the Messiah, celebrated in the church by his children, have in them a strength and power which nothing can withstand; they can abash infidelity, when at its greatest height, and strike hell itself dumb." (Horne)

v. Significantly, Jesus quoted this passage to His indignant accusers in Matthew 21:16, as Jesus did wonderful miracles in the temple area, and as He received the praise of children who cried out *Hosanna to the Son of David!* (Matthew 21:15).

b. **Because of Your enemies, that You may silence the enemy**: The reason *why* God displays His strength in unlikely vessels is because it works to **silence the enemy**; Satan and his fellow adversaries have nothing to say when God works so mightily in an otherwise weak person.

i. One dramatic example of this is the story of Job. In it, God silenced the accusations of Satan against both God and Job by the way that He sustained Job with His unseen hand in the midst of profound weakness.

ii. In quoting this passage in Matthew 21:15-16, Jesus told His accusers who *He* was and who *they* were. Since the **babes and nursing infants** praise God in Psalm 8, Jesus identified Himself as God. In this, Jesus also identified the indignant scribes and teachers as the **enemy and avenger** described in this psalm.

iii. "Aha! Aha! O adversary! To be overcome by behemoth or leviathan might make thee angry; but to be smitten out of infants' mouths causes thee to bite the dust in utter dishonor. Thou art sore broken, now that 'out of the mouth of babes and sucklings' thou art put to shame." (Spurgeon)

B. The surprising glory of mankind.

1. (3-5) Though seemingly insignificant, man is crowned with glory and honor.

When I consider Your heavens, the work of Your fingers,
The moon and the stars, which You have ordained,
What is man that You are mindful of him,
And the son of man that You visit him?
For You have made him a little lower than the angels,
And You have crowned him with glory and honor.

a. **When I consider Your heavens**: David knew the value of simply *considering* the glory of God's creation. He knew what it was like to look up into the starry sky and **consider** what a great God had made this vast, wonderful universe.

i. With the naked eye, one can see about 5,000 stars. With a four-inch telescope, one can see about 2 million stars. With a 200-inch mirror of a great observatory, one can see more than a billion stars. The universe is so big that if one were to travel at the speed of light, it would take 40 billion years to reach the edge of the universe. Considering the heavens makes us see the greatness of God.

ii. These great heavenly objects such as the **moon and the stars** are the work of God's **fingers**. "Notwithstanding the amazing magnitude of the sun, we have abundant reason to believe that some of the fixed stars are much larger: and yet we are told they are *the work of* GOD'S FINGERS! What a *hand*, to move, form, and launch these globes!" (Clarke)

b. **What is man that You are mindful of him**: Considering the greatness of the heavens also made David consider the relative smallness and insignificance of man. David wondered why such a big, great God would be **mindful** of such small beings.

i. "We gave you but a feeble image of our comparative insignificance, when we said that the glories of an extended forest would suffer no more from the fall of a single leaf, than the glories of an extended universe would suffer though the globe we tread upon, and all that it inherits, should dissolve." (Chalmers, cited in Spurgeon)

ii. God is so big that He makes the universe with His fingers; man is so small that he is dwarfed by the universe. Yet David did not doubt that God *was* **mindful** of man; he simply said "**You are mindful of him**" and only wondered *why*. Before we share David's question, we should first share his assured confidence that *God is mindful of us*; He thinks of us and considers what we do.

iii. "Sorry, sickly man, a mass of mortalities, a map of miseries, a mixture or compound of dirt and sin...and yet God is mindful of him." (Trapp)

iv. "David's question can be asked with many nuances. In Psalm 144:3-4 it mocks the arrogance of the rebel; in Job 7:17 it is a sufferer's plea for respite; in Job 25:6 it shudders at human sin. But here it has no tinge of pessimism; only astonishment that *thou are mindful* and *thou dost care*." (Kidner)

c. **And the son of man that You should visit him**: Indeed, using the poetic method of repetition, David repeated the idea in a stronger way. **Son of man** is a title that emphasizes the "humanness" of man, and we might say that **visit him** is yet stronger than **are mindful of him**.

i. David was confident that God not only carefully thought about man, but that He had some kind of personal connection and contact with men (**that You visit him**). He thinks about us and acts in our lives.

ii. Morgan considered the use of the terms **man** and **son of man** as a "contrast between the stately splendor of the moon and the stars, and man – *Enosh* – frail man – and the son of man *Ben-Adam* – of apparently earthly origin. The contrasts are graphic." (Morgan)

d. **For You have made him a little lower than the angels**: David saw that God made man **a little lower than the angels**, and this is evident in the way that man is beneath the angels in present glory, power, and nearness to God.

i. The word translated **angels** is *Elohim*, and most often refers to God Himself. There are some (such as Boice) who believe that David meant to say that man is a *little lower than God*, stressing the idea that man is made in God's image.

ii. Yet the ancient translators of the Bible from Hebrew to Greek understood *elohim* here to speak of angelic beings; more importantly, that was how the writer to the Hebrews understood it. "The Hebrew for [**angels**] is simply 'God' or 'gods' ('Elohim'). It may refer to angelic beings." (VanGemeren)

iii. Significantly, David did not say that man was "a little higher than the beasts," though one could say that is true. Theologians since Thomas Aquinas have noted that man is in a middle position between the angels and the animals: lower than the angels yet higher than the animals. Yet David rightly makes us look upward and not downward, though many think of mankind as more animal than angelic, David wrote that **You have made him a little lower than the angels**.

iv. "Although made in God's image and ordained to become increasingly like the God to whom they look, men and women have turned their backs on God. And since they will not look upward to God, which is their privilege and duty, they actually look downward to the beasts and so become increasingly like them." (Boice)

v. This very passage is quoted in Hebrews 2:5-9 to reinforce and build upon this exact point. In it he notes that man's low estate relates only to this world, and not the world to come (Hebrews 2:5). More pointedly, the writer of Hebrews used this passage from Psalm 8 to show that Jesus really did add a genuinely *human* nature to His divine nature and thus also became **a little lower than the angels**.

e. **You have crowned him with glory and honor**: Though for a **little** while set lower than the angels, man's destiny is one day to be **crowned** with a **glory and honor** that surpasses even the angels. It is the destiny of redeemed men and women to one day be lifted above the angels (1 Corinthians 6:3, Revelation 1:6, 5:10).

i. "*Little* can sometimes mean 'for a little while' in both Hebrew and Greek, which is the sense probably implied in [Hebrews]." (Kidner)

ii. "A little lower in nature, since they are immortal, and but a little, because time is short; and when that is over, saints are no longer lower than the angels." (Spurgeon)

iii. God's glory is *above the heavens*; yet He put this same **glory and honor** on man as a crown. "This is an effective way of identifying man with God and of saying that he has been made in God's image, reflecting God's glory in a way other parts of the creation do not." (Boice)

iv. As the writer of Hebrews points out, it seems that this divine call and gift given to man of great dominion over the whole earth is tragically unfulfilled; fallen man seems so weak and incapable of dominion over his own thoughts and desires, much less crowned with glory and honor. Yet, as Hebrews properly says, *but we see Jesus* (Hebrew 2:9).

v. "In Him we have had the full revelation of the greatness of man. But we have seen more than that. We have seen Him 'crowned with glory and honour, that by the grace of God He should taste death for every man.' That vision creates our confidence that man will at last realize the Divine purpose." (Morgan)

vi. "Satan is no doubt filled with scorn of man when he looks at him and measures him with himself. 'Is this the creature that is to be set over all the works of God's hands, made of earth and water, phosphates and metals? I am nobler far than he. Can I not flash like lightning, while he must creep about the world to find himself a grave?'" (Spurgeon)

2. (6-9) The dominion of man and the excellence of God.

You have made him to have dominion over the works of Your hands;
You have put all *things* **under his feet,**
All sheep and oxen –
Even the beasts of the field,
The birds of the air,
And the fish of the sea
That pass through the paths of the seas.
O Lord, **our Lord,**
How excellent *is* **Your name in all the earth!**

a. **You have made him to have dominion over the works of Your hands**: David understood the mandate given to Adam and His descendants at creation (Genesis 1:26-28 and 9:2). By both God's decree and through superior ability, man indeed has **dominion** over the other creatures and resources of the earth.

i. "In this section of the psalm, allusions to the first chapter of Genesis are inescapable, which shows that David was thoroughly acquainted with this book." (Boice) Perhaps this knowledge of God's word came from David's mother, whom he twice in Psalms refers to as a *maidservant* of the Lord (Psalm 86:16 and 116:16).

ii. As part of this authority, mankind has the responsibility to wisely manage the creatures and resources of this earth in a way that gives God glory and is good for man. It means that it is wrong to see man as *merely* part of the ecosystem (thus denying his God-ordained **dominion**). It is also wrong for man to abuse the ecosystem, thus making him a bad manager of that which ultimately belongs to God (Psalm 24:1). The mandate of **dominion** asks man to use the creatures and resources of the earth, but to use them wisely and responsibly.

b. **You have put all things under his feet**: Here, David developed the idea introduced in the first line of Psalm 8:6. The **dominion** of man extends to **all things**, including **sheep, oxen…beasts of the field, the birds of the air, and the fish of the sea.**

> i. The Apostle Paul quoted this passage in 1 Corinthians 15:27. Paul quoted it in much the same way that the writer of Hebrews did in Hebrews 2:5-9, showing that this promise of dominion is now only incompletely fulfilled among men. Yet it will be ultimately fulfilled in Jesus, the ultimate Man, and will be one day also completely fulfilled in His resurrected followers.

> ii. In light of all this, it is a great tragedy when a man is captured and held in bondage by the things of this world. We were born to have **dominion over** such material things, instead of being in bondage to them.

c. **O Lord, our Lord, how excellent is Your name in all the earth**: When David thought about how vast a dominion God had given to man, it made him praise God all over again. That this humble creature – humble in light of the majesty of the universe, humble in light of its present standing under angelic beings – should be given such authority is a demonstration of both the excellence and the goodness of God.

> i. David understood that the position of man in creation says far more about the glory of God than saying anything about the glory of man. Understanding it all should make us praise God, not man. "For man's dominion over nature, wonderful though it is, takes second place to his calling as servant and worshipper, to whose very children the *name* of the Lord has been revealed." (Kidner)

> ii. There are three wonderful and important truths about man found in this psalm; when these truths are denied or neglected, man never is what God made him to be.
> - God made man.
> - God made man something glorious.
> - God made man for a high and worthy destiny.

> iii. All three of these principles are rooted in *what God has made man*; they do not exist nor are they fulfilled from the plan or work of man. That is why this glorious psalm about man is even more so a psalm about God. "The most striking feature of Psalm 8…is its description of man and his place in the created order. But the psalm does not begin by talking about man. It begins with a celebration of the surpassing majesty of God." (Boice)

iv. "He made us to have dominion by the word of creation. He made us kings unto God by his blood. His name shall, therefore, be honoured through all the earth." (Meyer)

v. "Even thou, silly worm, shalt honour him, when it shall appear what God hath done for thee, what lusts he hath mortified, and what graces he hath granted thee." (Spurgeon)

Psalm 9 – God Remembers, Man Forgets

The title of this psalm reads **To the Chief Musician. To the tune of "Death of the Son." A Psalm of David**. *The title indicates for us that David wrote this psalm to God Himself (generally regarded as the "Chief Musician") to a popularly known tune in his day (in Hebrew,* Muth Labben*). In this psalm, David celebrates the help and goodness of God with a big vision for the nations.*

While most believe the title Muth Labben *refers to a tune; others suggest that it refers to an instrument upon which the song was played. Some (as in the New King James Version) associate the title with the phrase* **The Death of the Son**, *and apply that title as the ancient Chaldee version does: "Concerning the death of the Champion who went out between the camps," referring to Goliath. Perhaps David wrote this psalm remembering the victory over Goliath from the vantage point of many years since that triumph.*

"From this point in the Psalter up to Psalm 148 the versions differ over the numbering of the psalms, since the LXX *[Septuagint] and Vulgate, followed by the Roman church, count Psalms 9 and 10 as a single poem, while the Protestant churches follow the Hebrew reckoning."* (Derek Kidner)

A. Praising God for how He deals with an enemy.

1. (1-2) Singing praises to the God who does great things.

I will praise *You*, **O LORD, with my whole heart;**
I will tell of all Your marvelous works.
I will be glad and rejoice in You;
I will sing praise to Your name, O Most High.

> a. **I will praise You, O LORD, with my whole heart**: David recognized that God was worthy of praise with the **whole heart**. His entire being should be directed in affection towards God.

> > i. "Half heart is no heart." (Spurgeon)

52

ii. "We do not praise God with our lips very much, if at all. And when we do, if we do, we praise him halfheartedly.... It is more often true that Christians complain of how God has been treating them, carry on excessively about their personal needs or desires, or gossip." (Boice)

b. **I will tell of all Your marvelous works**: Here, David described an important and often neglected way to praise God – to **tell of all** His **marvelous works**. Simply remembering and telling the great things God has done is a wonderful way to praise Him.

i. "Christians, so called, when they meet, seldom speak about God! Why is this? Because they have nothing to say." (Clarke)

ii. **Marvelous works**: "*Wonderful deeds* (or things) is a single Hebrew word, particularly frequent in the Psalms, used especially of the great redemptive miracles (*e.g.* Psalm 106:7, 22), but also of their less obvious counterparts in daily experience (*cf.* Psalm 71:17), and of the hidden glories of Scripture (Psalm 119:18)." (Kidner)

iii. David could see that "Today is as full of God to this man as the sacred yesterdays of national history, and his deliverances as wonderful as those of old." (Maclaren)

c. **I will be glad and rejoice in You**: David here described a second way to praise God, by simply finding and expressing gladness and joy **in** God. This is simply choosing to rest in and celebrate the goodness, greatness, and kindness of God.

d. **I will sing praise to Your name, O Most High**: Here, David listed a third way to praise God with the **whole heart**, by *singing* **praise** to the **name** of God. The idea is to honor and celebrate the character and nature of God, recognizing Him as the **Most High**.

i. **O Most High**: "God was so first called by Melchizedek, upon a like occasion as here by David, Genesis 14:19-20." (Trapp)

2. (3-5) David praises God for defending him against his enemies.

When my enemies turn back,
They shall fall and perish at Your presence.
For You have maintained my right and my cause;
You sat on the throne judging in righteousness.
You have rebuked the nations,
You have destroyed the wicked;
You have blotted out their name forever and ever.

a. **When my enemies turn back, they shall fall and perish at Your presence**: In the first two verses of this psalm, David described general reasons for praising God, reasons that are always valid. Now, he recounted a reason more specific to his present circumstances; he praised God for the way that the Most High defeated his **enemies**.

b. **For You have maintained my right and my cause**: David saw God move against his enemies by defending him on the *principle* of right and wrong in his conflict.

> i. This shows us that the God of David – that is, the God of the Bible – is not dispassionate regarding right and wrong among men; He is not always neutral in human conflict. It is entirely true that men may *think* God is on their side when He is not, and that it may be that God is against *both* parties in a dispute. Nevertheless, under inspiration of the Holy Spirit, David could say, "**For You have maintained my right and my cause.**"

> ii. Understanding this should not make us automatically claim that God is on *our* side in our battles or disputes; it should rather make us endeavor to be on *God's side*, by rigorously conforming ourselves to His word.

c. **You sat on the throne...You have rebuked the nations...You have blotted out their name forever and ever**: David saw God in action among **the nations**, righteously judging the wicked.

> i. By implication, we see that David also justified and defended the righteous – that is, himself, in the present situation.

> ii. "The past tenses of verses 5-8 are 'prophetic perfects,' a feature of the Old Testament: they describe coming events as if they have already happened, so certain is their fulfillment and so clear the vision." (Kidner)

3. (6-8) David celebrates the Lord's victory.

O enemy, destructions are finished forever!
And you have destroyed cities;
Even their memory has perished.
But the LORD shall endure forever;
He has prepared His throne for judgment.
He shall judge the world in righteousness,
And He shall administer judgment for the peoples in uprightness.

a. **O enemy, destructions are finished forever**: David shifted his focus from speaking directly to the LORD to addressing the enemies whom the LORD had defeated. David assured them that their evil work of destruction would end in futility.

i. "The metaphor of a judgment-seat is exchanged for a triumphant description of the destructions fallen on the land of the enemy, in all which God alone is recognised as the actor." (Maclaren)

b. **But the LORD shall endure forever**: We might have expected David to set *himself* in contrast to the wicked; yet he was wise and humble enough to know that God would judge the wicked more for being *His own* enemies instead of David's.

c. **He shall administer judgment for the peoples in uprightness**: David looked forward to the eventual and ultimate rule of God over all nations. This would be the perfect expression of God's righteous judgment.

i. "The psalm is a great pattern of praise on a far too much neglected level in our day. We praise God much for His mercy. That is right, but it is a good thing to recognize His righteous rule, and to praise Him for that." (Morgan)

ii. One thousand years after David's time, the Apostle Paul quoted this line on Mars Hill: **He shall judge the world in righteousness** (Acts 17:31).

B. Praising God for how He treats the oppressed.

1. (9-10) God is a trustworthy refuge.

The LORD also will be a refuge for the oppressed,
A refuge in times of trouble.
And those who know Your name will put their trust in You;
For You, LORD, have not forsaken those who seek You.

a. **The LORD also will be a refuge for the oppressed**: Here, David was grateful that God did more than judge the wicked; He also was a **refuge** and support for those **oppressed** by the wicked.

i. **Times of trouble**: According to Maclaren, this translates a rare word, and "occurs only here and in Psalm 10:1. It means a cutting off, *i.e.*, of hope of deliverance. The notion of distress intensified to despair is conveyed."

b. **Those who know Your name will put their trust in You**: David understood that the help of God wasn't given just because God favored some and opposed others. It was because His people *have relationship* with Him (**know Your name**), they have *faith* in Him (**put their trust in You**), and they *seek* Him (**who seek You**).

i. It is a serious trial to the child of God to feel **forsaken** by God. There are particular times when we are likely to feel that the Lord has forsaken us.

- When we have sinned.
- When we face great trouble.
- When we have some great job to do.
- When we feel our prayers are unanswered.

ii. Yet we can find refuge in seeking God, in knowing His name. "To 'know Thy name' is here equivalent to learning God's character as made known by His acts." (Maclaren)

iii. "We never trust a man till we know him, and bad men are better known than trusted. Not so the Lord, for where his name is poured out as an ointment, there the virgins love him, fear him, rejoice in him, repose upon him." (Trapp)

iv. "Men complain of their little faith: the remedy is in their own hands; let them set themselves to know God.... But for all this, you must make time. You cannot know a friend from hurried interviews, much less God. So you must steep yourself in deep, long thoughts of his nearness and his love." (Meyer)

2. (11-12) Singing praise to the God who remembers His people.

Sing praises to the LORD, who dwells in Zion!
Declare His deeds among the people.
When He avenges blood, He remembers them;
He does not forget the cry of the humble.

a. **Sing praises to the LORD:** David exhorted others to do what he had already done in this psalm – to praise the LORD, and to **declare His deeds among the people.**

i. "Singing and preaching, as means of glorifying God, are here joined together, and it is remarkable that, connected with all revivals of gospel ministry, there has been a sudden outburst of the spirit of song. Luther's Psalms and Hymns were in all men's mouths, and in the modern revival under Wesley and Whitfield, the strains of Charles Wesley, Cennick, Berridge, Toplady, Hart, Newton, and many others, were the outgrowth of restored piety." (Spurgeon)

ii. David here communicated something known among those who praise God. When they praise God, it is natural for them to draw others into similar praise.

b. **When He avenges blood, He remembers them; He does not forget the cry of the humble:** David called others to praise God for the same reasons he had praised Him earlier; notably, because God is a partisan on behalf of the oppressed and the humble. God even **avenges** their **blood.**

i. Numbers 35:33-34 tells us that the blood of unavenged murders pollutes the earth. The blood of Abel spoke to God (Genesis 4:10), and the blood of Nabal was seen by God (2 Kings 9:26). God has promised to avenge blood and remember the murdered. "The designation of God as 'making inquisition for blood' thinks of Him as the Goel, or Avenger. To seek here means to demand back...to demand compensation or satisfaction, and this finally comes to mean to avenge or punish." (Maclaren)

ii. It reminds us that God will remember and avenge the blood of His persecuted people. "O persecutors, there is a time a-coming, when God will make a strict enquiry after the blood of Hooper, Bradford, Latimer, Taylor, Ridley, etc. There is a time a-coming, wherein God will enquire who silenced and suspended such-and-such ministers, and who stopped the mouths of such-and-such, and who imprisoned, confined, and banished such-and-such, who were once burning and shining lights, and who were willing to spend and be spent that sinners might be saved, and that Christ might be glorified." (Spurgeon)

3. (13-14) A plea for mercy from the God who remembers.

Have mercy on me, O LORD!
Consider my trouble from those who hate me,
You who lift me up from the gates of death,
That I may tell of all Your praise in the gates of the daughter of Zion.
I will rejoice in Your salvation.

a. **Have mercy on me, O LORD:** David had just considered that God remembered the *cry of the humble*. Now, David wanted God to remember *him* in his season of **trouble (consider my trouble from those who hate me).**

i. **Gates of death...Your praise in the gates of the daughter of Zion:** "The contrast between the gates of death and the gates of the New Jerusalem is very striking; let our songs be excited to the highest and most rapturous pitch by the double consideration of whence we are taken." (Spurgeon)

b. **That I may tell of all Your praise:** David wanted God to rescue him so that he could give God all the more **praise**, and all the more passionately to **rejoice in** God's **salvation.**

i. Again, the idea is that David has much more than his own benefit and well-being in mind. Even his deliverance is a way for God to bring more glory to Himself. David did not see his rescue as the final goal; the goal was always God's greater glory.

ii. **I will rejoice in Your salvation**: "It is a good thing for the melancholy to become a Christian; it is an unfortunate thing for the Christian to become melancholy. If there is any man in the world that has a right to have a bright, clear face and a flashing eye, it is the man whose sins are forgiven him, and who is saved with God's salvation." (Spurgeon)

4. (15-16) The destiny of the wicked.

The nations have sunk down in the pit *which* they made;
In the net which they hid, their own foot is caught.
The LORD is known *by* the judgment He executes;
The wicked is snared in the work of his own hands. Meditation. Selah

a. **The nations have sunk down in the pit which they made**: David understood the triumph of God to be so complete that His enemies were ensnared in the same trap they set for others. Even the best plans and efforts of those who oppose God end up serving His purpose.

i. This pattern is demonstrated again and again in the Scriptures.

- Esau and Isaac plot against the purpose of God and end up serving it.

- Joseph's brothers fight against the plan of God only to further it.

- Haman built a gallows for Mordecai the Jew, only to be executed upon it himself.

- Judas betrayed Jesus and became himself a fulfillment of prophecy.

ii. This, of course, never justifies the evil that men do; though the betrayal of Judas sent Jesus to the cross, he himself was rightly called the *son of perdition* (the one destined for destruction) for his evil work (John 17:12).

iii. "There is nothing that a wicked man does that is not against his own interest. He is continually doing himself harm, and takes more pains to destroy his soul than the righteous man does to get his saved unto eternal life. This is a weighty truth; and the psalmist adds: *Higgaion; Selah*. Meditate on this; mark it well." (Clarke)

b. **The LORD is known by the judgment He executes**: The greatness of God is demonstrated by the way He can use the plans and efforts of the ungodly, while also bringing righteous **judgment** upon them.

C. Appealing to the God who judges in righteousness.

1. (17-18) God will deal with both the wicked and the humble.

The wicked shall be turned into hell,
***And* all the nations that forget God.**
For the needy shall not always be forgotten;
The expectation of the poor shall *not* perish forever.

a. **The wicked shall be turned into hell**: Here, as David approaches the conclusion of the psalm, he considered the *end* of the wicked – ultimate destruction in **hell**.

i. In the patterns of Hebraic poetry, the phrase "**and all the nations that forget God**" can be considered just another way of describing **the wicked** mentioned in the previous line. Yet it is a useful repetition, reminding us of the inherently great sin of *forgetting God*.

ii. What does the sinner forget about God?

- Man forgets the *infinite majesty and glory* of God.
- Man forgets the *mercies* of God.
- Man forgets the *laws* of God.
- Man forgets the *presence* of God.
- Man forgets the *justice* of God.

iii. Why does the sinner forget God?

- Man forgets God because *the thought of God makes him afraid*.
- Man forgets God because *the thought of God doesn't entertain him enough*.
- Man forgets God because *the thought of God makes it hard to carry on in sin*.

iv. "The forgetters of God are far more numerous than the profane or profligate, and according to the very forceful expression of the Hebrew, the nethermost hell will be the place into which all of them shall be hurled headlong. Forgetfulness seems a small sin, but it brings eternal wrath upon the man who lives and dies in it." (Spurgeon)

v. **The wicked shall be turned into hell**: "Hebrew, into into hell (twice), that is, into the nethermost hell, the lowest dungeon of hell.... R. Solomon's note here is, they shall be carried away from hell to judgment, and from judgment they shall be returned to the deepest pit of hell." (Trapp)

b. **For the needy shall not always be forgotten**: David expresses a beautiful contrast here. The wicked try to **forget God**; yet the **needy** and **poor** (here describing the godly who are oppressed by God's enemies) are **not...forgotten**.

i. **Shall not always be forgotten** reminds us that from the perception of the **needy** and **poor**, they may for a time feel forgotten. Yet the good God promises that they will not **always** feel this way, and their **expectation** will not forever be disappointed.

ii. There are few more painful things than feeling *forgotten* and feeling *disappointed*. To those in such pain, God makes these wonderful promises; that they **shall not always be forgotten**, and their **expectation** will not perish.

- You shall not always be forgotten at the mercy-seat; so keep praying.
- You shall not always be forgotten in the Word; so keep reading.
- You shall not always be forgotten from the pulpit; so keep hearing.
- You shall not always be forgotten at the Lord's Table; so keep receiving.
- You shall not always be forgotten in your service; so keep serving.
- You expect to have peace in Jesus; in Him you will have it.
- You expect to triumph over sin; in Him you will triumph.
- You expect to get out of trouble; in Him you will be delivered.
- You expect to grow strong in faith; in Him you will be strengthened.
- You expect to have spiritual joys and experiences; in Him you will have them.

iii. "The needy, and the poor, whose expectation is from the Lord, are never forgotten, though sometimes their deliverance is delayed for the greater confusion of their enemies, the greater manifestation of God's mercy, and the greater benefit to themselves." (Clarke)

2. (19-20) An appeal for God to glorify Himself among the nations.

Arise, O LORD,
Do not let man prevail;
Let the nations be judged in Your sight.
Put them in fear, O LORD,
***That* the nations may know themselves *to be but* men. Selah**

a. **Arise, O LORD, do not let man prevail**: Previously in this psalm, David expressed a firm confidence in God's judgment of the wicked and His vindication of the righteous. Yet David did not allow this expectation to make him *passive* or *fatalistic* in regard to the outworking of God's plan. Instead, he boldly prayed, "**Arise, O LORD, do not let man prevail.**"

i. "Prayers are the Church's weapons...whereby she is terrible as an army with banners; she prays down her enemies." (Trapp)

ii. "The word for *man*, in both verses, is one which tends to emphasize his frailty." (Kidner)

iii. "All the wealth of Croesus, the wisdom of Solon, the power of Alexander, the eloquence of Demosthenes, if added together, would leave the possessor but a man. May we ever remember this, lest like those in the text, we should be *put in fear.*" (Spurgeon)

b. **Let the nations be judged in Your sight...that the nations may know themselves to be but men**: David again expressed his confidence in God's judgment of the wicked. Yet this did not lead David to a hatred of mankind or unhealthy joy in judgment. His real hope was that the display of God's judgment would *teach* the nations their proper place before God (**to be but men**).

i. This is a place of humility, and as David has already noted in this psalm, the humble are remembered before God (Psalm 9:12). This was a prayer for God to *reach* the nations through the display of His judgment.

ii. "Strange, that man, dust in his original, sinful by his fall, and continually reminded of both by every thing in him and about him, should yet stand in need of some sharp affliction, some severe visitation from God, to bring him the knowledge of himself, and make him feel who and what he is." (Horne)

iii. "So the two parts of the psalm end with the thought that the 'nations' may yet come to know the name of God, the one calling upon those who have experienced His deliverance to 'declare among the peoples His doings,' the other praying God to teach by chastisement what nations who forget Him have failed to learn from mercies." (Maclaren)

iv. "What prayer, then, can we pray which is of more vital importance than that the nations may know themselves to be but men? Such knowledge must drive them to dependence upon God, and such dependence is the secret of national strength, and of national prosperity and permanence." (Morgan)

Psalm 10 – From Times of Trouble to Calm Confidence

Because this psalm has no title (in the midst of several psalms that do), and because it shares some similar themes with Psalm 9, some have thought that it was originally the second half of Psalm 9. There are more reasons to doubt this than to believe it; this psalm rightly stands on its own as a psalm of lament at the seeming prosperity of the wicked but ultimate confidence in the judgments of God.

"There is not, in my judgment, a Psalm which describes the mind, the manners, the works, the words, the feelings, and the fate of the ungodly with so much propriety, fullness, and light, as this Psalm." (Martin Luther, cited in Charles Spurgeon)

A. Questioning the success of the wicked.

1. (1-4) Questioning the seeming inactivity of God against the wicked.

> **Why do You stand afar off, O L**ord**?**
> ***Why* do You hide in times of trouble?**
> **The wicked in *his* pride persecutes the poor;**
> **Let them be caught in the plots which they have devised.**
> **For the wicked boasts of his heart's desire;**
> **He blesses the greedy *and* renounces the L**ord**.**
> **The wicked in his proud countenance does not seek *God;***
> **God *is* in none of his thoughts.**

a. **Why do You stand afar off, O L**ord**?** Here, the psalmist asked a question well known to those who follow God: the concern, the anxiety, over the seeming inactivity of God. The psalmist felt that God was **afar off** and did even **hide in times of trouble**.

i. "The presence of God is the joy of his people, but any suspicion of his absence is distracting beyond measure.... It is not the trouble, but the hiding of our Father's face, which cuts us to the quick." (Spurgeon)

ii. **Times of trouble**: According to Maclaren, this was a rare word in the ancient Hebrew vocabulary, used only here and in Psalm 9:9. "It means a cutting off, *i.e.*, of hope of deliverance. The notion of distress intensified to despair is conveyed."

b. **The wicked in his pride persecutes the poor**: This explains *why* the psalmist was so troubled by the seeming inactivity of God. He sees the **wicked**, proud man who not only **persecutes the poor** and approves other sinners (**blesses the greedy**), but he also sins against God (**renounces the LORD...does not seek God...God is in none of his thoughts**).

i. We immediately recognize that anyone who **renounces the LORD** is sinful. Yet the psalmist here puts the one who **does not seek God** and the one who does not think about God (**God is in none of his thoughts**) in the same category as the one who **renounces the LORD**.

ii. Men do not seek God; this is a great sin. Men do not think about God; this also is a great sin. Man has obligations to God as His creator and sovereign, and it is a sin to neglect them. Man commits these sins because of **his proud countenance**; ignoring God is an expression of our independence and perceived equality (or superiority) to Him.

iii. Poole observed that pride is in the heart, "yet it is manifested in the countenance, and is therefore oft described by lofty looks."

iv. "A brazen face and a broken heart never go together.... Honesty shines in the face, but villainy peeps out at the eyes." (Spurgeon)

v. It can be said of the proud, wicked man in this psalm, **God is in none of his thoughts**. At the same time, he cannot *not* think of God, as he does later in Psalm 10:11 and 13 (the thoughts, *God has forgotten; He hides His face; He will never see... You will not require an account*). Try as he may, he can't stop thinking about God.

c. **Let them be caught in the plots which they have devised**: This was the prayer of the psalmist regarding the wicked. In other psalms this is a confident expectation (such as Psalm 9:15); here it is a heartfelt prayer.

i. "There are none who will dispute the justice of God, when he shall hang every Haman on his own gallows, and cast all the enemies of his Daniels into their own den of lions." (Spurgeon)

2. (5-7) The pride of the wicked.

His ways are always prospering;
Your judgments *are* far above, out of his sight;
***As for* all his enemies, he sneers at them.**
He has said in his heart, "I shall not be moved;

I shall never be in adversity."
His mouth is full of cursing and deceit and oppression;
Under his tongue *is* trouble and iniquity.

a. **His ways are always prospering**: Here, the psalmist protested to God; not only did the wicked man seem to enjoy constant prosperity, but he did so because God's **judgments are far above, out of his sight**.

i. We can imagine the psalmist thinking, "If only God would demonstrate His judgment to this wicked man, he would change his ways." This may sound like a complaint against God and in some sense is; yet it should more so be seen as complete confidence in God's rule and authority. The psalmist recognized that the wicked could never prosper unless God allowed it; so he appealed to God to not allow it.

b. **He sneers at them..."I shall not be moved; I shall never be in adversity"...full of cursing and deceit and oppression**: The psalmist examined and exposed the sins of the wicked man, who is not afraid of his enemies. There is pride and sin in the wicked man's **heart**, in his **mouth**, and **under his tongue**. No wonder the psalmist wanted God to stop this kind of sinner!

i. We are impressed at how often the wicked *speech* of men – which is often today regarded as no sin at all – is regarded as sin in Psalms. "Cursing, lying, threatening, and troubling and evil speech are all destructive. They flow from one who does not believe that God will hold him or her accountable." (Boice)

ii. "Such cursing men are cursed men." (Trapp)

iii. "What a finished character! A blasphemer, a deceitful man, and a knave!" (Clarke)

iv. "He wants no prophet to teach him, no priest to atone for him, no king to conduct for him; he needs neither a Christ to redeem, nor a Spirit to sanctify him; he believes no Providence, adores no Creator, and fears no Judge." (Horne)

3. (8-11) The violence and blasphemy of the wicked.

He sits in the lurking places of the villages;
In the secret places he murders the innocent;
His eyes are secretly fixed on the helpless.
He lies in wait secretly, as a lion in his den;
He lies in wait to catch the poor;
He catches the poor when he draws him into his net.
So he crouches, he lies low,
That the helpless may fall by his strength.

He has said in his heart,
"God has forgotten;
He hides His face;
He will never see."

a. **He sits in the lurking places of the villages**: The psalmist continued his examination of the wicked man (or men) who had troubled him so. Key to the nature of this wicked man is *secrecy* (**lurking places...secret places... eyes are secretly fixed...lies in wait secretly...he lies low**).

b. **He murders the innocent**: Another characteristic of the wicked man is seen in how he is a bully, focusing his violence against the weak (**the innocent...the helpless...the poor**). He isn't manful or honorable enough to openly fight those who might effectively fight back.

> i. **The helpless**: "The pathetic state of his victims is shown in the reiterated word *hapless*, or 'poor wretch' (NEB), found only here (Psalm 10:8,10,14)." (Kidner)

> ii. "'Helpless' is a word only found in this psalm (vv. 8,10,14), which has received various explanations, but is probably derived from a root meaning *to be black*, and hence comes to mean *miserable, hapless*, or the like." (Maclaren)

c. **God has forgotten; He hides His face; He will never see**: For the psalmist, this made the murder, oppression, and bullying of the wicked man all the worse. He did it all cherishing the thought that God **has forgotten**, and would **never see** his wickedness against the poor and helpless.

> i. It is common for men to think that **God has forgotten** their sins simply because it seems, to those men, that they were committed a long time ago. "Is it not a senseless thing to be careless of sins committed long ago? The old sins forgotten by men, stick fast in an infinite understanding. Time cannot raze out that which hath been known from eternity." (Stephen Charnock, cited in Spurgeon)

> ii. We can fairly say that this added *blasphemy against God* to the wicked man's many sins against mankind. We can imagine the psalmist's blood boiling as he thought about this smiling, self-assured sinner and the pleasure he took in his sin.

> iii. We also notice a great difference between the *pain* in the believer who fears **God has forgotten** (as in Psalm 10:1), and the sinner who vainly hopes and takes false comfort in the idea that **God has forgotten**.

B. A prayer to God for protection and vindication.

1. (12-13) A call upon God to take action.

Arise, O LORD!
O God, lift up Your hand!
Do not forget the humble.
Why do the wicked renounce God?
He has said in his heart,
"You will not require *an account.*"

a. **Arise, O LORD**: The psalmist simply called upon God to *take action.* "LORD, this wicked man finds comfort in the idea that You won't do anything against him. **Arise, O LORD; lift up Your hand** against this wicked man!"

i. It is not stated in this untitled psalm, but it is often assumed that David wrote this psalm, because it is arranged in the midst of several psalms that are specifically attributed to David (Psalms 3-9; 11-32). Yet we know David to be a man of valiant action and warrior spirit, not the kind to stand passively back while the wicked murdered and terrorized the weak and helpless. The only exception to this would be if the wicked man were in a place of God-appointed authority, such as Saul was in Israel. Perhaps this psalm was a cry of David for *God* to stop Saul, because David knew that it was not his place to lift his hand against the LORD's anointed.

b. **Why do the wicked renounce God?** The psalmist answered his own question in the next lines. The **wicked renounce God** because they say in their **heart** that God **will not require an account**.

i. "The long-suffering of God, instead of leading such a one to repentance, only hardens him in his iniquity. Because sentence against an evil work is not executed speedily, he thinks it will not be executed at all." (Horne)

ii. This observation has an inherent prayer: "LORD, **require an account** from this wicked man who renounces You!"

2. (14-15) Asking for God's help in view of His kindness to the helpless.

But You have seen, for You observe trouble and grief,
To repay *it* by Your hand.
The helpless commits himself to You;
You are the helper of the fatherless.
Break the arm of the wicked and the evil *man;*
Seek out his wickedness *until* You find none.

a. **But You have seen, for You observe trouble and grief**: Upon further reflection, the psalmist recognized that God *has* indeed seen, because He sees and cares about the **trouble and grief** of the poor and helpless.

b. **To repay it by Your hand**: Here is the confidence of the psalmist in God's judgments. He most certainly *will* **repay** the wicked for their sins. God will indeed answer the **helpless** and be the **helper of the fatherless**.

c. **Break the arm of the wicked and the evil man**: The psalmist called upon God to help the weak by shattering the **wicked and the evil man**, and to thoroughly **seek out his wickedness until You find none**.

3. (16-18) Confidence in God's judgments.

The Lord is King forever and ever;
The nations have perished out of His land.
Lord, You have heard the desire of the humble;
You will prepare their heart;
You will cause Your ear to hear,
To do justice to the fatherless and the oppressed,
That the man of the earth may oppress no more.

a. **The Lord is King forever and ever**: The psalmist began with almost despair in his *times of trouble*; he ends with calm confidence in the reign of the Lord as an eternal **King**.

i. God had long been declared the King of Israel (Exodus 15:18), even when His people rejected His rule (1 Samuel 8:7-9). If David wrote this psalm (especially during a time of persecution from Saul), the words **the Lord is King forever and ever** would have special meaning, recognizing the reign of God even over the troubled and dysfunctional reign of Saul.

b. **The nations have perished out of His land**: Remembering the past victories of God against the cruel enemies of His people (in this case, the Canaanites who occupied **His land**) gave the psalmist greater confidence regarding the present help of the Lord.

i. "They are all either cut off or *converted*. This may refer to the *Canaanites*. What a mercy that we can say this of our own country! Once it was entirely heathen; now not one heathen family in the whole land." (Adam Clarke, speaking of his native England)

c. **You have heard the desire of the humble...You will prepare their heart...You will cause Your ear to hear**: This continues to express the calm confidence of the psalmist. God will not abandon the poor and needy, but will help and bless them.

i. "David does not say, 'Thou hast heard the *prayer* of the humble;' he means that, but he also means a great deal more. Sometimes, we have desires that we cannot express; they are too big, too deep; we cannot clothe them in language. At other times, we have desires which we dare not express; we feel too bowed down, we see too much of our own undesert to be able to venture near the throne of God to utter our desires; but the Lord hears the desire when we cannot or dare not turn it into the actual form of a prayer." (Spurgeon)

ii. With a wonderful phrase – **You will prepare their heart** – the psalmist reminds us that the *spiritual preparation of the heart* is a great gift, an answer to prayer, and a mark of God's blessing. "Surely none but the Lord can prepare a heart for prayer. One old writer says it is far harder work to raise the big bell into the steeple than to ring it afterwards. This witness is true. When the bell is well hung you can ring it readily enough; but in that uplifting of the heart lies the work and the labor." (Spurgeon)

iii. "The 'humble' and lowly, whatever they may suffer in the world, are the favourites of Jehovah: that he attends to the very 'desires' of their hearts: that such hearts 'prepared' to prayer, are so many instruments strung and tuned by the hand of heaven." (Horne)

iv. "Where God giveth a praying heart it is sure that he will show a pitying heart. If he prepare the heart, he will also bend his ear." (Trapp)

v. "See the economy of the grace of God: 1. God *prepares* the *heart*; 2. *Suggests the prayer*; 3. *Hears* what is prayed; 4. *Answers* the petition. He who has got a cry in his heart after God, may rest assured that that cry proceeded from a Divine preparation, and that an answer will soon arrive. No man ever had a cry in his heart after salvation, but from God. He who continues to cry shall infallibly be heard." (Clarke)

d. **To do justice...that the man of the earth may oppress no more**: The psalmist ends with assurance of God's **justice** applied to the wicked. What began with a sense of despair in *times of trouble* has ended with calm confidence in God's **justice** and victory.

i. **The man of the earth**: "Earthly and mortal men, who are made of the dust, and must return to it, such as the oppressors of the people are." (Poole)

ii. "Under the rule of God, the day must come when, 'That man who is of the earth may be terrible no more.' These were the concluding words of the song, and they constitute a fitting answer to its opening inquiry." (Morgan)

Psalm 11 – The Answer of Faith to the Advice of Fear

The title tells us both the author and the audience of the psalm: **To the Chief Musician. A Psalm of David.** *Some believe that* **the Chief Musician** *is the Lord GOD Himself, and others suppose him to be a leader of choirs or musicians in David's time, such as Heman the singer or Asaph (1 Chronicles 6:33, 16:5-7, and 25:6). This psalm records well-intentioned, but faithless advice of David's friends when he was a fugitive from King Saul. David lifted his eyes to the LORD to find faith in a time of testing. He knew the safest place to stand was in radical trust in God.*

A. The advice of fear.

1. (1) David reacts to the advice to flee.

In the LORD I put my trust;
How can you say to my soul,
"Flee *as* **a bird to your mountain"?**

a. **In the LORD I put my trust**: In the years before he took the throne of Israel, David lived the life of a fugitive. He was constantly hunted by King Saul and lived in constant danger. In such a time, his friends advised him, **"Flee as a bird to your mountain."** His friends meant well, but David knew it was the wrong thing to do.

b. **How can you say to my soul, "Flee as a bird to your mountain?"**: This expressed the near outrage in David's response to his friends. No matter how well-intentioned his friends were, they gave him the advice of fear. The advice of fear couldn't stand with the position of **trust** David had in the **LORD**.

i. "He would rather dare the danger than exhibit a distrust in the Lord his God." (Spurgeon)

2. (2-3) David remembers the words of fear in the mouths of his friends.

69

For look! The wicked bend *their* bow,
They make ready their arrow on the string,
That they may shoot secretly at the upright in heart.
If the foundations are destroyed,
What can the righteous do?

a. **For look! The wicked bend their bow, they make ready their arrow on the string**: In today's language, David's friends would say, "Look! There is a loaded gun to your head, and you have to run!"

b. **For look**: The advice given to David was well-meant, but ungodly. It was like when Peter advised Jesus to not go the way of the cross (Matthew 16:22-23). Peter meant well, but he was really being used by the devil.

i. We must always be careful with the advice we give to others. First, we must always mind our own business and not be busybodies (1 Thessalonians 4:11, 1 Timothy 5:13). Second, we can be too confident in our own perception of a situation. Job's friend confidently said, *"I will tell you, hear me; what I have seen I will declare"* (Job 15:17), but he was wrong. Our motive is good and right, but the advice is wrong.

c. **That they may shoot secretly at the upright in heart**: Here, David's friends are trying to make him afraid of a secret attack. When we fear the things we can't see, we are really walking in fear!

i. David's friends may have been using an element of manipulation here. They may have reasoned like this: "Look, for his own good, we have to get David out of here. It's justified for us to exaggerate things a little bit to get him to do what is right." But it wasn't justified. Manipulation is never right, even if it is for a good cause.

d. **If the foundations are destroyed, what can the righteous do?** These words in the mouths of David's friends were meant to be a warning. The idea was, "The very foundation of Saul's government is destroyed. What can a righteous one like you do, except flee?"

e. **What can the righteous do?** When David heard these words from his friends, his head probably told him there was something to them. But his heart told him that to heed this advice and to flee would be to compromise.

i. "He will use such plausible logic, that unless we once for all assert our immovable trust in Jehovah, he will make us like the timid bird which flies to the mountain whenever danger presents itself." (Spurgeon)

B. The answer of faith.

1. (4a) David answers by remembering where God is.

The LORD *is* in His holy temple,
The Lord's throne *is* in heaven;

a. **The LORD is in His holy temple**: Probably, David had in mind both the LORD's temple on earth (the tabernacle) and the LORD's temple in heaven. David reminded himself and his friends, "God hasn't gone anywhere. You can go to His temple and meet with Him." He may also have had the thought, "The LORD isn't going anywhere, so I won't either."

i. When the advice of fear comes upon us, we can only arrive at the answer of faith by spending time with the LORD. When we *think* about our problems, the advice of fear often overwhelms us. When we *pray* about our problems, the answer of faith assures our hearts.

ii. When we think of Jesus in the temple of heaven, we remember that He is praying for us. "What plots can men devise which Jesus will not discover? Satan has doubtless desired to have us, that he may sift us as wheat, but Jesus is in the temple praying for us, and how can our faith fail?" (Spurgeon)

b. **The LORD's throne is in heaven**: This was the source of David's confidence. It was not foolhardiness or self-reliance. Instead, David had confidence in a holy, all-powerful, all-knowing God.

i. David was asked, *What can the righteous do?* David answered with another question: "What *can't* the righteous do when the LORD God is still on His throne?"

ii. The problems were indeed bad. "But what were all these things to a man whose trust was in God alone?" (Spurgeon)

2. (4b-5) David answers by remembering what God sees.

His eyes behold, His eyelids test the sons of men.
The LORD tests the righteous,
But the wicked and the one who loves violence His soul hates.

a. **His eyes behold**: David didn't need to take the advice of fear, because God saw his situation. David had a greater cause than self-preservation, because he knew that God was looking at him and taking care of him.

b. **The LORD tests the righteous**: Again, David answered the question, *If the foundations are destroyed, what can the righteous do?* David answered, "The righteous can know that the LORD is testing them, and because a loving God is testing them, they can know they will not be pushed too far or forsaken. The righteous can know the LORD is in control."

c. **But the wicked and the one who loves violence His soul hates**: As God sees, He is not a detached observer. He cares; He sees the **wicked** and **hates** them. David is saying, "I don't need to flee to protect myself, because God in heaven is watching me and sees how sinful the conduct of my enemies is."

3. (6) David answers by remembering the destiny of the wicked.

Upon the wicked He will rain coals;
Fire and brimstone and a burning wind
***Shall be* the portion of their cup.**

> a. **Upon the wicked He will rain coals, fire and brimstone and a burning wind**: God will punish the wicked. This gave David confidence in the midst of the advice of fear. After all, if the ungodly persecute the righteous, how much more will the righteous God persecute the ungodly?

> b. **Fire and brimstone**: This gave the image of ultimate, eternal judgment. What did David have to fear from men destined for hell?

> c. **This shall be the portion of their cup**: The image of the **cup** as a container of judgment reminds us of Jesus' prayer in the garden: *O My Father, if it is possible, let this cup pass from Me; nevertheless, not as I will, but as You will* (Matthew 26:39). The cup Jesus dreaded was the cup that contained the wrath of God against sin, wrath that we deserved, but Jesus drank for us.

4. (7) David answers by remembering the love and favor of God.

For the LORD *is* righteous,
He loves righteousness;
His countenance beholds the upright.

> a. **For the LORD is righteous**: This was a comfort and encouragement to David. When we are rebelling against the LORD, His righteousness is no comfort to us. But David knew he was the innocent victim of persecution, and he knew the **righteous** LORD would take up his cause.

> b. **He loves righteousness**: David knew that as he walked righteously, he would *keep* [himself] *in the love of God* (Jude 21). It isn't that we must earn God's love by our personal righteousness; instead, our pursuit and practice of righteousness keeps us flowing in the benefits of God's love.

> > i. God's love extends everywhere. Nothing can separate us from God's love, and He loved us while we were still sinners (Romans 5:8). But we can deny ourselves the benefits of God's love.

> > ii. People who don't keep themselves in the love of God end up living as if they are on the dark side of the moon. The sun is always out there, always shining, but they are never in a position to receive the light or warmth of the sun. They are like the Prodigal Son of Luke 15, who

was always loved by the father, but for a time he did not benefit from that love.

c. **His countenance beholds the upright**: Scholars and translators debate if this means "God's upright people see Him" or "the LORD sees His upright people." Most modern translations think it speaks of God's people seeing Him: *Upright men will see his face* (NIV), *The upright will behold His face* (NASB), *The godly shall see his face* (LB). However, it really doesn't matter, because both are true.

> i. God shines His face on His people. This speaks of "an eye of approbation, and true and tender affection, and watchful and gracious providence; which is oft signified by God's *beholding* or *looking* upon men." (Poole) In fact, the last line of the priestly blessing of Numbers 6:26 is, *The LORD lift up His countenance upon you, And give you peace.*

> ii. God's people will see Him. *I will see Your face in righteousness* (Psalm 17:15). *Blessed are the pure in heart, for they shall see God* (Matthew 5:8). In fact, the desire to behold God is one of the greatest motivations to an upright life and heart.

> iii. All in all, when David considers the greatness of God, the care of God, and the vision of God, it all outweighs the danger. For David, trusting God was the safest move of all. His friends may or may not have meant well, but David would not receive their advice of fear. Instead, he would answer with faith.

Psalm 12 – The Words of Man and the Word of God

The title of this psalm reads, **To the Chief Musician. On an eight-stringed harp. A Psalm of David**. *The title is like many others in this general section of psalms, simply stating the audience, the instrument, and the author of the psalm. In this psalm David complains about the vicious words of his adversaries, and in contrast praises the pure and precious Word of God.*

A. The problem of flattering lips.

1. (1-2) The disappearance of the godly man and his unfortunate replacement.

Help, LORD, for the godly man ceases!
For the faithful disappear from among the sons of men.
They speak idly everyone with his neighbor;
***With* flattering lips *and* a double heart they speak.**

a. **Help, LORD, for the godly man ceases**: The exact circumstances under which David wrote this psalm are unknown, and it could have been during many different periods in his life. David knew what it was like to feel that **the faithful disappear from among the sons of men**.

i. David was a warrior and a fierce soldier, but we see here that he also had to deal with the battles of gossip and the backbiting of idle and deceptive talkers. David knew what it was like to feel all alone in this kind of battle, where it seemed that no one would speak up and defend him. Instead, he took his case to the LORD. We sense that David probably would have preferred to battle with swords and shields than among the gossips and backbiters surrounding him.

b. **With flattering lips and a double heart they speak**: Instead of the **godly man**, David saw around him those who spoke with idle chatter (**they speak idly everyone with his neighbor**), and who were two-faced liars (**flattering lips...a double heart**).

74

i. This psalm may have come from the time in David's life when he was in the court of King Saul, but was a target for the mad jealousy of the king. We can easily imagine a vicious whispering campaign against David among those who wanted to gain favor with the misguided king.

ii. The essence of **flattering lips** is that they *say what people want to hear*. There are many such talkers today, even within the church – those who know the *right* answer for every occasion but speak with no honesty or transparency of heart. They constantly speak what people hope to hear or what is assumed to be proper instead of their true thoughts, feelings, and deeds.

iii. "Daniel says that flattery will be a tool of that wicked world ruler who will arise at the last day (Daniel 11:32)." (Boice)

iv. "'*They speak with a double heart.*' The original is, 'A heart and a heart': one for the church, another for the change; one for Sundays, another for working-days; one for the king, another for the pope. A man without a heart is a wonder, but a man with two hearts is a monster." (Thomas Adams, cited in Spurgeon)

2. (3-5) A plea for God to judge those who speak wickedly.

May the LORD cut off all flattering lips,
***And* the tongue that speaks proud things,**
Who have said,
"With our tongue we will prevail;
Our lips *are* our own;
Who *is* lord over us?"
"For the oppression of the poor, for the sighing of the needy,
Now I will arise," says the LORD;
"I will set *him* in the safety for which he yearns."

a. **May the LORD cut off all flattering lips**: David felt somewhat helpless against these destructive chatterers; he found his refuge in the LORD, to whom he appealed to **cut off...the tongue that speaks proud things**.

i. Benjamin Franklin once wrote, "Since I cannot govern my own tongue, tho' within my own teeth, how can I hope to govern the tongues of others?" David felt this same frustration with the idle and destructive tongues of others.

ii. "Better to have the tongue touched with a live coal from the altar than cut out." (Maclaren)

b. **With our tongue we will prevail...Who is lord over us?** David despised these destructive tongues, not only for what they said, but also for the pride that made them so difficult to stop. It was as if they freely said, "You can never make us stop talking as we please."

i. "*With our tongues we will prevail*; by raising and spreading slanders and evil reports concerning him, whereby both Saul will be highly and implacably enraged against David, and the hearts of the people alienated from him." (Poole)

ii. For the one who professes to be a follower of Jesus Christ, there is only one answer to this question, **Who is lord over us?** Jesus Christ is our Lord, and He owns us body, soul, and spirit. We are bought with a price and are therefore obligated to glorify God in our bodies, including our **lips** and **tongue** (1 Corinthians 6:20).

c. **Now I will arise**: These destructive talkers spoke as they pleased, but they could not stop the LORD God from speaking as *He* pleased. In a wonderful and dramatic way, the LORD announced that He would act on behalf of the **poor** and **needy** victimized by these proud, unstoppable talkers.

i. "Think of God arising in his might. When he ariseth, he shakes terribly the earth; nothing stands before him when he once arises. Poor, sick, needy, sorrowing, sighing child of God, it is you who can bring him into this marvellous state of activity." (Spurgeon)

d. **I will set him in the safety for which he yearns**: David believed that this was God's word *for him*. He was one of the **poor** and **needy** yearning for safety from these destructive critics and talkers.

B. The words of God and the wickedness of men.

1. (6-7) The pure words of the LORD.

The words of the LORD are pure words,
Like silver tried in a furnace of earth,
Purified seven times.
You shall keep them, O LORD,
You shall preserve them from this generation forever.

a. **The words of the LORD are pure words**: In contrast to the idle, two-faced, lying, and proud lips of David's adversaries, God's words are **pure**, as if they were fine **silver…purified seven times**.

i. "What a contrast between the vain words of man, and the pure words of Jehovah. Man's words are yea and nay, but the Lord's promises are yea and amen." (Spurgeon)

ii. "The words of Jehovah are holy in his precepts, just in his laws, gracious in his promises, significant in his institutions, true in his narrations, and infallible in his predictions. What are thousands of gold and silver compared to the treasures of the sacred page!" (Horne)

iii. This means that the word of God can be *trusted* in every sense. It is good, pure, and tested thoroughly. We can trust that God has tested His own word; but it has also been tested by students, scholars, critics, and doubters through the centuries – and the *Word of God still stands.* It is like a mighty anvil that has worn out countless hammers that have pounded upon it.

iv. "The Bible has passed through the furnace of persecution, literary criticism, philosophic doubt, and scientific discovery, and has lost nothing but those human interpretations which clung to it as alloy to precious ore. The experience of saints has tried it in every conceivable manner, but not a single doctrine or promise has been consumed in the most excessive heat." (Spurgeon)

v. "After more than two centuries of facing the heaviest guns that could be brought to bear, the Bible has survived – and is perhaps the better for the siege. Even on the critics' own terms – historical fact – the Scriptures seem more acceptable now than when the rationalists began the attack." (Time Magazine, cited in Boice)

vi. "Do sinners talk of vanity? Let saints then speak of Jesus and his gospel. Do they talk impure words? Then let the faithful use the pure words of God, which like silver, the more used, the more melted in the fire, the more precious will they be." (Robert Hawker, cited in Spurgeon)

vii. "As silver enriches its owner, so does the Word of God enrich its lovers. Nothing so strengthens the intellect, clears the judgment, enlarges the views, purifies the taste, quickens the imagination, and educates the whole man." (Meyer)

b. **You shall keep them, O LORD, You shall preserve them**: This was David's declaration of confidence in God's ability to **preserve** His own words. He did not only give His word to mankind; His providential hand has protected the existence and integrity of His word through the centuries.

i. There are some manuscripts and Bible translations that render this *You shall keep us, O LORD, You shall preserve us.* Yet, according to VanGemeren, there is legitimate manuscript support for the rendering **You shall keep them...You shall preserve them**. We can take it as true that God will **keep** and **preserve** both His Word and His people.

ii. "The psalmist breaks out into praise of the purity of His words, and declares that Jehovah will 'keep them,' and 'preserve them.' The 'them' refers to the words. There is no promise made of widespread revival or renewal. It is the salvation of a remnant and the preservation of His own words which Jehovah promises." (Morgan)

iii. God *has* kept and *will* **keep** and **preserve** His Word. "The French atheist Voltaire…once said, 'In twenty years Christianity will be no more. My single hand shall destroy the edifice it took twelve apostles to rear.' He wrote that in fifty years no one would remember Christianity. But in the year he wrote that, the British Museum paid the Russian government five hundred thousand dollars for a Bible manuscript while one of Voltaire's books was selling in the London book stalls for just eight cents." (Boice)

iv. "Give up no line of God's revelation…. Brethren, we cannot endure this shifty theology. May God send us a race of men who have backbones! Men who believe something, and would die for what they believe. This Book deserves the sacrifice of our all for the maintenance of every line of it." (Spurgeon)

2. (8) The way of the wicked.

The wicked prowl on every side,
When vileness is exalted among the sons of men.

a. **The wicked prowl on every side**: David knew that the existence and exaltation of God's pure word would not *eliminate* the **wicked**. They would still exist and **prowl on every side** as they could, but never with the assurance of final victory.

i. "Here we return to the fount of bitterness, which first made the Psalmist run to the wells of salvation, namely, the prevalence of wickedness." (Spurgeon)

b. **When vileness is exalted among the sons of men**: We might feel that this psalm ends on a sad, depressing note. Yet David was utterly realistic in his outlook. He knew that even with the precious and pure word of God available to men, many of the **sons of men** would still prefer that **vileness is exalted**.

i. "If 'vileness is set on high among the sons of men,' it is because the sons of men prefer it to the stern purity of goodness. A corrupt people will crown corrupt men and put them aloft." (Maclaren)

ii. We might say that David almost left it as a challenge. Let the **sons of men** exalt **vileness**; he would exalt the pure and precious Word of God. Eventually all would see the winner of this contest. Let these wicked men do their worst – God helping him, David would do his best and see the victory of the LORD.

Psalm 13 – Enlighten My Eyes

The title tells us both the author and the audience of the psalm: **To the Chief Musician. A Psalm of David.** *Some believe that* **the Chief Musician** *is the Lord GOD Himself, and others suppose him to be a leader of choirs or musicians in David's time, such as Heman the singer or Asaph (1 Chronicles 6:33, 16:5-7, and 25:6). This is a psalm of transition. Starting in discouragement and despair, David finishes in a place of trust, joy, and encouragement.*

A. David's despair.

1. (1) David's despair with the LORD.

How long, O LORD?
Will You forget me forever?
How long will You hide Your face from me?

> a. **How long, O LORD?** It seems that every child of God has asked this question at one time or another, and that every follower of God has felt neglected by God – or at least that he has waited a long time for God to do what needs to be done.

> > i. "If the reader has never yet found occasion to use the language of this brief ode, he will do so ere long, if he be a man after the Lord's own heart." (Spurgeon)

> > ii. **How long?** "This question is repeated no less than four times. It betokens very intense desire for deliverance, and great anguish of heart.... It is not easy to prevent desire from degenerating into impatience. O for grace that, while we wait on God, we may be kept from indulging a murmuring spirit!" (Spurgeon)

> > iii. **How long** is the critical question. Often we faint under the simple *length* of our trials. We feel we could endure almost anything if we knew when it would come to an end; yet sometimes we are tried under problems that make us cry out, "**How long?**"

iv. "Whenever you look into David's Psalms, you may somewhere or another see yourselves. You never get into a corner but you find David in that corner. I think that I was never so low that I could not find that David was lower; and I never climbed so high that I could not find that David was up above me, ready to sing his song upon his stringed instrument, even as I could sing mine." (Spurgeon)

b. **Will You forget me forever? How long will You hide Your face from me?** The pain in David's heart came from a sense that God had forgotten him and that God was distancing Himself from him. No doubt, David had faced worse circumstances but had faced them more bravely when he had sensed the presence of God with him. Yet now, feeling distant from God, it did not take much to send David into despair.

i. God will never forget us: *But Zion said, "The LORD has forsaken me, and my Lord has forgotten me." Can a woman forget her nursing child, and not have compassion on the son of her womb? Surely they may forget, yet I will not forget you. See, I have inscribed you on the palms of My hands.* (Isaiah 49:14-16)

ii. "The final absence of God is hell itself. 'Depart from me, ye cursed,' is worse than 'into everlasting fire.' To be punished from the presence of the Lord is the hell of hells, 2 Thessalonians 1:9." (Trapp)

c. **Forget.... Hide Your face**: Of course, God did not **forget** David. God did not **hide** His **face from** David – but David felt like it. When we have such strong feelings, then the feelings create their own reality. David *felt* God had forgotten him, and *felt* God was hiding. So, in a sense, it was true for David – but true according to *feelings*, not according to *fact*.

i. There is a balance in life when it comes to feelings. Some people *ignore* feelings and think that feelings should have nothing to do with our relationship with God. This is an extreme viewpoint, because God has given us feelings as an expression of His image in us. We can feel anger, love, care, sorrow, and many other feelings, because God feels those feelings. In this sense, feelings are a gift from God and a sign that we are made in His image.

ii. On the other side, some live their lives *ruled* by feelings. They believe whatever reality their feelings present them. The problem with this is that though we have feelings because we are made in the image of God, our feelings are affected by our fallenness. We can't *trust* our feelings because of this. In this sense, it was all right for David to feel these feelings, and good to take them to God, but he should never accept the reality of feelings as "real" reality.

iii. "This is a lesson of profound value. If the heart be overburdened and Jehovah seems to hide His face, let the story of woe be told to Him. It is a holy exercise. Men may not understand it. They may even charge us with failing faith." (Morgan)

2. (2) David's despair with himself and others.

How long shall I take counsel in my soul,
Having **sorrow in my heart daily?**
How long will my enemy be exalted over me?

a. **How long shall I take counsel in my soul**: No wonder David was discouraged! Taking counsel in his own soul had led him to **sorrow in** his **heart daily**. When I am discouraged and depressed, the answer is not in looking inside myself, but in looking to the LORD.

i. Many times when I am confronted with problems, I find this to be true: The more I *think* about the problems, the more depressed I get. But when I *pray* about the problems, a glorious sense of release and peace comes.

ii. Thinking about our troubles is hard work. Trouble is often like a pill God wants us to just swallow, but we make it worse by keeping it in our mouths and chewing it.

iii. Spurgeon proposed a sermon on the phrase, "**How long should I take counsel in my soul, having sorrow in my heart daily?**" He suggested that the sermon would have these points: "*Self-torture*, its cause, curse, crime, and cure."

b. **How long will my enemy be exalted over me?** This mentions the third way that David was depressed. David didn't want to lose in any area he was attacked and see his **enemy...exalted over** him. David was depressed in three ways:

• First, in his relationship with God.

• Second, within himself.

• Third, in regard to his enemies.

i. This was not a purely selfish desire. David knew he was the LORD's man, with a special calling to lead God's people. In this sense, David's enemies were the LORD's enemies, and enemies against the people of God.

ii. David's feeling that God had abandoned him was connected to his sense of depression. Boice helpfully lists several sources of spiritual depression:

- Temperament may incline one to depression.

- Illness can drain the physical strength and lead to depression.

- Exhaustion can also leave one quite open to depression and the feeling of abandonment.

- The let-down after some great effort, fueled by coming down off of an adrenaline high, can often lead to depression.

- Pressure from spiritual and natural enemies can push us toward depression.

B. David's dependent prayer.

1. (3) David prays for his relationship with God.

Consider *and* hear me, O LORD my God;
Enlighten my eyes,
Lest I sleep the *sleep of* death;

a. **Consider and hear me**: We should not think that David meant two different things when he said, "**Consider and hear me**." He used the Hebrew method of repetition to show emphasis. David desperately cried out to God, asking the LORD to **hear** him.

 i. David felt God was not listening before (*Will You forget me forever? How long will You hide Your face from me?* Psalm 13:1). Yet he should continue to cry out because God is honored when we persistently and desperately cry out to Him.

 ii. God often waits until our prayers are desperate before He answers us. The cause of the powerlessness of much of our prayer is lack of desperation; too often we almost pray with the attitude of wanting God to care about things we really don't care too much about.

 iii. Desperate prayer has power not because it in itself persuades a reluctant God. Instead, it demonstrates that our heart cares passionately about the things God cares about, fulfilling Jesus' promise *If you abide in Me and My words abide in you, you will ask what you desire and it shall be done for you* (John 15:7).

b. **Enlighten my eyes**: David had the wisdom to know that though he felt powerful feelings, he wasn't seeing reality. His vision was clouded and dark, so he cried out to God, "**Enlighten my eyes**."

 i. This was a great prayer. We need the light of God to shine upon us and to give us His wisdom and knowledge. No matter what problem we are in, we should cry out with all our heart, "**Enlighten my eyes**."

ii. The Apostle Paul knew the importance of having our eyes enlightened by the Lord. This is what he prayed for Christians: *that the God of our Lord Jesus Christ, the Father of glory, may give to you the spirit of wisdom and revelation in the knowledge of Him,* **the eyes of your understanding being enlightened***; that you may know what is the hope of His calling, what are the riches of the glory of His inheritance in the saints, and what is the exceeding greatness of His power toward us who believe, according to the working of His mighty power* (Ephesians 1:17-19).

c. **Lest I sleep the sleep of death**: If we are not enlightened by God, we will surely fall asleep. And often, spiritual **sleep** leads to spiritual **death**.

i. Paul may have had this verse in mind when he wrote of our need for the light of Jesus: *Awake, you who sleep, arise from the dead, and Christ will give you light* (Ephesians 5:14).

2. (4) David prays for victory over his enemies.

Lest my enemy say, "I have prevailed against him";
***Lest* those who trouble me rejoice when I am moved.**

a. **Lest my enemy say**: David knew one of the worst parts about losing to anyone is hearing him boast after he has defeated you. He did not want his **enemy** to **rejoice** when he was brought low.

b. **Lest those who trouble me rejoice when I am moved**: Knowing how his enemies would gloat over his fall, David was even more determined to not be **moved**.

i. "Awareness of God and the enemy is virtually the hallmark of every psalm of David; the positive and negative charges which produced the driving force of his best years." (Kidner)

C. David's declaration.

1. (5a) David's trust in God's mercy.

But I have trusted in Your mercy;

a. **I have trusted**: David, after his prayer, came to a place of confidence and trust. **I have trusted** speaks in the past tense; it is as if David remembered that he really did trust God, and he cleared away the fog from his sleepy eyes as God enlightened his eyes.

b. **In Your mercy**: At this place of discouragement, David could not trust in God's justice, or in God's law, or in God's holiness. Those things might condemn him because his feelings had made him not see clearly. But he could always trust in God's **mercy**. When you can't trust anything else, trust in God's mercy.

i. "He begins his prayer as if he thought God would never give him a kind look more.... But by the time he had exercised himself a little in duty, his distemper wears off, the mists scatter, and his faith breaks out as the sun in its strength." (William Gurnall, cited in Spurgeon)

2. (5b-6a) David's joy in the LORD and His salvation.

My heart shall rejoice in Your salvation.
I will sing to the LORD,

a. **My heart shall rejoice**: Now, David was still in the realm of feelings (**rejoice**). But he directed his feelings instead of having his feelings direct him (**shall rejoice**). He told his heart to get busy rejoicing!

b. **In Your salvation**: This is what David rejoiced in. David, if he could rejoice in nothing else, could rejoice in the salvation God gave him. This is solid ground for any believer. If you are saved, you can **rejoice**, and tell your heart to start rejoicing.

c. **I will sing to the LORD**: David knew rejoicing is wonderfully expressed in singing. So, he would **sing to the LORD**. Singing to the LORD would both *express* his joy and *increase* his joy.

i. "There is not half enough singing in the world...I remember a servant who used to sing while she was at the wash-tub. Her mistress said to her, 'Why, Jane, how is it that you are always singing?' She said, 'It keeps the bad thoughts away.'" (Spurgeon)

ii. David moved from being depressed and feeling abandoned by God, to singing joy. "The fact that we feel abandoned itself means that we really know God is there. To be abandoned you need somebody to be abandoned by. Because we are Christians and have been taught by God in the Scriptures, we know that God still loves us and will be faithful to us, regardless of our feelings." (Boice)

3. (6b) With enlightened eyes, David sees God's goodness.

Because He has dealt bountifully with me.

a. **Because He has dealt bountifully with me**: As David thought about it, he had good reason to rejoice and sing, because God had been good to him. If we will only think about it, every person on this earth has reason to rejoice, because in some way God has been good to everyone.

b. **He has dealt bountifully with me**: What a transition! In the beginning of the psalm, David was overwhelmed by his feelings and believed that God forgot him and was hiding from him. He had trouble with God, with himself, and with others. Yet now he sees how God had **dealt bountifully**

with him. Because his eyes were enlightened, David could now see God's goodness, and what a change in perspective that was!

i. Before God can enlighten our eyes, we must agree that we don't see everything. We need to realize that our feelings are not giving us full and accurate information. But if we will do this, and cry out to the LORD, He will enlighten our eyes and bring us from a place of despair to a place of trust, joy, and confidence!

ii. "[In times of trouble, the Lord] would with one Scripture or another, strengthen me against all; insomuch that I have often said, *Were it lawful, I could pray for greater trouble, for the greater comfort's sake.*" (John Bunyan, cited in Spurgeon)

Psalm 14 – Fallen Man and a Faithful God

This psalm is simply titled **To the Chief Musician. A Psalm of David.** *With this title, we have the author (***David***) and the intended audience (***the Chief Musician***), whom we can take to represent more than a choir leader such as Asaph; it looks to the ultimate Musician of the universe, God Himself. "The thought of the whole psalm is the safety of godliness, and the peril of ungodliness." (G. Campbell Morgan)*

A. The sad condition of the man who rejects God.

1. (1) David's analysis of the God-rejecting man.

The fool has said in his heart,
"*There is* no God."
They are corrupt,
They have done abominable works,
There is none who does good.

> a. **The fool has said in his heart, "There is no God"**: David looked at those who denied the existence of God and came to the conclusion that they are *fools*. The idea behind this ancient Hebrew word translated **fool** is more *moral* than *intellectual*. David did not have in mind those not smart enough to figure God out (no one is that smart); he had in mind those who simply reject God.

> > i. From the italics in the New King James Version we can see that what the fool actually says is, "**No God.**" "That is, 'No God for me.' So his is a practical as well as theoretical atheism. Not only does he not believe in God, he also acts on his conviction." (Boice)

> > ii. David says this because of the plain evidence that there is a God: evidence in both *creation* and *human conscience* that Paul described in Romans 1. The fact that some men insist on denying the existence of God does not erase God from the universe; it instead speaks to their

86

own standing as *fools*. As Paul wrote in Romans 1:22, *Professing to be wise, they became fools.*

iii. "The Hebrew word for *fool* in this psalm is *nabal,* a word which implies an aggressive perversity, epitomized in the Nabal of 1 Samuel 25:25." (Kidner)

iv. The God-denying man is a **fool** because:

- He denies what is plainly evident.
- He believes in tremendous effect with no cause.
- He denies a moral authority in the universe.
- He believes only what can be proven by the scientific method.
- He takes a dramatic, losing chance on his supposition that there is no God.
- He refuses to be persuaded by the many powerful arguments for the existence of God.

v. There are many powerful arguments for the existence of God; among them are these:

- *The Cosmological Argument*: The existence of the universe means there must be a creator God.
- *The Teleological Argument*: The existence of design in the universe means there must be a designer God.
- *The Anthropological Argument*: The unique nature and character of humanity means there must be a relational God.
- *The Moral Argument*: The existence of morality means there must be a governing God.

vi. "Which is cause, and which is effect? Does atheism result from folly, or folly from atheism? It would be perfectly correct to say that each is cause and each is effect." (Morgan)

b. **The fool has said in his heart**: David not only found *what* the fool said to be significant; *where* he said it is also important (**in his heart**). The God-denying man David has in mind is not merely troubled by intellectual objections to the existence of God; **in his heart** he wishes God away, typically for fundamentally moral reasons.

i. John 3:20 explains it this way: *For everyone practicing evil hates the light and does not come to the light, lest his deeds should be exposed.*

ii. This means that the man David had in mind is not an atheist for primarily intellectual reasons. "Honest intellectual agnosticism does not necessarily produce immorality; dishonest emotional atheism always does." (Morgan)

iii. When we speak with one who denies God, we should not only – or even primarily – speak to his head, but also to his **heart**. "Let the preacher aim at the heart, and preach the all-conquering love of Jesus, and he will by God's grace win more doubters to the faith of the gospel than any hundred of the best reasoners who only direct their arguments to the head." (Spurgeon)

iv. The phrasing of **said in his heart** also reminds us that it is possible for one to *say in his mind* that there is a God, yet deny it in his **heart** and life. One may believe in God in theory, yet be a *practical atheist* in the way he lives.

v. 1 Samuel 27:1 tells us what David **said in his heart** on one occasion: *Now I shall perish someday by the hand of Saul. There is nothing better for me than that I should speedily escape to the land of the Philistines; and Saul will despair of me, to seek me anymore in any part of Israel. So I shall escape out of his hand.* Was this not David, in some sense, also denying God and speaking as a **fool**?

vi. "Practical denial or neglect of His working in the world, rather than a creed of negation, is in the psalmist's mind. In effect, we say that there is no God when we shut Him up in a far-off heaven, and never think of Him as concerned in our affairs. To strip Him of His justice and rob Him of His control is the part of a fool. For the Biblical conception of folly is moral perversity rather than intellectual feebleness, and whoever is morally and religiously wrong cannot be in reality intellectually right." (Maclaren)

c. **They are corrupt, they have done abominable works**: David here considers the *result* of denying God. It leads men into *corruption* and **abominable works**. This isn't to say that every atheist lives a dissolute life and every God-believer lives a good life; yet there is a marked difference in moral behavior between those who take God seriously and those who do not.

d. **There is none who does good**: As David considered the sin of the God-denier, he looked out over the landscape of humanity and concluded that **there is none who does good**. He did not mean that there is no human good in this world, but that fallen man is so fallen that he does not by instinct do **good**, and even the **good** he may do is tinged with evil.

- We are born with both the will and the capacity to do evil; no one has to teach a child to do bad things.

- The path of least resistance usually leads us to do bad, not to do good.

- It is often easier to encourage others to do bad things, instead of good things.

- Many of our good deeds are tinged with selfish, bad motives.

    i. "This is no exaggeration, since every sin implies the effrontery of supposedly knowing better than God, and the corruption of loving evil more than good." (Kidner)

2. (2-3) Heaven's analysis of fallen humanity.

The LORD looks down from heaven upon the children of men,
To see if there are any who understand, who seek God.
They have all turned aside,
They have together become corrupt;
***There is* none who does good,**
No, not one.

a. **The LORD looks down from heaven upon the children of men**: While man may wish to forget about God, God never forgets about man. He is always observing man, looking **down from heaven upon the children of men**.

    i. In man's rejection of God, there is often the wish that God would *just leave us alone*. This is an unwise wish, because all human life depends upon God (Acts 17:28; Matthew 5:45). This is an *impossible* wish, because God has rights of a creator over His creation.

    ii. "The words remind us of God descending from heaven to observe the folly of those building the tower of Babel (Genesis 11:5) or looking down upon the wickedness of the race prior to his judgment by the flood." (Kidner)

b. **To see if there are any who understand, who seek God**: When God does look down from heaven, one thing He looks for is if there is any *understanding* or *seeking* among humanity.

    i. God looks for this not primarily as an *intellectual* judgment; He doesn't wonder if there are any smart enough to figure Him out. He looks for this more as a *moral* and *spiritual* judgment: if there are men who **understand** His heart and plan, and who **seek** Him for righteousness sake.

    ii. We deceive ourselves into thinking that man, on his own, really does **seek God**. Don't all the religions and rituals and practices from the beginning of time demonstrate that man does indeed **seek God**?

Not at all. If man initiates the search then he doesn't seek the true God, the God of the Bible. Instead he seeks an idol that he makes himself.

iii. "You have gone through this form of worship, but you have not sought after God. I am sick of this empty religiousness. We see it everywhere; it is not communion with God, it is not getting to God; indeed, God is not in it at all." (Spurgeon, from a sermon on Romans 3)

c. **They have all turned aside, they have together become corrupt**: When God looks, this is what He finds. He finds that man has **turned** away from God and has therefore **become corrupt**.

i. Poole on **turned aside**: "Or, *are grown sour*, as this word signifies."

ii. "The Hebrews have the same word for sin and a dead carcase; and again the same word for sin and stench." (Trapp)

d. **There is none who does good, no, not one**: When God finds **none who does good**, it is because there *are* none. It isn't as if there were some and God couldn't see them. David here observes and remembers that man is truly, profoundly, deeply *fallen*.

i. David's use of "**there is none who does good**" suddenly broadens the scope beyond the atheist to include *us*. "'After all, we are not atheists!' we might say. But now, as we are let in on God's perspective, we see that we are too included. In other words, the outspoken atheist of verse 1 is only one example of mankind in general." (Kidner)

ii. "What a picture of our race is this! Save only where grace reigns, there is none that doeth good; humanity, fallen and debased, is a desert without an oasis, a night without a star, a dunghill without a jewel, a hell without a bottom." (Spurgeon)

B. God's defense of His righteous people.

1. (4-6) God defends the **generation of the righteous**.

Have all the workers of iniquity no knowledge,
Who eat up my people *as* they eat bread,
And do not call on the Lord?
There they are in great fear,
For God *is* with the generation of the righteous.
You shame the counsel of the poor,
But the Lord is his refuge.

a. **Have all the workers of iniquity no knowledge**: David first considered the profound fallenness of man; now he deals with the fate of God's people in such a fallen world. God's people might seem like the weak fools, but David understood that it is **the workers of iniquity** who have **no knowledge**.

> i. "The question has almost a tone of surprise, as if even Omniscience found…wonder in men's mysterious love of evil." (Maclaren)

b. **Who eat up my people as they eat bread**: It *looks* like the **workers of iniquity** are strong and have the upper hand. David wondered if the people of God are abandoned to the fools and the corrupt of this world, to those who **do not call on the LORD**.

> i. "*As they eat bread*, i.e. with as little regret or remorse, and with as much greediness, and delight, and constancy too, as they use to eat their meat." (Poole)

> ii. **And do not call on the LORD**: "Practical atheism is, of course, prayerless." (Maclaren)

c. **There they are in great fear, for God is with the generation of the righteous**: After asking the question, David now answers it with great wisdom. The **workers of iniquity** seem strong and confident, but they are actually **in great fear**, because they can't erase the consciousness that **God is with the generation of the righteous**.

> i. "A panic terror seized them: 'they feared a fear,' as the Hebrew puts it; an undefinable, horrible, mysterious dread crept over them. The most hardened of men have their periods when conscience casts them into a cold sweat of alarm." (Spurgeon)

> ii. As strong as they may wish to deny it, they live under the cloud of knowing that *they are battling against God*, and can therefore never win.

d. **You shame the counsel of the poor, but the LORD is his refuge**: David here announces it to the **workers of iniquity** previously mentioned – that they may work against the **poor**, but God has a refuge for them that cannot be breached. They are fighting against God and will never succeed.

> i. Spurgeon considered the ways that the **poor** takes **counsel**.

> > • He takes counsel with his own weakness and sees that he must depend upon God.

> > • He takes counsel with his observations and sees the end of the wicked.

> > • He takes counsel with the Bible and trusts it to be the Word of God.

- He takes counsel with his own experience and sees that God answers prayer.

ii. Spurgeon used this verse to consider the ways that Christians should stand strong though they are shamed and mocked by the **workers of iniquity**. "You young men in the great firms of London, you working men that work in the factories – you are sneered at. Let them sneer. If they can sneer you out of your religion, you have not got any worth having. Remember you can be laughed into hell, but you can never be laughed out of it." (Spurgeon)

iii. "'Oh! but they will point at you.' Cannot you bear to be pointed at? 'But they will chaff you.' Chaff – let them chaff you. Can that hurt a man that is a man? If you are a molluscous creature that has no backbone, you may be afraid of jokes, and jeers, and jests; but if God has made you upright, stand upright and be a man." (Spurgeon)

2. (7) Longing for the LORD's salvation.

Oh, that the salvation of Israel *would come* out of Zion!
When the LORD brings back the captivity of His people,
Let Jacob rejoice *and* Israel be glad.

a. **Oh, that the salvation of Israel would come out of Zion**: David *knew* that the LORD was a refuge for His people and that the workers of iniquity would never win. Yet that was hard to see at the present time, so David expressed his great longing that God would bring the victory and deliverance He had promised to His people.

b. **When the LORD brings back the captivity of His people**: This was not the Babylonian Captivity, many generations after David's time. Here **captivity** is used in a general sense, speaking of any time or situation where God's people are oppressed and bound.

i. "We take that phrase 'turns the captivity' in the sense in which it admittedly bears in Job 42:10 and Ezekiel 16:53, namely that of deliverance from misfortune." (Maclaren)

c. **Let Jacob rejoice and Israel be glad**: David anticipates the coming deliverance, and calls the people of God to be joyful in consideration of it.

Psalm 15 – *The Character of the One God Receives*

This psalm is simply titled **A Psalm of David**. *In it, David meditates over the character of the man received into the presence of God. We have no precise occasion for this psalm, but it may well have been on the bringing of the ark of the covenant into Jerusalem (2 Samuel 6). This was a time when David was very much concerned with the questions asked and answered in this psalm.*

A. The question presented: Who can come before God?

1. (1a) Who can come to the tabernacle of God?

LORD, who may abide in Your tabernacle?

> a. **LORD, who may abide in Your tabernacle?** In one sense, David's question here is figurative. Though he, like the sons of Korah, may have wished to live in the house of God (Psalm 84:2-4; 84:10), it was impossible for him because David was not a priest.

> > i. The word translated **abide** can be better thought of as *sojourn*; it describes a visit, receiving the hospitality of a tent-dwelling host. This opening is understood in light of the customs of hospitality in the ancient Near East.

> > ii. "In the gracious hospitality of the antique world, a guest was sheltered from all harm; his person was inviolable, his wants all met. So the guest of Jehovah is safe, can claim asylum from every foe and share in all the bountiful provision of His abode." (Maclaren)

> b. **Abide in Your tabernacle:** The **tabernacle** of God was the great tent of meeting that God told Moses and Israel to build for Him during the Exodus (Exodus 25-31). This tabernacle survived through several centuries, and at David's time seems to have been at Gibeon (1 Chronicles 16:39-40).

> > i. Since the **tabernacle** was the place where man met with God through the work of the priests and the practice of sacrifice, David's longing to

abide in Your tabernacle was actually a desire to **abide** in the presence of God.

ii. David has in mind the life that lives in the presence of God – who walks in close fellowship with God because the heart, the mind, and the life are all in step with the heart, mind, and life of God.

2. (1b) Who can come to the hill of God's temple?

Who may dwell in Your holy hill?

a. **Who may dwell in Your holy hill?** In one sense, David here simply uses the Hebrew technique of repetition to ask the same question as in the first part of the verse.

i. The word **dwell** here has a more permanent sense than the word *abide* in the previous line. It is as if David wrote, "Who may be received as a guest into God's tent, enjoying all the protections of His hospitality? Who may live as a citizen in His holy hill?"

b. **Your holy hill**: Yet in another sense, David asked a second, more intense question. At this time, the **tabernacle** of God was at Gibeon (1 Chronicles 16:39 and 21:29). Depending upon when David wrote this psalm, it may very well be that the *ark of the covenant* was in Jerusalem (2 Samuel 6:17) and even at the **holy hill** of Moriah, where God had told David to build the temple (2 Samuel 24:18-21; 1 Chronicles 21:28-22:5, 2 Chronicles 3:1).

i. Since the tabernacle was not at God's **holy hill** in David's time (though the ark of the covenant was), David has two different – yet similar – places in mind.

B. The character of the one who can come before God.

1. (2-3) His character among his friends and neighbors.

He who walks uprightly,
And works righteousness,
And speaks the truth in his heart;
He *who* does not backbite with his tongue,
Nor does evil to his neighbor,
Nor does he take up a reproach against his friend;

a. **He who walks uprightly**: In describing the character of the man who can live in God's presence, David begins with two general descriptions (**walks uprightly, and works righteousness**).

i. In one sense David speaks from an Old Covenant perspective. Though the Old Covenant gave an important place to sacrifice and atonement through blood, it also based blessing and cursing on obedience (Leviticus 26, Deuteronomy 28). The disobedient could not expect blessing, including the blessing of God's presence.

ii. The New Covenant gives us a different ground for blessing and relationship with God: the finished work of Jesus Christ on the cross. Under the New Covenant, faith rather than performance is the basis for blessing.

iii. Nevertheless, David's principle is also accurate under the New Covenant in this sense: the conduct of one's life is a reflection of his fellowship with God. As John wrote: *If we say that we have fellowship with Him, and walk in darkness, we lie and do not practice the truth* (1 John 1:6). We might say that under the Old Covenant a righteous walk was the *precondition* for fellowship with God; under the New Covenant a righteous walk is the *result* of fellowship with God, founded on faith.

iv. "The Christian answer to the psalmist's question goes deeper than his, but is fatally incomplete unless it include his and lay the same stress on duties to men." (Maclaren)

v. "David responds to the question of verse 1 with *representative* answers. This means that the items listed in verse 2-5 are not all-inclusive." (Boice) We also see this from similar passages such as Psalm 24:3-4 and Isaiah 33:14-17, which are not identical in the items listed.

b. **Speaks the truth in his heart; he who does not backbite with his tongue**: David here understood that an upright and righteous life is known by the way someone *speaks*. As Jesus said in Matthew 12:34: *Out of the abundance of the heart the mouth speaks.*

i. "I think more damage has been done to the church and its work by gossip, criticism, and slander than by any other single sin. So I say, don't do it. Bite your tongue before you criticize another Christian." (Boice)

ii. Clarke wrote this about the word **backbite**: "He is a *knave*, who would rob you of your *good name*; he is a *coward*, that would speak of you in your *absence* what he dared not to do in your *presence*; and only an ill-conditioned *dog* would fly at and *bite* your *back* when your *face* was *turned*. All these *three ideas* are included in the term; and they all meet in the *detractor* and *calumniator*. His tongue is the tongue of a *knave*, a *coward*, and a *dog*."

c. **Nor does evil to his neighbor, nor does he take up a reproach against his friend**: David also knew that righteousness is expressed in the *way we treat one another*. We might have thought David would have given greater priority to religious obligations such as sacrifice or purification ceremonies

– which certainly have their place, but are useless without the practical godliness of being good and honest and honorable to neighbors and friends.

i. In these words of David, we also see the deeper work of Jesus Christ, who commanded us to not only love our **neighbor** and **friend**, but also to love our enemies and those who spitefully use us (Matthew 5:44).

2. (4-5a) His character among difficult people.

In whose eyes a vile person is despised,
But he honors those who fear the LORD;
He *who* swears to his own hurt and does not change;
He *who* does not put out his money at usury,
Nor does he take a bribe against the innocent.

a. **In whose eyes a vile person is despised**: David knew that we cannot love good unless we also oppose evil. As it says in Proverbs 8:13: *The fear of the LORD is to hate evil.* Yet this righteous man also **honors those who fear the LORD**; he makes his judgments about men on a godly basis, not from favoritism, flattery, or corruption.

i. "Who rejected the wicked, however rich and honourable; and chose the well inclined, however poor and contemptible in the world." (Horne)

ii. "He doth not admire his person, nor envy his condition, nor court him with flatteries, nor value his company and conversation, nor approve of or comply with his courses; but he thinks meanly of him; he judgeth him a most miserable man, and a great object of pity he abhors his wicked practices, and labours to make such ways contemptible and hateful to all men as far as it lies in his power." (Poole)

iii. **Honors those who fear the LORD**: "We must be as honest in paying respect as in paying our bills. Honour to whom honour is due. To all good men we owe a debt of honour, and we have no right to hand over what is their due to vile persons who happen to be in high places." (Spurgeon)

b. **He who swears to his own hurt and does not change**: The idea behind this is the man keeps his promises even when it is no longer to his advantage to do so.

i. "Joshua and the elders kept their oath to the Gibeonites, though to their inconvenience." (Trapp)

ii. "The law prohibited the substitution of another animal sacrifice for that which had been vowed (Leviticus 27:10); and the psalm uses the same word for 'changeth,' with evident allusion to the prohibition, which must therefore have been known to the psalmist." (Maclaren)

c. **He who does not put out his money at usury, nor does he take a bribe against the innocent**: David described the man who is wants to live a righteous life when it comes to *money*. Many people who would be considered godly in other areas of their lives still have not decided to use their money in a way that honors God and shows love and care to others.

> i. **Usury** "is condemned in the Bible, not in general (*cf.* Deuteronomy 23:20; Matthew 25:27) but in the context of trading on a brother's misfortunes, as a comparison between Deuteronomy 23:19 and Leviticus 25:35-38 makes clear." (Kidner)

> ii. "I am convinced that the concern of this verse is not with receiving interest for money loaned, though it seems to say that, but rather with whom the interest is taken from. In other words, the verse concerns greed eclipsing justice.... The best Old Testament illustration of the abuse verse 5 is talking about is in Nehemiah 5, where all the wealthy were taking advantage of the poor among the exiles when all should have been helping one another." (Boice)

> iii. It is easy – and proper – to look at this list and see where we fall short. Yet seeing our sin in this psalm should drive us to Jesus. We see this whole psalm through the grid of the New Covenant; we see Jesus as having perfectly fulfilled the requirements of the law and the standards of this psalm. We see that by faith His obedience is accounted as ours, and that we are being transformed into His image, thus the fulfillment of this psalm should more and more mark our life.

3. (5b) The blessing that comes from this character.

He who does these *things* shall never be moved.

a. **He who does these things**: David has in mind the basic performance-based system of the Old Covenant. The one who has pleased God with this kind of performance can expect blessing from God.

> i. "To continue in sin is to frustrate the very purpose of God in grace. To do that is to be excluded from His tent, to be shut out from the holy mountain." (Morgan)

b. **Shall never be moved**: In the Old Covenant system, this stability of life is a blessing from God given to the obedient. Under the New Covenant, the promise of stability and security is given to those who abide in faith, such faith being evident through a life lived in general obedience.

i. The idea behind **shall never be moved** is that this righteous one will be a guest in the tent of God forever (as in Psalm 61:4). In New Testament words, we could express it like this: *And the world is passing away, and the lust of it; but he who does the will of God abides forever* (1 John 2:17).

Psalm 16 – The Benefits of a Life-Commitment to God

This psalm is titled **A Michtam of David**. The title **Michtam** is commonly understood as golden; others think it is related to a word meaning to cover. Since the psalms with this title (16, 56-60) are written from times of peril, some think the idea is of covering the lips in the sense of secrecy, as if this were a secret or silent psalm given in a time of crisis. This is a wonderful song relating how David found the secret of contentment and great gladness even in pressing times; it also powerfully predicts Jesus and His work for us.

A. David's confidence in God.

1. (1-3) What David's soul said to the LORD.

Preserve me, O God, for in You I put my trust.
***O my soul,* you have said to the LORD,**
"You *are* my Lord,
My goodness is nothing apart from You."
As for the saints who *are* on the earth,
"They are the excellent ones, in whom is all my delight."

> a. **Preserve me, O God, for in You I put my trust**: It seems that David wrote this psalm from a time of trouble, because he asked for preservation, knew that he would not be moved (Psalm 16:8), and had confidence in some kind of resurrection (Psalm 16:10). Yet the *tone* of this psalm is not despair or complaint; it is settled joy. Despite his trouble, David had a praising confidence in his God.

> > i. "This was a most powerful plea, for to trust God is the highest honour we can do him, it is to set the crown upon his head." (Trapp)

> > ii. "Preserve me from the world; let me not be carried away with its excitements; suffer me not to be before its blandishments, nor to fear its frowns. Preserve me, from the devil; let him not tempt me

99

above what I am able to bear. Preserve me from myself; keep me from growing envious, selfish, high-minded, proud, slothful. Preserve me from those evils into which I see others run, and preserve me, from those evils into which I am myself most apt to run; keep me from evils known and from evils unknown." (Spurgeon)

b. **You are my Lord**: This is what David's **soul** had **said to the** Lord. David happily said that Yahweh (**Lord**) was his master (**Lord**).

i. David knew how to speak to his own soul; Psalms 42:5 and 43:5 are other examples. It is a good thing to speak good things to our own soul.

c. **My goodness is nothing apart from You**: David knew that his very best – all of his goodness – was **nothing** apart from God.

- It was **nothing** when it came to making David righteous before God; he needed God to bring His righteousness to David.

- It was **nothing** because David's **goodness** was itself a gift of God; therefore apart from Him, it was **nothing**.

- It was **nothing** because David's **goodness**, as precious as it was, was of small value without his relationship with God.

    i. "I receive all good from thee, but no good can I return to thee; wherefore I acknowledge thee to be most rich, and myself to be most beggardly." (Greenham, cited in Spurgeon)

d. **As for the saints who are on the earth**: David proclaimed regarding God's people on this earth, **"They are the excellent ones, in whom is all my delight."** David *delighted* in the people of God, despite all their failings, scandals, and embarrassments.

i. This is an obvious failing for many followers of Jesus Christ today. They are so negative about the people of God that they find themselves unable to see any excellence in God's people, unable to **delight** in them.

ii. "This is a practical matter, for it is a way by which we can measure our relationship to the Lord. Do you love other Christians? Do you find it good and rewarding to be with them? Do you seek their company? This is a simple test. Those who love the Lord will love the company of those who also love him." (Boice)

2. (4-6) The folly of idolatry and the blessing of honoring the Lord.

Their sorrows shall be multiplied who hasten *after* another *god*;
Their drink offerings of blood I will not offer,
Nor take up their names on my lips.

O LORD, *You are* the portion of my inheritance and my cup;
You maintain my lot.
The lines have fallen to me in pleasant *places;*
Yes, I have a good inheritance.

a. **Their sorrows shall be multiplied who hasten after another god**: David understood that those who served other gods found many **sorrows** in life.

i. David knew that his life, lived for God, was not an easy one. He experienced many hardships because he remained faithful to God. Nevertheless, he also knew that life lived for **another god** was even *more difficult*. It was the attitude of Peter in John 6:66-69, when he said "Lord, to whom shall we go?"

ii. "There is a distinct echo of the story of the Fall in the phrase, *multiply their sorrows*, since very similar words were spoken to Eve in the Hebrew of Genesis 3:16. There could hardly be a more ominous allusion to what follows from apostasy." (Kidner)

b. **Their drink offerings of blood I will not offer**: David allowed his knowledge of the *futility* of pagan beliefs to affect his behavior. Therefore, he would not follow the pagans in their vain practices.

i. "Many heathens sacrificed to their idols (that is, to devils) with man's blood, against all laws of humanity and piety." (Trapp) In addition, the priests of Baal offered their own blood to their false god; some Roman Catholics and Muslims also whip themselves to blood, offering their blood to their twisted conception of God.

c. **O LORD, You are the portion of my inheritance and my cup; You maintain my lot**: After stating that there was nothing found in the pagan gods, David explained the good he received from Yahweh.

i. **You are the portion of my inheritance**: David was the youngest son in a family with many sons. He could expect no **inheritance** from his family; yet he took joy and comfort in the fact that God was **the portion** of his **inheritance**, and he knew that he had a **good inheritance**. The **lines** that marked out his inheritance had **fallen** to him **in pleasant places**.

ii. God said to the priests in the days of Moses: "I am your portion and your inheritance" (Numbers 18:20). David understood that this was a promise given not only to the priests, but also to all who would trust God to be the portion of their inheritance. "Every godly man has the same possession and the same prohibitions as the priests had. Like them he is landless, and instead of estates has Jehovah." (Maclaren)

iii. **You maintain my lot**: This described the **portion** of David's inheritance. David was confident that God would **maintain** what He had first given to him.

iv. This attitude did not come easily or always to David. He complained to Saul in 1 Samuel 26:19: *for they have driven me out this day from sharing in the inheritance of the LORD, saying, "Go, serve other gods."* Yet here in this psalm, he comes back to the conclusion that the LORD *is* his inheritance and *will* maintain his lot.

v. David's words here speak of *contentment*. He is content with what God has given him. A mark of our age – especially with the Baby Boom generation and perhaps even more with those following – is discontentment, boredom, and restlessness. The generation with short attention spans, the constant need for excitement and adrenaline rushes, and 24-hour-a-day entertainment, needs to know by experience what David knew.

B. The benefits of David's confidence.

1. (7-8) The benefits of guidance and security.

I will bless the LORD who has given me counsel;
My heart also instructs me in the night seasons.
I have set the LORD always before me;
Because *He is* at my right hand I shall not be moved.

a. **I will bless the LORD who has given me counsel**: The false gods of the nations could never give **counsel** the way the LORD gave it to David. When David needed guidance, God gave it to him, and therefore David praised God.

b. **My heart also instructs me in the night seasons**: David's heart was instructed first by God and His Word, and therefore his heart could also instruct him in the ways of God. This is an example of the benefits that come from the transformation of thinking spoken of in Romans 12:1-2.

i. Solomon says in Psalm 127:1-2 that it *can be* vain to stay up late to try to figure out your problems. Yet David, Solomon's father, knew the joy of communing with God **in the night seasons** and receiving guidance from Him.

ii. "Methinks I hear a sweet still voice within me, saying, This is the way, walk in it; and this in the night season, when I am wrapped in rest and silence." (Trapp)

c. **I have set the LORD always before me**: This speaks of a *decision* David made to put God first in his life. He determined that God would always be his focus, his perspective.

i. In the ultimate sense, only Jesus did this perfectly. He was always in the intimate presence of His Father. "The method taken by Christ, as man, to support himself in time of trouble, and persevere unto the end, was to maintain a constant and actual sense of the presence of Jehovah...he then feared not the powers of earth and hell combined for his destruction." (Horne)

d. **Because He is at my right hand I shall not be moved**: This was the plain result of David's decision to put God first. There was a standing and security in David's life that would not have otherwise existed.

2. (9-11) The benefits of joy and preservation.

Therefore my heart is glad, and my glory rejoices;
My flesh also will rest in hope.
For You will not leave my soul in Sheol,
Nor will You allow Your Holy One to see corruption.
You will show me the path of life;
In Your presence *is* fullness of joy;
At Your right hand *are* pleasures forevermore.

a. **Therefore my heart is glad, and my glory rejoices**: David continued to describe the benefits of his decision to *set the LORD always before* him (Psalm 16:8). This decision brought a *gladness* and a *glory* to David's life.

i. For those who do not live out a true commitment to God, it is easy for them to think of what such a commitment *costs* them. This is not entirely bad, because this kind of decision to *set the LORD always before* one's self does have a cost, and the cost should be counted and appreciated. It may cost certain pleasures, popularity, anonymity, family relationships, life goals, career choices, financial priorities, and so forth.

ii. Yet David also tells us some of the *benefits* of such a life decision: **my heart is glad, and my glory rejoices**. There was happiness and a glory David knew by this life commitment that he would not have known otherwise.

iii. David could maturely understand both the costs and the benefits, and sing a song of praise about his life decision.

b. **My flesh also will rest in hope. For You will not leave my soul in Sheol**: David described a further benefit of his life decision to *set the LORD always before* him. It was the confidence of God's care and blessing in the life beyond. David had the settled **hope** (a confidence, not a simple wish) that God would not leave his **soul** in the grave (**Sheol**), but that his life would continue on in the presence of God.

i. This statement is a wonderful declaration of trust in some sort of resurrection and afterlife. Yet, Psalms contains both such confident statements and other more doubtful words about the life beyond (such as in Psalm 6:5 and 88:11). This cloudy understanding of the afterlife in the Old Testament does not surprise the reader of the New Testament, who knows that Jesus Christ brought *life and immortality to light* (2 Timothy 1:10).

c. **Nor will You allow Your Holy One to see corruption**: Wonderfully (and perhaps unknowingly), David spoke beyond himself. In one sense David was indeed the **Holy One** of God, whose soul would not be left in the grave. Yet in a greater and more literal sense, only Jesus Christ fulfills this in His resurrection.

i. This was perceived by Peter on the Day of Pentecost, who said that these words went beyond David who was obviously dead, buried in a grave, and whose body had long ago decayed into dust (Acts 2:25-31).

ii. In quoting and applying this passage from Psalm 16 to the death, burial, and resurrection of Jesus, Peter showed an inspired understanding of the work of Jesus on the cross. He understood that because Jesus bore our sin without becoming a sinner, He remained the **Holy One**, even in His death. Since it is incomprehensible that God's Holy One should be bound by death, the resurrection was absolutely inevitable. As Peter said: *It was not possible that He should be held* by death (Acts 2:24).

iii. The fact that Jesus remained God's **Holy One** despite the ordeal of the cross demonstrates that Jesus *bore the penalty* of human sin without *becoming a sinner* Himself. It also shows that this *payment* of sins was perfect and complete, the only type of payment a **Holy One** could make. In these ways (as Peter understood), the resurrection *proves* the perfection of Jesus' work on the cross.

iv. We might imagine Jesus applying this promise to Himself in the agony before and during the crucifixion, and even afterwards. "It was as though our Lord had stayed his soul upon these words as He left this world and entered the unseen...He sang, as He went, this hymn of immortal hope." (Meyer)

d. **You will show me the path of life; in Your presence is fullness of joy**: With these words David seemed to understand that the benefits of this life commitment to God were received in both this life, and the life beyond.

    i. The **path of life** is something enjoyed by the believer both now, and in eternity. God gives us eternal life to enjoy as a present gift, extending into eternity.

    ii. **In Your presence is fullness of joy**: This was a joy David could experience now (in the context of his previously mentioned gladness and rejoicing), but also ultimately receive when in the more immediate **presence** of God.

    iii. Peter also quoted these lines in his message on the Day of Pentecost. They show that instead of being punished for His glorious work on the cross, Jesus was *rewarded*, as prophetically described in this psalm.

e. **At Your right hand are pleasures forevermore**: David had full confidence that his life with God – both now and **forevermore** – would be marked by the highest and best **pleasures**. This is life lived above shallow entertainments and excitements.

    i. These **pleasures** are enjoyed at a *place*: "We are also told that heaven is to be enjoyed at the right hand of God. The right hand, even on earth, is the place of favor, and the place of honor, and the place of security. The right-hand place is always regarded as the place of dignity and nobility in all courts. God is not going to give his people any left-handed heaven, but they are to dwell at his right hand for evermore." (Spurgeon)

    ii. **At Your right hand are pleasures forevermore**: This tells that both in this life and the life beyond, true **pleasures forevermore** are found at the **right hand** of God, not in separation from Him.

    iii. In his fictional work *The Screwtape Letters*, C.S. Lewis wrote in the voice of a senior devil, complaining about the "unfair advantage" that God has against the devils as they do their dark work: "He's a hedonist at heart. All those fasts and vigils and stakes and crosses are only a façade. Or only like foam on the sea shore. Out at sea, out in His sea, there is pleasure, and more pleasure. He makes no secret of it; at His right hand are 'pleasures forevermore'. Ugh! I don't think He has the least inkling of that high and austere mystery to which we rise in the Miserific Vision. He's vulgar, Wormwood. He has a bourgeois mind. He has filled His world full of pleasures. There are things for humans to do all day long without His minding in the least – sleeping, washing, eating, drinking, making love, playing, praying, working.

Everything has to be *twisted* before it's any use to us. We fight under cruel disadvantages. Nothing is naturally on our side."

iv. The conclusion of this psalm is especially wonderful when we consider how it began. "The refugee of verse 1 finds himself an heir, and his inheritance beyond all imagining and all exploring." (Kidner)

v. When we go back to the first verse, we remember that this life of gladness and rejoicing and fullness of joy *is not* a problem-free life. It is a life that may be challenged and face attack on many levels. Yet in that a life commitment to God has been made and is enjoyed, it is a secure, happy, blessed life.

Psalm 17 – Shelter Under the Shadow of His Wings

The title of this psalm is simply **A Prayer of David**. *We can't attach it to a specific time in David's life, because there are too many possible points where this connects with his general circumstances. This psalm is remarkable for its trust in God, its lack of confidence in self, and its glorious heavenly hope.*

A. A plea to be heard in time of crisis.

1. (1-2) David presents his cause to the Lord.

Hear a just cause, O Lord,
Attend to my cry;
Give ear to my prayer *which is* not from deceitful lips.
Let my vindication come from Your presence;
Let Your eyes look on the things that are upright.

a. **Hear a just cause, O Lord:** As is common in Psalms, David again prayed from a time of crisis. Here he began his appeal to God by declaring the *justice* of his **cause**. He believed God had every reason to **attend to** his **cry** because his **cause** was just.

i. It is entirely possible for someone to think that his cause is just when it is not; or for both parties in a fight to each be absolutely convinced that his own cause is just. We cannot automatically apply these words of David to ourselves and immediately judge our cause as just.

ii. Yet we can look at our cause as impartially and dispassionately as possible, looking at it from the perspective of others to the best of our ability, and be more concerned with what is truly **just** than simply what favors us.

iii. "A cry is our earliest utterance, and in many ways the most natural of human sounds; if our prayer should like the infant's cry be more natural than intelligent, and more earnest than elegant, it will be none

107

the less eloquent with God. There is a mighty power in a child's cry to prevail with a parent's heart." (Spurgeon)

b. **Give ear to my prayer which is not from deceitful lips**: Even as David was convinced regarding the justice of his cause, he was also careful to speak honestly about his problem. The idea is that David has not deceived so as to deserve his current problem, and that he was not withholding facts that would undermine his cause.

i. In Psalm 139:23-24, David prayed: *Search me, O God, and know my heart; try me, and know my anxieties; and see if there is any wicked way in me, and lead me in the way everlasting.* This wonderful prayer – to know one's own heart and hidden motives and sins – is the kind of thing that David prayed *before* he prayed this psalm. He comes to God here with some confidence through a *tested* conscience.

ii. **Deceitful lips**: "They have Jacob's voice, but Esau's hands; they profess like saints, but practise like Satans; they have their long prayers, but short prayings." (Bales, cited in Spurgeon)

c. **Let my vindication come from Your presence**: David did not want a vindication that came from *himself.* In his long struggle with King Saul, David had several opportunities to set things right himself, but he refused and waited until **vindication** came from the **presence** of God.

i. This was an important way that David left his problem to the LORD. "God, I refuse to take matters into my own hands. I will wait for **vindication** to **come from Your presence**; I want to know that this is Your work and not mine."

d. **Let Your eyes look on the things that are upright**: David phrased his request in a way that put more emphasis upon God's justice than on his own cause. He did believe that his cause was just; but he spoke in a manner that gave more importance to the **things that are upright**.

i. David's idea was something like this: "LORD, I believe my cause is just and I have searched my own heart for deceit. Yet I wait for Your vindication, and I want You to do and to promote what is right. If I'm not on Your side, move me so that I am."

ii. "I desire nothing that is unreasonable or unjust, but that thou wouldst judge righteously between me and mine enemies, and vindicate my own honour and faithfulness in making good thy promise to me." (Poole)

2. (3-4) A plea from a tested heart.

You have tested my heart;
You have visited *me* in the night;
You have tried me and have found nothing;
I have purposed that my mouth shall not transgress.
Concerning the works of men,
By the word of Your lips,
I have kept away from the paths of the destroyer.

a. **You have tested my heart**: David *invited* the test in the previous verses; here he speaks as having *passed* the test (**You have tried me and have found nothing**).

i. Clarke assumes (probably rightly) that this psalm comes from the context of Saul hunting David. "Thou hast seen me in my most *secret* retirements, and knowest whether I have *plotted* mischief against him who now wishes to take away my life." (Clarke)

ii. It takes some level of patience and maturity to let God test one's heart in this manner. We must accept the fact that we might be wrong and that someone else may be right in the matter. We must be more interested in God's justice and His standard of right and wrong than we are in winning our cause. We must come to God and His word with a heart ready to be convicted and corrected.

iii. There are three questions for everyone to ask: "Do I allow God to test **my heart**? Can I be corrected? Will I listen to others when they tell me that I may be wrong?"

iv. David *did* allow God to test his heart, and therefore he came with great confidence in prayer. "Open and unconfessed sin is a great prayer barrier. An upright life is a strong basis for appeals." (Boice)

v. Boice suggests these questions for examining our heart before prayer:

- Are we being disobedient?
- Are we being selfish?
- Are we neglecting some important duty?
- Is there a wrong we should first make right?
- Are our priorities in order?

b. **I have purposed that my mouth shall not transgress**: David was careful to not speak in a sinful way about his crisis. He could speak in a way that might deceive others or himself, and promote his own cause at the expense of God's justice; yet David **purposed** that it would not be so.

i. "The strong professions of heart-cleanness and outward obedience which follow are not so much denials of any sin as avowals of sincere devotion and honest submission of life to God's law." (Maclaren)

c. **By the word of Your lips, I have kept away from the paths of the destroyer**: This was one reason why David was good at this kind of strong self-analysis. He lived by the words of God's **lips**; he knew and loved and lived God's **word**.

i. It was this word that **tried** David and **found nothing**. It was this word that gave David the wisdom and the strength to keep **away from the paths of the destroyer**.

ii. David learned and displayed this lesson over and over again during his long crisis with King Saul. David had to protect himself, his family, and his men from Saul without becoming himself a twisted, self-interested **destroyer** like Saul.

B. A plea for protection.

1. (5) Hold up my steps.

Uphold my steps in Your paths,
***That* my footsteps may not slip.**

a. **Uphold my steps**: David felt that he was in danger of falling or slipping into disaster; he needed God to hold up his steps, so that his **footsteps may not slip**.

i. "The word of God affords us direction, but the grace of God must enable us to follow its direction, and that grace must be obtained by prayer." (Horne)

ii. "What! Slip in God's ways? Yes, the road is good, but our feet are evil, and therefore slip, even on the King's highway." (Spurgeon)

b. **In Your paths**: This again shows the significant humility of David's prayer. He wants to be upheld, but only on *God's* **paths**. Included in this is the unspoken prayer, "LORD, if I am not on Your path, please put me there. I want to be in **Your paths**, not my own."

2. (6-9) Keep me safe by Your power.

I have called upon You, for You will hear me, O God;
Incline Your ear to me, *and* hear my speech.
Show Your marvelous lovingkindness by Your right hand,
O You who save those who trust *in You*
From those who rise up *against them.*
Keep me as the apple of Your eye;
Hide me under the shadow of Your wings,

From the wicked who oppress me,
***From* my deadly enemies who surround me.**

a. **I have called upon You, for You will hear me**: David's calm confidence in the midst of his crisis is encouraging. Though his problems were not gone yet, he still was confident that God would **hear** when he **called**.

i. Boice explained how this psalm is a great pattern of prayer. "It models prayer by the way the psalmist uses arguments to make his appeal to God. He does not merely ask for what he wants or needs. He argues his case, explaining to God what God should answer."

ii. We don't make such arguments in prayer because we can, through brilliant or persuasive arguments, convince God to do something that He doesn't really want to do. Instead, it is "because arguments force us to carefully think through what we are asking and to sharpen our requests." (Boice)

b. **Show Your marvelous lovingkindness by Your right hand**: This is the first appearance in Psalms of the wonderful word, **lovingkindness**. David asked that this special love be shown to him by the special power of God (**Your right hand**).

i. Kidner on **lovingkindness**: "*Steadfast love*, or 'true love' (NEB) is that faithfulness to a covenant, to which marital devotion gives some analogy. It is the word which older versions translated 'lovingkindness', before its connection with covenanting and its strong element of fidelity were fully appreciated."

ii. "This is the love by which he enters into a favorable relationship with his people, promising to be their God." (Boice)

iii. Yet David spoke of more than **lovingkindness** here; he spoke of **marvelous lovingkindness**, and that **by Your right hand**. "The wonder of extraordinary love is that God should make it such an ordinary thing, that he should give to us 'marvellous lovingkindness,' and yet should give it so often that it becomes a daily blessing, and yet remains marvellous still." (Spurgeon)

iv. Many of us ask for or only expect God's *moderate* lovingkindness. We make our prayers, our faith, and our expectations small. David here shows us a pattern to expect and ask from God **marvelous lovingkindness**.

v. "Do you not see that you have been a marvellous sinner? Marvellously ungrateful have you been; marvellously have you aggravated your sins; marvellously did you kick against a mother's tears; marvellously did you defy a father's counsels; marvellously have you laughed at death;

marvellously have you made a covenant with death and a league with hell...'Oh!' saith he, 'God will never have mercy on me; it is too great a thing to hope, too great a wonder to expect!' Young man, here is a new prayer for you, 'Show thy marvellous loving-kindness.'" (Spurgeon)

c. **Keep me as the apple of Your eye**: The phrase "**apple of Your eye**" was used to describe something precious, easily injured and demanding protection. David wanted to be kept by God as if he were something *valuable* and even *fragile*.

i. "No part of the body more precious, more tender, and more carefully guarded than the eye; and of the eye, no portion more peculiarly to be protected than the central apple, the pupil, or as the Hebrew calls it, 'the daughter of the eye.' The all-wise Creator has placed the eye in a well-protected position; it stands surrounded by projecting bones like Jerusalem encircled by mountains. Moreover, its great Author has surrounded it with many tunics of inward covering, besides the hedge of the eyebrows, the curtain of the eyelids, and the fence of the eyelashes; and, in addition to this, he has given to every man so high a value for his eyes, and so quick an apprehension of danger, that no member of the body is more faithfully cared for than the organ of sight." (Spurgeon)

ii. This figure of speech is also used in Deuteronomy 32:10, Proverbs 7:2, and Zechariah 2:8. To be kept as the apple of the eye means:

- To be kept with many guards and protections.
- To *always* be kept safe.
- To be kept from the small things, like dust and grit.
- To always be kept sensitive and tender.
- To be kept clear and unobstructed.
- To be kept as something beautiful *and* eminently useful.

d. **Hide me under the shadow of Your wings**: This is another powerful figure of speech. The idea is of how a mother bird shields her young chicks from predators, from the elements, and from dangers by gathering them under her wings.

i. This figure of speech is also used in three other psalms (Psalms 36:7, 57:1, and 63:7). Jesus used this same word picture to show His love and desired care for Jerusalem in Matthew 23:37.

ii. "Even as the parent bird completely shields her brood from evil, and meanwhile cherishes them with the warmth of her own heart, by covering them with her wings, so do thou with me, most condescending God, for I am thine offspring, and thou hast a parent's love in perfection." (Spurgeon)

iii. Taken together, these two phrases are powerful pictures of God's care for His people. "He who has so fenced and guarded that precious and tender part, the pupil of the eye, and who has provided for the security of a young and helpless brood under the wings of their dam, is here entreated to extend the same providential care and parental love to the souls of his elect." (Horne)

e. **From the wicked who oppress me, from my deadly enemies who surround me**: The threat in David's life was *real*. He faced not only **oppression** that made his life difficult, but also **deadly enemies** who wanted to end his life.

i. In the midst of these real threats, David did the right thing: he *prayed*. "Fears that have become prayers are already more than half conquered." (Maclaren)

ii. Boice quotes a Bible teacher who had the habit of praying a certain prayer when he felt he was under attack: "Lord, your property is in danger."

3. (10-14) Defeat my proud and arrogant enemies.

They have closed up their fat *hearts;*
With their mouths they speak proudly.
They have now surrounded us in our steps;
They have set their eyes, crouching down to the earth,
As a lion is eager to tear his prey,
And like a young lion lurking in secret places.
Arise, O LORD,
Confront him, cast him down;
Deliver my life from the wicked with Your sword,
With Your hand from men, O LORD,
From men of the world *who have* their portion in *this* life,
And whose belly You fill with Your hidden treasure.
They are satisfied with children,
And leave the rest of their *possession* for their babes.

a. **They have closed up their fat hearts**: David here begins to describe the deadly enemies who oppressed him so. They were insensitive (**fat hearts**), and spoke **proudly**.

i. "The meaning plainly is, that pride is the child of plenty, begotten by self-indulgence, which hardens the hearts of men against the fear of God, and the love of their neighbours.... Let every man take care, that, by pampering the flesh, he does not raise up an enemy of this stamp against himself." (Horne)

b. **Surrounded us in our steps...set their eyes...crouching down to the earth, as a lion**: David described the dangerous, wild, beast-like actions of his enemies. They would destroy him as a **lion** destroys its prey.

c. **Arise, O LORD, confront him, cast him down**: David declared his dependence on God to protect him. It wasn't because David was afraid of such lion-like enemies; as a young boy David had bested both the bear and the lion (1 Samuel 17:33-37). It was because David needed to see his enemy defeated by the hand of God, not the hand of David.

i. **Confront him**: "Hebrew, *prevent his face*, i.e., go forth against him, and meet and face him in battle, as enemies used to do." (Poole)

ii. This psalm has no firm connection to any particular recorded event in David's life, but it is not hard to see it belonging to the long period when Saul hunted David. During that time David refused to strike out against Saul when he had the opportunity, because he knew that *God* must strike against Saul, and not David himself.

d. **Deliver my life from the wicked...from men of the world who have their portion in this life**: David recognized that one characteristic of his enemies was that they looked much more to **this life** than they did to eternity.

i. And, they may very well have had some satisfactions in this life: **whose belly You fill...they are satisfied with children, and leave the rest of their possession for their babes**. Spurgeon explained it like this: "Their sensual appetite gets the gain which it craved for. God gives to these swine the husks which they hunger for. A generous man does not deny dogs their bones; and our generous God gives even his enemies enough to fill them, if they were not so unreasonable as never to be content."

4. (15) The settled confidence of prayer.

As for me, I will see Your face in righteousness;
I shall be satisfied when I awake in Your likeness.

a. **As for me**: David here set himself in contrast to his enemies, who looked only to this life and not to eternity.

i. "This superb verse soars straight up from the prosperous lowlands of verse 14, where all was earthbound." (Kidner)

ii. "I do not envy this their felicity, but my hopes and happiness are of another nature. I do not place my portion in earthly and temporal treasures, as they do, but in *beholding God's face*." (Poole)

iii. "The smell of the furnace is upon the present psalm, but there is evidence in the last verse that he who wrote it came unharmed out of the flame." (Spurgeon)

b. **I will see Your face**: David was confident not only of life after death, but that he would one day **see** the **face** of God. The idea is not merely of *contact* with God, but of unhindered fellowship with God.

c. **See Your face in righteousness**: The idea is that David would have a righteousness that would enable him to see the face of God, to have this unhindered relationship with Him.

i. From a New Covenant perspective, we can say that this **righteousness** is the gift of God, granted to those who receive the person and work of Jesus by faith.

d. **I shall be satisfied when I awake**: David knew that the transition from this life to the next was like *waking*. He knew that the world beyond was *more* real and less dreamlike than our own.

i. We tend to think of heaven and its realities as an uncertain, cloudy dream world. In truth it is more real than our present environment, which by contrast will seem uncertain and cloudy when we **awake** in God's presence.

ii. "The moment is at hand when we shall awake and start up and declare ourselves fools for having counted dreams as realities, whilst we were oblivious to the eternal realities." (Meyer)

iii. Though David's focus was on eternity, this verse does not ignore the present day. There is a real sense in which these realities – closer fellowship with God, His righteousness in our life, a life truly awake, a life more and more conformed to His image – can in greater and greater measure be ours in this life. We should remember that eternal life begins *now*.

e. **When I awake in Your likeness**: David did not have a sophisticated understanding of heaven; one might say that no one in the Old Testament really did. Yet he did know that when he saw God's face, when he received His righteousness, when he awoke in heaven's reality, that he would be **in** God's **likeness**.

i. David seemed to anticipate what Paul would write some 1,000 years later: *For whom He foreknew, He also predestined to be conformed to the image of His Son* (Romans 8:29). The destiny of God's people is to be conformed into the image of God, as perfectly displayed in Jesus Christ His Son.

ii. This – and perhaps only this – would make David **satisfied**. The implication is that he would never be **satisfied** until:

- He saw God's **face**, enjoying unhindered relationship with Him.
- He received God's **righteousness**.
- He would **awake** in and live in heaven's reality.
- He was conformed into God's **likeness**.

iii. "The mind will be satisfied with his truth, the heart with his love, the will with his authority. We shall need nothing else." (Meyer)

Psalm 18 – Great Praise from a Place of Great Victory

This is a long psalm; there are only three psalms longer in the entire collection (78, 89, and 119). Its length is well suited to its theme, as described in the title. The title itself is long, with only one longer in the psalter (Psalm 60): **To the Chief Musician. A Psalm of David the servant of the Lord, who spoke to the Lord the words of this song on the day that the Lord delivered him from the hand of all of his enemies and from the hand of Saul. And he said:**

In the title David tells us whom the psalm was written for: God Himself, who is **the Chief Musician.** *He tells us more about himself, that we should consider him* **the servant of the Lord.** *He tells us the occasion for the writing of the psalm – possibly not only the immediate aftermath of Saul's death (described in 1 Samuel 31; 2 Samuel 1), but also of the period leading to David's enthronement (2 Samuel 2-5). He tells us also something about Saul, who out of great, undeserved kindness on David's part, is not explicitly counted among the enemies of David* (**from the hand of all of his enemies and from the hand of Saul**).

This psalm is virtually the same as the psalm sung by David at the very end of his life, as recorded in 2 Samuel 22. It is likely that David composed this song as a younger man; yet in his old age David could look back with great gratitude and sing this song again, *looking at his whole life.*

A. God's past deliverance for David.

1. (1-3) David praises the God of his deliverance.

I will love You, O Lord, my strength.
The Lord is my rock and my fortress and my deliverer;
My God, my strength, in whom I will trust;
My shield and the horn of my salvation, my stronghold.
I will call upon the Lord, *who is worthy* **to be praised;**
So shall I be saved from my enemies.

a. **I will love You, O LORD**: This was a triumphant declaration made in a season of great triumph. It is true that David *decided* to love the LORD, but even more true that he simply felt *compelled* to love the LORD who delivered him so wonderfully.

i. Since he was taken from the sheepfold and anointed the future king of Israel, David had lived some 20 or so years as a fugitive, and as a man who had lost everything. He lost his safety, he lost his youth, he lost his family, he lost his career, he lost his rights, he lost his connection with the covenant people of God, he lost his comforts, and at times he even lost his close relationship with God. Despite all, he remained steadfast to the Lord, and God – in His timing – delivered David and fulfilled the long-ago promise of his anointing.

ii. In saying, "**I will love You**," David used a somewhat unusual word. "This word for *love* is an uncommon one, impulsive and emotional. Found elsewhere only in its intensive forms, it usually expresses the compassionate love of the stronger for the weaker." (Boice)

iii. "Hebrew, I will love thee dearly and entirely...from the very heart-root." (Trapp)

iv. "The precluding invocation in vv. 1-3 at once touches the high-water mark of Old Testament devotion, and is conspicuous among its noblest utterances. Nowhere else in Scripture is the form of the word employed which is here used for 'love.' It has special depth and tenderness." (Maclaren)

v. David said, "**I will love You**" to the God who delivered him, not only for rescuing him *from* his trial, but for all God did in and through the trials to make him what he was. David wasn't bitter against God, as if he said, "Well, it's about time You delivered me." Instead he was grateful that the years of trouble had done something good and necessary in his life.

b. **The LORD is my rock and my fortress and my deliverer**: David knew this to be true before, but he knew it by *faith*. Now David sang from a perspective that knew this by experience in a greater way than ever before.

i. When David said, "**The LORD is my rock**," he likely meant it in more than one sense. A rock was of help to the ancient Judean in several ways.

- It could provide essential shade, always needed in the merciless sun and heat of the desert (as in Isaiah 32:2).

- It could provide shelter and protection in its cracks and crevasses (as in Exodus 33:22 and Proverbs 30:26).

- It could provide a firm place to stand and fight, as opposed to sinking sand (as in Psalm 40:2).

c. **My God, my strength, in whom I will trust**: David knew the triumph of God's **strength** over the *long* trial. Many people fall under the excruciating *length* of an extended season of trial, and David *almost* did (1 Samuel 27; 29-30).

i. That fact that David saw his God as his **strength** reminds us of the promise later expressed through Paul: *Be strong in the Lord and in the power of His might* (Ephesians 6:10).

d. **My shield and the horn of my salvation, my stronghold**: As David listed honoring name for God upon honoring name (we can count nine just in these first few verses), we get the feeling of a *flood* of praise and emotion from David. He can't say enough about who God is and the great things He has done for David.

i. It is revealing that David can speak so eloquently about his God and what God has done for him. As Maclaren says, "The whole is one long, loving accumulation of dear names." This means that David both *knew* God and had *experienced* God.

ii. In these nine titles, we see what God was for David:

- His **strength**, the One who empowered him to survive against and defeat his enemies.
- His **rock**, which indicates a place of shelter, safety, and a secure standing.
- His **fortress**, a place of strength and safety.
- His **deliverer**, the One who made a way of escape for him.
- His **God**, "my *strong God*, not only the object of my adoration, but he who puts strength in my soul." (Clarke)
- His **strength**, but this uses a different Hebrew word than in Psalm 18:1. According to Clarke, the idea behind this word is *fountain, source, origin.*
- His **shield**, who defends both his head and his heart.
- His **horn**, meaning his strength and defense.
- His **stronghold**, his high tower of refuge where he could see an enemy from a great distance and be protected from the adversary.

iii. "When he was conscious that the object of his worship was such as he has pointed out in the above *nine* particulars, it is no wonder that he resolves to *call upon him*; and no wonder that he expects, in consequence, to be saved from his enemies; for who can destroy him whom such a God undertakes to save?" (Clarke)

e. **I will call upon the LORD, who is worthy to be praised; so shall I be saved from my enemies**: In previous psalms David cried out to God from times of intense crisis; now he cries out to God with the same strength to praise Him for His deliverance. It is sad to say that many are far more passionate in asking for help than they ever are in giving thanks or praise.

i. The thought, "**So shall I be saved from my enemies**" did not always come easily for David. Not very long before this great season of victory, he said to himself: *Now I shall perish someday by the hand of Saul. There is nothing better for me than that I should speedily escape to the land of the Philistines* (1 Samuel 27:1). This shows that there were times when David deeply doubted the final victory he now enjoyed; but it also shows that in the end, his faith – and more importantly, God's strength – was greater than his weakness.

ii. Therefore, at this point, it is all a song of praise for David. "To be saved singing is to be saved indeed. Many are saved mourning and doubting; but David had such faith that he could fight singing, and win the battle with a song still on his lips." (Spurgeon)

2. (4-6) The danger that made David cry out to the LORD.

The pangs of death surrounded me,
And the floods of ungodliness made me afraid.
The sorrows of Sheol surrounded me;
The snares of death confronted me.
In my distress I called upon the LORD,
And cried out to my God;
He heard my voice from His temple,
And my cry came before Him, *even* **to His ears.**

a. **The pangs of death surrounded me, and the floods of ungodliness made me afraid**: David described two threats: first, the threat of **death**, and second the **floods of ungodliness**. The overwhelming presence of **ungodliness** was a significant trial to David.

i. This reminds us that despite the fact that David was a true warrior, he was also a sensitive soul who was troubled by the deeds and words of the ungodly.

b. **The sorrows of Sheol surrounded me**: This was another way of saying that David was threatened with death. **Sheol** is another word for the grave or death.

c. **He heard my voice from His temple**: This was long before the later building of the temple in the days of Solomon. The city of Jerusalem wasn't even in Israeli control at the time David wrote this (not until 2 Samuel 5:6-10). Yet David knew that *God* had a **temple**, a heavenly temple that was the model for the tabernacle and the later temple (Exodus 25:9, 25:40), and that God heard prayer from heaven.

i. What did God hear **from His temple**? God heard David's cry (**cried out to my God**). "This same poor man cried, and the cry set Jehovah's activity in motion. The deliverance of a single soul may seem a small thing, but if the single soul has prayed it is no longer small, for God's good name is involved." (Maclaren)

3. (7-15) The majestic deliverance God brought to David.

Then the earth shook and trembled;
The foundations of the hills also quaked and were shaken,
Because He was angry.
Smoke went up from His nostrils,
And devouring fire from His mouth;
Coals were kindled by it.
He bowed the heavens also, and came down
With darkness under His feet.
And He rode upon a cherub, and flew;
He flew upon the wings of the wind.
He made darkness His secret place;
His canopy around Him *was* dark waters
And thick clouds of the skies.
From the brightness before Him,
His thick clouds passed with hailstones and coals of fire.

The Lord thundered from heaven,
And the Most High uttered His voice,
Hailstones and coals of fire.
He sent out His arrows and scattered the foe,
Lightnings in abundance, and He vanquished them.
Then the channels of the sea were seen,
The foundations of the world were uncovered
At Your rebuke, O Lord,
At the blast of the breath of Your nostrils.

a. **Then the earth shook and trembled**: David describes the dramatic deliverance God brought to him. It was marked by earthquakes, the indignation of God (**He was angry**), **smoke** and **fire**, and the personal intervention of God (**He rode upon a cherub, and flew**).

i. "When a monarch is angry, and prepares for war, his whole kingdom is instantly in commotion. Universal nature is here represented as feeling the effects of its sovereign's displeasure, and all the visible elements are disordered." (Horne)

ii. **Smoke went up from His nostrils**: "A violent Oriental method of expressing fierce wrath. Since the breath from the nostrils is heated by strong emotion, the figure portrays the Almighty Deliverer as pouring forth smoke in the heat of his wrath and the impetuousness of his zeal." (Spurgeon)

iii. **He rode upon a cherub, and flew**: David here emphasized the *speed* of God's deliverance. "As swiftly as the wind. He came to my rescue with all speed." (Poole) We may fairly wonder if it seemed speedy to David at the time.

iv. This terminology of David emphasizes the judgment of God; but since the judgment is directed against David's enemies, it means deliverance for David. God won this victory against David's *strong enemy*, against those *who hated* David (Psalm 18:16-17).

v. There is a larger principle here: understanding that deliverance for a righteous person or people often means judgment against those who oppress them.

b. **The Lord thundered from heaven**: David set phrase upon phrase in describing the great work of God on his behalf. According to David's description, God moved heaven, sky, earth, and sea to deliver David.

i. When David described help coming to him through earthquakes, thunder, storms, and lightning, he clearly used poetic images from the way God delivered Israel from Egypt, at Mount Sinai, and during the conquest of Canaan under Joshua. Yet it is also entirely possible – if not probable – that he also literally saw such phenomenon sent from God to protect and fight for him. Though such events are not recorded in 1 or 2 Samuel, we remember that there were long periods of David's life (such as when he was hunted as a fugitive from Saul) of which we have few descriptions of events. He must have experienced God's deliverance again and again in a variety of ways.

ii. The way David describes it all leaves us with two impressions. First, he really believed those things happened as recorded in the Bible. Second, he saw the same God do similar things for him in his own day.

iii. Significantly, we might say that David could only really see this *once his deliverance was accomplished*. In the midst of his trial, David had many reasons and occasions to wonder where the delivering hand of

God was. God's deliverance is always seen most clearly looking back; looking forward it is often only seen by faith.

4. (16-19) David set in safety.

He sent from above, He took me;
He drew me out of many waters.
He delivered me from my strong enemy,
From those who hated me,
For they were too strong for me.
They confronted me in the day of my calamity,
But the LORD was my support.
He also brought me out into a broad place;
He delivered me because He delighted in me.

a. **He took me; He drew me out of many waters. He delivered me from my strong enemy**: David felt that he was drowning when the strong hand of God picked him **out of many waters**. Like a man caught up in a flood, David knew that his enemies **were too strong for** him, but that God could deliver him.

i. "Some will not see the hand of God, but I warrant you, brethren, those who have been delivered out of the deep waters will see it. Their experience teaches them that God is yet among us." (Spurgeon)

b. **He also brought me out into a broad place**: The strong hand of God not only plucked David from the flood, but it also set him in a safe place.

c. **He delivered me because He delighted in me**: We can say that David meant this in two ways. First, he **delighted in** David in the sense that He chose him, anointed him, and set His *marvelous lovingkindness* (Psalm 17:7) upon David. Second, he **delighted in** David because he lived a righteous life, as explained in the following verses.

i. "Deliverance from sin, deliverance from evil propensities, deliverance from spiritual enemies – each deliverance bears evidence of God's love to us…. How much he delights in you it is not possible to say. The Father delights in you, and looks upon you with doting love; like as a father takes pleasure in his child, so does he rejoice over you." (Spurgeon)

5. (20-24) God delivered David because of his righteousness.

The LORD rewarded me according to my righteousness;
According to the cleanness of my hands
He has recompensed me.
For I have kept the ways of the LORD,
And have not wickedly departed from my God.

For all His judgments *were* before me,
And I did not put away His statutes from me.
I was also blameless before Him,
And I kept myself from my iniquity.
Therefore the LORD has recompensed me according to my righteousness,
According to the cleanness of my hands in His sight.

a. **The LORD rewarded me according to my righteousness**: During his long season of affliction under Saul, David was challenged to respond in unrighteous ways. He had many opportunities to strike out against Saul as a matter of self-defense. Yet David consistently conducted himself in **righteousness** and knew that God **rewarded** him because of it.

b. **I have kept the ways of the LORD, and have not wickedly departed from my God…. I was also blameless before Him, and I kept myself from my iniquity**: This was not a claim of sinless perfection on David's part. In fact, the year or so before the death of King Saul was spent in some significant measure of spiritual and moral compromise (1 Samuel 27; 29-30). Yet through it all David kept a core of integrity towards God, was correctable despite his failings, and most importantly did not fail in the greatest test: to not give in to the temptation to gain the throne through killing or undermining Saul.

i. We believe this psalm – twice recorded in Scripture, with minor variations, both here and in 2 Samuel 22 – actually speaks from two contexts. Here, according to the title, it was sung first from David's victory over Saul and receiving of the throne of Israel. In 2 Samuel 22 David sang it as a grateful retrospect over his entire life. He can say "**I have kept the ways of the LORD, and have not wickedly departed from my God**" in both contexts, but with somewhat different meaning. It meant one thing to say it *before* his sin with Bathsheba and against Uriah; it was another thing to say it *after* that sin.

ii. Spurgeon explained how the statement could be true both before and after the scandal with Bathsheba: "Before God the man after God's own heart was a humble sinner, but before his slanderers he could with unblushing face speak of the '*cleanness of his hands*' and the righteousness of his life."

iii. Nevertheless, we can largely agree with Adam Clarke: "The times in which David was most afflicted were the times of his greatest uprightness. *Adversity* was always to him a time of spiritual prosperity."

c. **I kept myself from my iniquity**: Some think this is arrogance or pride on David's part. Spurgeon quotes one commentator who protested, "Kept himself! Who made man his own keeper?" Yet we know there is certainly a sense in which we must keep ourselves from sin, even as Paul spoke of a man cleansing himself for God's glory and for greater service (2 Timothy 2:21).

i. We may see a *personal danger* in the words, **my iniquity**. It shows that there is iniquity in every person, and that we must be on special guard against our own tendencies to sin, to practice **iniquity**. It is true that all we like sheep have gone astray; but we have also turned each one to our *own* way. Our iniquity may be in us from birth; it may have been educated into us by a bad family or by bad company. Our iniquity may come to us through temptations, through adversity, or through prosperity – even by our blessings.

ii. These words of David also tell us of *a special guard*. David was determined to **keep** himself from his iniquity. "Be resolved in the power of the Holy Spirit that this particular sin shall be overcome. There is nothing like hanging it up by the neck, that very sin, I mean. Do not fire at sin indiscriminately; but, if thou hast one sin that is more to thee than another, drag it out from the crowd, and say, 'Thou must die if no other does. I will hang thee up in the face of the sun.'" (Spurgeon)

iii. One may object: "Yet David *did not* keep himself from his iniquity, and some years after this he sinned with Bathsheba, and he grievously sinned against Uriah." That is true, and David was disciplined greatly for that sin. Nevertheless, we never hear of him sinning in a similar way *after* his repentance from that terrible transgression. There is a real sense in which after his repentance, David *did* keep himself from his iniquity. As Benjamin Franklin wrote: "Many princes sin with David, but few repent with him."

d. **Therefore the LORD has recompensed me according to my righteousness**: David resisted the remarkably strong temptation to depose Saul and take the throne promised to him by either violence or intrigue. This was the consistent expression of **righteousness** that the LORD rewarded by giving David a throne that could not be taken *from him*.

i. David here simply testified to his clean conscience, which is a good and wonderful thing. "A godly man has a clear conscience, and knows himself to be upright; is he to deny his own consciousness, and to despise the work of the Holy Ghost, by hypocritically making himself out to be worse than he is?" (Spurgeon)

6. (25-27) An abiding principle of God's dealing with man.

With the merciful You will show Yourself merciful;
With a blameless man You will show Yourself blameless;
With the pure You will show Yourself pure;
And with the devious You will show Yourself shrewd.
For You will save the humble people,
But will bring down haughty looks.

a. **With the merciful You will show Yourself merciful**: David understood a basic principle of God's dealing with men; that God often treats a man in the same way that man treats others.

i. Jesus explained this principle in the Sermon on the Mount: *For with what judgment you judge, you will be judged; and with the measure you use, it will be measured back to you* (Matthew 7:2). Human nature wants to use a *small* measure of mercy with others, but wants a *large* measure of mercy from God. Jesus told us to expect the same measure from God that we give to others.

ii. "Note that even the merciful need mercy; no amount of generosity to the poor, or forgiveness to enemies, can set us beyond the need of mercy." (Spurgeon)

iii. "The attitude of God towards men is created by their attitude towards Him." (Morgan) This principle works in a positive way; those who show great mercy are given great mercy. It also works in a negative way: **with the devious You will show Yourself shrewd**. One illustration of this was how God used the **shrewd** Laban to educate the **devious** Jacob (Genesis 27-28).

iv. It is significant that this appears in the psalm that celebrates David's victory over Saul. Both sides of this principle (God's dealing with the **merciful** and the **devious**) were mightily illustrated in the lives of David and Saul through their ongoing conflict.

v. Translators have had trouble with the second half of Psalm 18:26, because it communicates a difficult concept. It's easy say that if a man is pure towards God, then God will be pure to him. But you can't say that if a man is wicked towards God, then God will be wicked towards him, because God can't do wickedness. So, "David expresses the second half of the parallel by a somewhat ambiguous word, the root meaning of which is 'twisted.' The verse actually says, 'To the twisted (or crooked) you will show yourself twisted (or crooked)'.... The idea seems to be that if a person insists in going devious ways in his dealings with God, God will outwit him, as that man deserves." (Boice)

vi. Leviticus 26:23-24 promises such a thing: *And if by these things you are not reformed by Me, but walk contrary to Me, then I also will walk contrary to you, and I will punish you yet seven times for your sins.*

b. **You will save the humble people, but will bring down haughty looks**: God loves to give grace to the humble, and likewise resists the proud (James 4:6; 1 Peter 5:5).

i. **Humble people**: The idea behind the Hebrew word *ani* refers to the poor, afflicted, and needy ones. God's care for these **humble people** is found in several psalms (Psalm 10:2, 22:24, 35:10, 68:10), though the Hebrew word *ani* may be translated differently in different places.

B. God's present and future power for David.

1. (28-30) God gives His light and word to empower David.

For You will light my lamp;
The LORD my God will enlighten my darkness.
For by You I can run against a troop,
By my God I can leap over a wall.
As for **God, His way** *is* **perfect;**
The word of the LORD is proven;
He *is* **a shield to all who trust in Him.**

a. **For You will light my lamp**: David now moves from joyful thanks for the past to confidence in the future. The same God who brought him to the throne would give him the **light** he needed to rule and **enlighten** his **darkness**.

b. **For by You I can run against a troop, by my God I can leap over a wall**: This gives thanks for past victories, and thanks God for present strength. One might think that after the 20-some years of living as a fugitive from Saul, David would simply be exhausted. This was not the case; God empowering him, he felt strong enough to accomplish superhuman feats.

i. "*By thee I have* broken through the armed troops of mine enemies. I have scaled the walls of their strongest cities and castles, and so taken them." (Poole)

ii. "With faith, how easy all exploits become! When we have no faith, though, to fight with enemies, and overcome difficulties, is hard work indeed; but, when we have faith, oh, how easy our victories! What does the believer do? There is a troop, – well, he runs in faith, then, to fight with enemies, and overcome difficulties is hard wall, what about that? He leaps over it. It is amazing how easy life becomes when a man has faith. Does faith diminish difficulties? Oh, no, it increaseth them; but it increaseth his strength to overcome them. If thou hast faith, thou shalt have trials; but thou shalt do great exploits, endure great privations, and get triumphant victories." (Spurgeon)

c. **His way is perfect; the word of the LORD is proven**: David spoke of the great things he could do as empowered by God, but he came back to the thought of the greatness of God. He considered the perfection of **His way**, and the **proven** character of His **word**.

> i. **The word of the LORD is proven**: "Literally *tried in the fire*. It has stood all tests; and has never failed those who pleaded it before its author." (Clarke)

> ii. David could say "**the word of the LORD is proven**" from his personal experience. The word given to David – that he would be the next king of Israel, plus hundreds of smaller promises – had been **proven** true.

> iii. Many do not know this from their own experience because they will never allow themselves to be put in a situation where God *must* prove His word true. David knew the truth of this from the extreme circumstances of his life.

2. (31-36) God gives David strength and skill.

For who *is* God, except the LORD?
And who *is* a rock, except our God?
***It is* God who arms me with strength,**
And makes my way perfect.
He makes my feet like the *feet of* deer,
And sets me on my high places.
He teaches my hands to make war,
So that my arms can bend a bow of bronze.

You have also given me the shield of Your salvation;
Your right hand has held me up,
Your gentleness has made me great.
You enlarged my path under me,
So my feet did not slip.

> a. **For who is God, except the LORD?** David here celebrated the reality of the God of Israel against the illusions of the gods of the nations. The Philistines, the Moabites, the Edomites, and all the rest had their gods; but only Yahweh (**the LORD**) **is God**.

> > i. "Vain were the idols of the ancient world, Baal and Jupiter; as vain are those of modern times – pleasure, honour, and profit. They cannot bestow content, or make their votaries happy below; much less can they deliver from death, or open the everlasting doors above." (Horne)

b. **It is God who arms me with strength…. He makes my feet like the feet of deer**: David knew by experience the **strength** of God given to him, and also the skill to use such strength. This skill was like the skill that **deer** have, who can run effortlessly upon the **high places**.

i. David sang about the way God helped him make war (as in 2 Samuel 8). God gave him **strength**, helped him run swiftly and on a secure path (**makes my way perfect…feet like the feet of deer**), made him strong enough to **bend a bow of bronze**, and gave him **the shield of Your salvation**. As a warrior, David knew God as one who helped him make war triumphantly. As God gave David what he needed (physical strength and skill), God will also give us what we need.

ii. Kidner suggests that the **bow of bronze** was actually a wooden bow that was reinforced with metal.

c. **Your right hand has held me up; Your gentleness has made me great**: David was held by the *strength and skill* of God's **right hand**, and made **great** by the **gentleness** of God.

i. We don't often think of someone being made **great** by the **gentleness** of God. It is easy to underestimate the power of God's **gentleness**, and we often want a more evidently spectacular work from God. Yet David – this great warrior – received from and responded to the **gentleness** of God.

ii. We can say this was the **gentleness** of God in at least two respects. It was the **gentleness** that God *showed to* David, and the **gentleness** that David *learned from* God and *showed to* others. "While it was the gentleness God exercised that allowed David his success, it was the gentleness God taught him that was his true greatness." (Kidner)

iii. God had shown His gentleness to David in many ways, and there were even more ways after his victory over Saul and taking of the throne.

- God's gentleness was great to David when he was a despised member of his family, neglected, ignored, tending the sheep in solitude.
- God's gentleness was great to David when He consoled his soul when Saul began to envy and hate him.
- God's gentleness was great to David when He gave him a friend like Jonathan.
- God's gentleness was great to David when He allowed him to have the holy bread at the tabernacle as he was fleeing from Saul.

- God's gentleness was great to David when He told Abigail about Nabal, thereby keeping David from slaughtering a foolish man and his family.

- God's gentleness was great to David when He granted him the self-control to spare Saul's life – *twice*.

- God's gentleness was great to David when He protected him even when he was foolish, such as when he acted like a madman in the court of a Philistine ruler.

- God's gentleness was great to David when He prevented him fighting on behalf of the Philistines against Saul and Israel.

- God's gentleness was great to David when He comforted him after David had lost all at Ziklag; where David encouraged himself in the LORD and afterwards recovered all.

iv. We notice also what this **gentleness** of God did: it made David **great**. We can say that the **gentleness** of God makes every believer **great** also, more than they often consider.

- In this world, some people are thought to be great because of their royal birth; who has a greater claim to royal birth than the son or daughter of the King of Kings?

- In this world, some people are thought to be great because of their election; what greater election is there than to be the elect of God?

- In this world, some people are thought to be great because of their wealth; who has greater riches than the children and heirs of the God who owns all?

- In this world, some people are thought to be great because of their victories; who has achieved greater victory than the one who is in unity with Jesus Christ, the greatest champion of all?

- In this world, some people are thought to be great because of their influence; who has greater influence than the child of God who can move the hand of God with his faithful and righteous prayers?

- In this world, some people are thought to be great because of their discoveries; who has discovered anything greater than the nature of the infinite and eternal God?

- In this world, some people are thought to be great because of their history; who has a greater heritage than a member of the body of Christ as it spans through the ages and generations?

- In this world, some people are thought to be great because of their destiny; who has a more glorious and amazing destiny than the heirs of His glory, those who are His own inheritance?

3. (37-42) God gives David victory over his enemies.

I have pursued my enemies and overtaken them;
Neither did I turn back again till they were destroyed.
I have wounded them,
So that they could not rise;
They have fallen under my feet.
For You have armed me with strength for the battle;
You have subdued under me those who rose up against me.
You have also given me the necks of my enemies,
So that I destroyed those who hated me.
They cried out, but *there was* none to save;
***Even* to the LORD, but He did not answer them.**
Then I beat them as fine as the dust before the wind;
I cast them out like dirt in the streets.

a. **I have pursued my enemies and overtaken them**: Here David had in mind those other than Saul. David knew that as King of Israel he would have to face enemies from surrounding nations, and here he celebrated the past victories God gave him against his **enemies**.

b. **Neither did I turn back again till they were destroyed…. You have also given me the necks of my enemies**: David fought as a true warrior, and sought to utterly defeat the enemies of Israel on the field of battle. He properly believed that God gave him the victory over these enemies.

i. "Thou hast made me a complete conqueror. *Treading on the neck* of an enemy was the triumph of the conqueror, and the utmost disgrace of the vanquished." (Clarke)

ii. "Of David we may say, as one did of Julius Caesar, you may perceive him to have been an excellent soldier by his very language; for he wrote with the same spirit he fought." (Trapp)

4. (43-49) God establishes David's throne.

You have delivered me from the strivings of the people;
You have made me the head of the nations;
A people I have not known shall serve me.
As soon as they hear of me they obey me;
The foreigners submit to me.
The foreigners fade away,
And come frightened from their hideouts.

The LORD lives!
Blessed *be* **my Rock!**
Let the God of my salvation be exalted.
It is **God who avenges me,**
And subdues the peoples under me;
He delivers me from my enemies.
You also lift me up above those who rise against me;
You have delivered me from the violent man.
Therefore I will give thanks to You, O LORD, among the Gentiles,
And sing praises to Your name.

a. **You have delivered me from the strivings of the people**: David knew that taking the throne of Israel was more than just a matter of removing Saul. There were also the **strivings of the people**, of those who did not immediately support David as king over a united Israel (2 Samuel 2-5).

b. **You have made me the head of the nations; a people I have not known shall serve me**: David also knew that God would raise him up not only as the King of Israel, but as a regional power with authority over neighboring nations who brought him tribute.

i. Isaiah 55:3-5 (and other passages) tell us that this promise will have an even greater fulfillment in the millennial kingdom of Jesus Christ, when David will be the king over the millennial Israel, which will be exalted above the other nations of the earth.

ii. **As soon as they hear of me they obey me**: We could say that Psalm 18:44 tells us how we should obey Jesus. This not only tells us of the obligation of the believer, but also that one *can* immediately come to Jesus Christ, be converted, and live obediently to God. No probation period is necessary.

iii. "If any of you have thought that trusting Christ does not involve obeying him, you have made a great mistake. They do very wrong who cry up believing in Christ, and yet depreciate obedience to him, for obeying is believing in another form, and springs out of believing." (Spurgeon)

c. **The LORD lives! Blessed be my Rock**: All of this made David love and honor the LORD more than ever. He gave praise to God for the great things He had done. He had truly **delivered** David **from the violent man**, most notably the murderous Saul who hunted him.

i. "If we begin with 'The Lord is my Rock,' we shall end with 'Blessed be my Rock.'" (Maclaren)

d. Therefore I will give thanks to You, O LORD, among the Gentiles, and sing praises to Your name: On one level, this was David praising God for his deliverance and safety among his neighboring kingdoms. On a second level, Paul quotes this in Romans 15:8-12 as the first of four Old Testament prophesies demonstrating that the work of Jesus Christ was not only for the Jewish people, but for the Gentiles also.

i. "And therefore David is here transported beyond himself, even to his seed forever, as it is expressed in Psalm 18:50, and speaks this in special relation to Christ." (Poole)

ii. "While David may have thought only of Yahweh's fame spread abroad, his words at their full value portray the Lord's anointed (Psalm 18:50), ultimately the Messiah, praising Him *among* – in fellowship with – a host of Gentile worshippers." (Kidner)

iii. "At this point we are encouraged to look back over the entire psalm for messianic meanings." (Boice) We can see many pictures of Jesus and His work in this psalm:

- Psalm 18:1-6 suggests His death (*the pangs of death encompassed me...the sorrows of Sheol surrounded me; the snares of death confronted me*).

- Psalm 18:7-18 suggests His resurrection (*the earth shook and trembled; the foundations of the hills also quaked and were shaken.... He sent from above, He took me; He drew me out of many waters. He delivered me from my strong enemy*).

- Psalm 18:19-27 suggests His exaltation (*I have kept the ways of the LORD.... I was also blameless before Him.... Therefore the LORD has recompensed me according to my righteousness*).

- Psalm 18:28-42 suggests His victory (*For by You I can run against a troop.... I have pursued my enemies and overtaken them*). Jesus was strong enough to run against a troop and be victorious; the enemies against Jesus were strong and disciplined; yet Christ confronted them and defeated them. Jesus was great enough to jump over a wall: the wall of God's holy law that separated us from Him. He didn't destroy the wall; instead with His holy life He jumped over it and fulfilled the law on our behalf.

- Psalm 18:43-50 suggests His kingdom (*You have made me the head of the nations.... The foreigners submit to me.... You also lift me up above those who rise against me.... Therefore I will give thanks to You, O LORD, among the Gentiles*).

iv. While the use of Psalm 18:49 in Romans 15:9 does show that the Holy Spirit spoke of Jesus and His work here, it also has a unique application to David himself. "There is a sense in which it applies particularly to David, well observed by *Theodoret*: 'We see,' says he, 'evidently the fulfilment of this prophecy; for even to the present day David praises the Lord among the Gentiles by the mouth of true believers; seeing there is not a town, village, hamlet, country, nor even a desert, where Christians dwell, in which God is not praised by their singing the Psalms of David.'" (Clarke)

5. (50) God blesses His anointed king.

Great deliverance He gives to His king,
And shows mercy to His anointed,
To David and his descendants forevermore.

a. **Great deliverance He gives to His king**: David could say this with confidence, not only that God would give him **deliverance**, but also more importantly that he was **His king**. David knew this because he did all that he could to make sure that *he* did not seize or usurp the throne. He let God give it to him in time. David therefore had the blessed benefit of knowing that he was *God's* king, and not one of his own making.

b. **And shows mercy to His anointed**: David perhaps thought back some 20 years before, when he was first **anointed** for the throne that he now received. It had been a long, but important journey between the time of his anointing and his receiving the throne.

c. **To David and his descendants forevermore**: Here David understood something by either intuition or by faith, something that would not be specifically promised to him until later. The promise was that David (and not Saul) would begin a hereditary monarchy in Israel, and that **his descendants** would also sit on the throne of Israel. This was the promise to build a house for David that God explicitly made in 2 Samuel 7:1-17.

Psalm 19 – The Heavens, the Word, and the Glory of God

The title tells us both the author and the audience of the psalm: **To the Chief Musician. A Psalm of David.** *Some believe that the Chief Musician is the Lord* GOD *Himself, and others suppose him to be a leader of choirs or musicians in David's time, such as Heman the singer or Asaph (1 Chronicles 6:33, 16:5-7, and 25:6).*

"This Psalm reflects, more than any other, the beauty and splendor of the Hebrew poetry found in the Psalter. C.S. Lewis wrote, 'I take this to be the greatest poem in the Psalter and one of the greatest lyrics in the world.'" (Willem VanGemeren)

A. The message from the heavens.

1. (1-4a) The message from the heavens is broad.

The heavens declare the glory of God;
And the firmament shows His handiwork.
Day unto day utters speech,
And night unto night reveals knowledge.
***There is* no speech nor language**
***Where* their voice is not heard.**
Their line has gone out through all the earth,
And their words to the end of the world.

> a. **The heavens declare the glory of God**: David looked to the heavens – not the spiritual heaven where God is enthroned, but the heavens of the blue sky and the night sky – and he clearly saw **the glory of God** declared.

> > i. He could see it in the blue sky, with the glory of the sun and clouds and the beauty of sunrises and sunsets.

> > ii. He could see it in the night sky, with the brightness of the moon, the awe of the starry sky and the cloudy spread of the distant galaxies.

iii. These together – with their size, their awe, their grandeur – shouted to David and all who would see, "The God who created all this is glorious, and this is evidence of His glory."

- He is glorious in His size, having created something so big.

- He is glorious in His engineering, having created something that works together so well.

- He is glorious in His artistry, having created something so beautiful.

- He is glorious in His goodness and kindness, having created something for all humanity to see.

b. **And the firmament shows His handiwork**: David repeated the idea in the previous line. "**Firmament**" is a poetic way of referring to the heavens or the sky, and they show the **handiwork** of God.

c. **Day unto day utters speech, and night unto night reveals knowledge**: The day sky and the night sky speak to us, and reveal knowledge about the glory, wisdom, and creative greatness of God.

i. **Utters speech**: "This is stronger in the Hebrew text than it appears to be in English, for the image is literally of a gushing spring that copiously pours forth sweet, refreshing waters of revelation." (Boice)

ii. **Reveals knowledge**: "*Knowledge* is well matched with *night*, since without the night skies man would have known, until recently, nothing but an empty universe." (Kidner) If God had not placed the stars in the night sky, the blackness of night would have communicated powerfully to all humanity, ancient and modern, "There is nothing and no one out there."

iii. "Though all preachers on earth should grow silent, and every human mouth cease from publishing the glory of God, the heavens above will never cease to declare and proclaim his majesty and glory. They are for ever preaching; for, like an unbroken chain, their message is delivered from day to day and from night to night." (Tholuck, cited in Spurgeon)

iv. "Day bids us labour, night reminds us to prepare for our last home; day bids us work for God, and night invites us to rest in him; day bids us look for endless day, and night warns us to escape from everlasting night." (Spurgeon)

d. **There is no speech nor language where their voice is not heard**: The glory of God in the visible heavens is for all to see; it is communicated to all mankind, no matter what their **language**. It is a message that has **gone out through all the earth**.

> i. The Apostle Paul expanded this idea in Romans 1. He explained that God's *invisible attributes are clearly seen, being understood by the things that are made, even His eternal power and Godhead, so that they are without excuse* (Romans 1:20). Paul told us that because this testimony had gone out through all creation, all men are *without excuse* for rejecting the God who gave us such clear (and beautiful) evidence of His power and wisdom.

> ii. "Should a man live underground, and there converse with the works of art and mechanism, and should afterwards be brought up into the open day, and see the several glories of the heaven and earth, he would immediately pronounce them the works of such a Being as we define God to be." (Aristotle, cited in Spurgeon)

> iii. "For the scientist who has lived by his faith in the power of reason, the story ends like a bad dream. He has scaled the mountains of ignorance; he is about to conquer the highest peak; as he pulls himself over the rock, he is greeted by a band of theologians who have been sitting there for centuries." (Astronomer and physicist Robert Jastrow, cited in Boice)

2. (4b-6) The message from the heavens is strong and glorious.

In them He has set a tabernacle for the sun,
Which *is* like a bridegroom coming out of his chamber,
And rejoices like a strong man to run its race.
Its rising *is* from one end of heaven,
And its circuit to the other end;
And there is nothing hidden from its heat.

> a. **In them He has set a tabernacle for the sun**: David poetically described the nighttime sky as a dwelling place – a tent, a **tabernacle** – for **the sun**. The sun comes out of its "tent" every day to cross the heavens, and returns to its **tabernacle** at night.

> > i. "God has assigned it its place to occupy and its *course* to run; the whole sky its mere *tent* and track." (Kidner)

> b. **Like a bridegroom coming out of his chamber, and rejoices like a strong man to run its race**: The sun makes its course through the sky with strength and joy, like a man in his prime or an athlete running a race.

> > i. "All would agree that the psalm, if it glances at mythology, repudiates it. The sun may be 'like' a bridegroom or a runner; it is in fact no more than a glorious part of God's 'handiwork.'" (Kidner)

c. **Its rising is from one end of heaven…there is nothing hidden from its heat**: The sun covers the whole sky, and its strength extends everywhere. It is a wonderful example of the glory of God declared in the heavens.

B. The message from the Word of God.

1. (7-9) The glorious character of God's word, described seven ways.

The law of the LORD is perfect, converting the soul;
The testimony of the LORD is sure, making wise the simple;
The statutes of the LORD are right, rejoicing the heart;
The commandment of the LORD is pure, enlightening the eyes;
The fear of the LORD is clean, enduring forever;
The judgments of the LORD are true *and* righteous altogether.

a. **The law of the LORD**: Here David abruptly shifted from praising the God who reveals Himself in creation to praising the same God for revealing Himself in His word. It is as if David said, "Creation tells us much about God, but His word tells us much more."

i. "'Two things', according to Kant, 'fill the mind with ever new and increasing admiration and awe…the starry heavens above and the moral law within.' The psalm transcends the second of these themes by looking to the divine law revealed." (Kidner)

ii. One reason the word is a greater revelation than creation is that it tells us much more about God. It reveals Him as the covenant God of love, as reflected in the structure of this psalm. In Psalm 19:1-6, God is referred to as *El* – the most generic word for God in the Hebrew language (even more generic than the commonly used *Elohim*). Yet here at Psalm 19:7-9, God is referred to as *Yahweh* (**the LORD**), the God of covenant love and faithfulness to His people.

iii. "He is wisest who reads both the world-book and the Word-book as two volumes of the same work, and feels concerning them, 'My Father wrote them both.'" (Spurgeon)

iv. David then explains seven glorious statements about the word of God: how wonderful and effective it is. As is common in other places – especially the great Psalm 119 – David used a variety of expressions to refer to the word of God (**law, testimony, statutes, commandment, fear, judgments**). It is best to see these as poetic terms describing God's written revelation in general, rather than one specific type of revelation (such as only the laws given in the Mosaic law).

b. **The law of the LORD is perfect, converting the soul**: The word of God is **perfect**. It gives us *all things that pertain to life and godliness* (2 Peter 1:3). While it does not give us all knowledge, all the knowledge it gives is true and **perfect**. Understood in its literary context, God's word is never wrong in science or history or the understanding of either divine or human nature.

> i. Part of the perfection of God's word is that it is effective; it does the work of **converting the soul**. There is power in the reading and hearing and studying of the word of God that goes beyond intellectual benefit; it actually changes for the better – *converts* – **the soul**.

> ii. The Hebrew word translated here as **converting** is perhaps better understood as *reviving* – that is, bringing new life to the soul. "First, God's word 'revives.' Its restorative quality gives healing to the whole person by assuring forgiveness and cleansing and by giving life to the godly." (VanGemeren)

c. **The testimony of the Lord is sure, making wise the simple**: The word of God is **sure**, being reliable and certain. As the psalmist would write in Psalm 119:89, *Forever, O Lord, Your word is settled in heaven.*

> i. "*Sure*, by its passive form, can mean not only what is firm but what is confirmed: *cf.* 'verified' in Genesis 42:20." (Kidner)

> ii. Because it is so sure and certain, it does the work of **making wise the simple**. Many people of simple education or upbringing have tremendous wisdom unto life and godliness because they study and trust the **sure** word of the Lord.

d. **The statutes of the Lord are right, rejoicing the heart**: God's word and the commands contained within are **right**. They are morally **right**, they are practically **right**, and they are universally **right**. They are **right** because it is the revelation of a God who is holy, true, and always **right**.

> i. **Are right**: "To make *straight, smooth, right, upright*, opposed to *crookedness* in mind or conduct; showing what the man should be, both *within* and *without*." (Clarke)

> ii. The one who knows the word of God and the God of the word *rejoices* in this. He finds joy, actual pleasure in the truth of God and relationship with God revealed in His word.

e. **The commandment of the Lord is pure, enlightening the eyes**: Because God's word comes from a God who is Himself **pure** and holy, the word itself is **pure**. A pure God can communicate no other way. We never have to worry about the word of God leading people into sin or impurity; if it seems to have happened, it is evidence that the scriptures have been twisted (2 Peter 3:16).

i. This pure word will *enlighten* **the eyes**. It will bring the cheer and comfort and knowledge and confidence that a light in the midst of darkness brings.

f. **The fear of the LORD is clean, enduring forever**: The word of God is **clean**, and therefore is **enduring forever**. It will never fade or corrode, diminishing because of impurity. It is **clean** and it makes clean.

i. Here David called the word of God the "**fear of the LORD**." It is deeply connected to the awe and majesty of God Himself. One who reads and hears and studies the word of God, meeting Him in His word, will have an appropriate appreciation of God's awe and majesty – **the fear of the LORD**.

g. **The judgments of the LORD are true and righteous altogether**: David summarized this beautiful chain of seven pearls, each describing some aspect of the word of God. Here he declared that the words of God **are true and righteous altogether**; there is nothing false or unrighteous in His word.

i. There is no applied aspect to this statement as in the previous five. For David, it was enough to simply say it: "**true and righteous altogether**." Perhaps David assumed we would be wise and logical enough to apply it ourselves: "Therefore read it, study it, meditate on it, love it, live it."

ii. Remember that King David wrote this with only a fraction of what we have today as the word of God; his portion was not as glorious as the complete revelation of God. David would have had the first five books of Moses (Genesis through Deuteronomy); Joshua, Judges, a few psalms; and perhaps Job and Ruth. We can only imagine what King David would have written about Isaiah or Hosea or the entire Psalter, much less any of the books of the New Testament. We can say with confidence that God's word *is far more glorious than King David knew!*

2. (10-11) The great value of God's word.

More to be desired *are they* than gold,
Yea, than much fine gold;
Sweeter also than honey and the honeycomb.
Moreover by them Your servant is warned,
***And* in keeping them *there is* great reward.**

a. **More to be desired are they than gold**: King David insisted that the value of God's word – His written revelation to man – was more valuable and desirable than **gold** itself. David wanted no amount of money or wealth to command his attention and affection more than the word of God.

i. King David was a massively wealthy man, yet he is rarely known for his riches. He is much more known for his great heart towards God. His son Solomon was even more wealthy than David, and was known for his riches – yet not nearly as much for his heart towards God and his love of God's word.

ii. If it weren't enough to say that God's word should be more desirable than **gold**, King David amplified the point by saying, "**Yea, than much fine gold**."

iii. "This is strictly true; but who believes it? By most men *gold* is preferred both to *God* and his *judgments*; and they will barter every heavenly portion for gold and silver!" (Clarke)

b. **Sweeter also than honey and the honeycomb**: For King David, God's word was not only to be held in greater esteem than material wealth, but also greater than experiences of the senses. **Honey** is sweet and pleasant to eat, but God's word is **sweeter** still.

c. **Moreover by them Your servant is warned, and in keeping them there is great reward**: David here gave two reasons why the word of God was greater than material wealth or sensual pleasures.

i. God's word gives instruction – *warning* – that wealth or pleasures do not give (**is warned**).

- Warning is needed for sins we are susceptible to.
- Warning is needed for dangers we cannot see.
- Warning is needed for dangers we cannot appreciate.
- Warning is needed for dangers far off in the future.
- Warnings are often *rejected*.

ii. God's word gives benefit – **reward** – greater than wealth or pleasures (**great reward**).

d. **In keeping them there is great reward**: It is also true that there is **great reward** *for* keeping the Word of God; but that is not what the psalmist said here. Here David noted the reward **in keeping them**. There is a sense in which obedience becomes its own reward, because we live the way God wants us and designed us to live.

i. One of the great rewards of keeping the word of God is peace of mind. "A quiet conscience is a little heaven. A martyr was fastened to the stake, and the sheriff who was to execute him expressed his sorrow that he should persevere in his opinions, and compel him to set fire to the pile. The martyr answered, 'Do not trouble yourself, for I am not troubling myself. Come and lay your hand upon my heart, and see if it does not beat quietly.' His request was complied with, and he was found to be quite calm. 'Now,' said he, 'lay your hand on your own heart, and see if you are not more troubled than I am; and then go your way, and, instead of pitying me, pity yourself.'" (Spurgeon)

3. (12-13) The desire for inward cleansing.

Who can understand *his* errors?
Cleanse me from secret *faults.*
Keep back Your servant also from presumptuous *sins;*
Let them not have dominion over me.
Then I shall be blameless,
And I shall be innocent of great transgression.

a. **Who can understand his errors?** In the previous verse David reflected on the warnings found in the word of God, and in the great reward found in obeying God's word. This made him reflect on the times and ways he had ignored the warnings and not kept the word.

i. In asking "**Who can understand his errors?**" David understood that he had ignored and disobeyed God's word even more than he was aware of. What he knew was enough to make him concerned; his actual **errors** before God were still worse.

ii. Notably, the fact that we cannot **understand** our **errors** does not excuse us from them. We are still accountable for such **errors** and **faults** before God and must trust in His atonement to cleanse us from these **errors** and **secret faults**.

b. **Cleanse me from secret faults**: David wisely prayed this prayer, knowing that he could not know just how many his **errors** were before God. He needed cleansing even from the sins and **faults** that were secret to him.

i. "We desire the inner purity of heart. But this is peculiarly God's prerogative. It is his work to cleanse the thoughts of our hearts by the inspiration of his Holy Spirit. 'Cleanse THOU me.'" (Meyer)

ii. **Secret faults**: "From those which I have committed, and have forgotten; from those for which I have not repented; from those which have been committed in my heart, but have not been brought to act in my life; from those which I have committed without knowing that they were sins, sins of *ignorance*; and from those which I have committed in private, for which I should blush and be confounded were they to be made public." (Clarke)

c. **Keep back Your servant also from presumptuous sins**: David added this because he knew that his problem was greater than **secret faults** and unknown **errors**. Without God's help (which he here prayed for), he was also perfectly capable of committing **presumptuous sins**, sins done in a proud and knowing way.

    i. Things that make sin **presumptuous**:··

- When we know better.
- When friends have warned us.
- When God Himself has warned us.
- When we have warned others against the same sins.
- When we plan and relish our sin.

    ii. The description of **errors** and **secret faults** and **presumptuous sins** reminds us that sin has a progression.

- It goes from passing temptation to chosen thought (**errors**).
- It goes from chosen thought to object of meditation.
- It goes from object of meditation to wished-for fulfillment.
- It goes from wished-for fulfillment to planned action (**secret faults**).
- It goes from planned action to opportunity sought.
- It goes from opportunity sought to performed act.
- It goes from performed act to repeated action.
- It goes from repeated action to delight (**presumptuous sins**).
- It goes from delight to new and various ways.
- It goes from new and various ways to habit.
- It goes from habit to idolatry, demanding to be served.
- It goes from idolatry to sacrifice.
- It goes from sacrifice to slavery.

    iii. All along this continuum the Holy Spirit – and hopefully our conscience – say, "No – stop!" All along this continuum, we are given *the way of escape* by God (1 Corinthians 10:13), if we will only take it. Yet if we do not, and we end up in slavery to sin, it legitimately questions the state of our soul (1 John 3:6-9).

    iv. Because of this great danger, David prayed **keep back Your servant also from presumptuous sins**. "Will you just note, that this prayer was the *prayer of a saint*, the prayer of a holy man of God? Did David need to pray thus? Did the 'man after God's own heart' need to cry, 'Keep back thy servant?' Yes, he did." (Spurgeon)

d. **Let them not have dominion over me**: Indeed, King David not only knew that he was capable of such sins, but that they could potentially have **dominion over** him. His prayer was rightly placed; his love of God's word and his dependence upon God in prayer would help him stay free from the dominion of enslaving sin.

i. This prayer is even more fitting for one who relates to God on the basis of the New Covenant. As Paul wrote, *For sin shall not have dominion over you, for you are not under law, but under grace* (Romans 6:14).

e. **Then I shall be blameless**: David knew that when sin was addressed in his life – dealing both with inward, secret sin *and* outward, presumptuous, enslaving sin – then he could be **blameless** and **innocent of great transgression**.

i. This was not a claim of sinless perfection, either achieved or to attain to before resurrection. David knew well that he needed to be *cleansed*, and trusted in God's perfect sacrifice – prefigured by the animal sacrifices he practiced in the Mosaic system. David understood blamelessness and innocence on a human, relative level and not in an absolute sense according to the Divine measure.

4. (14) A prayer of surrender and purity.

Let the words of my mouth and the meditation of my heart
Be acceptable in Your sight,
O LORD, my strength and my Redeemer.

a. **Let the words of my mouth, and the meditation of my heart be acceptable in Your sight**: David closed this glorious psalm with a humble surrender of his mouth and heart to God. He knew that real godliness was not only a matter of what a man did, but also of what he said and thought in his heart.

i. This was not a proud proclamation that David *knew* he was innocent and blameless; it was a plea to be made so by the transforming power of God.

ii. **Acceptable in Your sight**: "The psalm ends, not on the note of avoiding sin, but on that of offering back to God the mind's fitting response to His own words, as a pure sacrifice (*cf.* Hosea 14:2). This is the probable implication of *acceptable*, a term often found in sacrificial contexts." (Kidner)

b. **O Lᴏʀᴅ, my strength and my Redeemer**: King David looked to the Lord Gᴏᴅ to be his strength and redemption. He knew that he needed a **Redeemer**, and that the faithful God would rescue him.

    i. **Strength** can also be translated as *Rock*. God's strength is like a mighty rock that rescues us and gives us a firm standing place.

    ii. **Redeemer** is that great Hebrew word *goel*, the kinsman-redeemer. It was the *goel* who bought his relative out of slavery, who rescued him in bankruptcy and total loss. King David looked to God Himself as his kinsman-redeemer.

    iii. "If our Rock were not our Redeemer, we should be without hope. If our Redeemer were not our Rock, still might we be afraid. It is good that we never forget the mutual interpretation of these two revelations of God." (Morgan)

    iv. This psalm has run a glorious course. It begins with recognizing the glory of God in creation, and then the glory of His written revelation. Next to this great God and His great works, David knew himself to be small and sinful. Yet this great God would also be David's **strength** and **Redeemer** as David put his trust in Him.

    v. The glorious God of creation and revelation was also the glorious God of personal relationship and redemption for His people. King David knew this; so should we.

Psalm 20 – The Lord Saves His Anointed

The title of this psalm is the same as several others: **To the Chief Musician. A Psalm of David.** *Yet the psalm itself is different, notably because it is in the voice of a multitude that prays on behalf of the King of Israel as he is ready to go into battle. This is seen in the way the psalm speaks in the first-person plural (We) in Psalm 20:1-5 and 20:7-9. The first-person singular (I) of 20:6 is likely the response of either David himself or the High Priest on his behalf.*

Yet since this is **A Psalm of David**, *perhaps David took a moment of spontaneous prayer by the people on his behalf and shaped it into a song to remember and recall the spiritual strength and glory of that moment.*

A. The people pray for the King.

1. (1-2) May the Lord answer and help.

May the Lord answer you in the day of trouble;
May the name of the God of Jacob defend you;
May He send you help from the sanctuary,
And strengthen you out of Zion;

> a. **May the Lord answer you**: This was a prayer from a multitude or congregation (based on the use of *we* in 20:5) that God would answer the prayers of one, who in context is the king readying for battle.
>
> > i. We know that "**you**" refers to one person, because it is in the singular. "*You* is singular throughout, identified in verse 6 as the Lord's anointed." (Kidner)
> >
> > ii. The picture is that of King David, before battle – perhaps something like the battle with the Syrians in 2 Samuel 10 – at the tabernacle of God and offering prayers and sacrifices. Here the onlooking multitude responds to the king's prayer with the cry, "**May the Lord answer you in the day of trouble**."

iii. "It is one of the most stirring of the Psalms, by its tense awareness of life-and-death issues soon to be resolved." (Kidner)

iv. With the eye of faith, we see that this also speaks to the great battle fought by one greater than King David – by Jesus, the Son of David and the King of Kings. We can imagine this prayer being offered prophetically for Jesus as He pointed Himself toward the cross, where He would fight the greatest battle against sin, death, and Satan's power.

b. **Answer you in the day of trouble...defend you...send you help... strengthen you**: After the pattern of Hebrew poetry, this idea is intensively expressed by the use of repetition with slight variation. David was about to lead Israel into battle, and he needed the help of God in each of these ways.

i. Because King David was about to lead Israel as a whole into battle, the language is full of references appealing to the LORD as the God of Israel.

- **The LORD**: Using *Yahweh*, the covenant name of God.

- **The God of Jacob**: Remembering Israel's patriarch.

- **From the sanctuary**: Calling to mind the tabernacle, the center of Israel's worship.

- **Out of Zion**: Referring to the hills of Jerusalem.

ii. "This word for *sanctuary* is simply 'holiness', a synonym here for *Zion*, where already God's ark, but not yet His Temple, signified His presence." (Kidner)

iii. The prayer that God would **strengthen you out of Zion** is fitting for more than the field of battle. It is also appropriate for the church pulpit, which is a field of battle in a spiritual sense. "This verse is a benediction befitting a Sabbath morning, and may be the salutation either of a pastor to his people, or of a church to its minister." (Spurgeon)

2. (3) May the LORD receive sacrifice.

May He remember all your offerings,
And accept your burnt sacrifice. Selah

a. **May He remember all your offerings**: Sacrifice was commonly made at important moments, such as on the eve of battle. This is a prayer that the LORD would see and receive the sacrifices King David would make before war.

i. **All your offerings**: "The *minchah*, which is here mentioned, was a *gratitude-offering*. It is rarely used to signify a bloody sacrifice." (Clarke)

b. **May He remember...and accept your burnt sacrifice**: This reminds us that *not all* sacrifices are accepted before God. If they were not offered with faith and in accordance with the Levitical system, they would not be remembered or accepted by God.

i. **Burnt sacrifice**: "The *olah* here mentioned was a *bloody sacrifice*. The blood of the victim was spilt at the altar, and the flesh consumed." (Clarke)

ii. The place of *faith* was important in the Old Testament sacrificial system. The one who brought the offering had to trust in the ultimate, perfect sacrifice that God would one day provide, the one that each animal sacrifice pointed towards (Genesis 22:8, 22:14).

iii. "The prayer for acceptance of the burnt offering is very graphic, since the word rendered 'accept' is literally 'esteem fat.'" (Maclaren)

c. **Selah**: The idea in the Hebrew for this word (occurring 74 times in the Old Testament) is for a *pause*. Most scholars think it speaks of a reflective pause, a pause to meditate on the words just spoken. It may also be a musical instruction, or a musical interlude of some kind.

i. *We* take this **Selah** as an opportunity to consider Jesus, and see that this prayer was appropriate for Him as He faced the cross. The prayer was worthy to be prayed – that God would indeed **remember** and **accept** the offering Jesus made on the cross, which could rightly be called a **burnt sacrifice**, as it was burned with the fire of God's righteous judgment, and Jesus held nothing back in this **sacrifice**.

3. (4) May the LORD grant fulfillment.

May He grant you according to your heart's *desire*,
And fulfill all your purpose.

a. **May He grant you according to your heart's desire**: In this moment, King David had one desire – to defend the people of God and the kingdom in covenant with God. Therefore it was good to pray, "**May He grant you according to your heart's desire.**"

i. When our desires are in accord with the plan and will of God for us, we can pray this same prayer with confidence. We can also look for God to bring our desires more and more into conformity with His, in the course of our Christian growth.

b. **And fulfill all your purpose**: Since David's **purpose** was victory for the people of God, this was a good and necessary prayer to pray.

i. We see this statement also applied to the great desire and purpose for the King of Kings as He went to battle to accomplish our salvation. We look to Jesus, struggling in the Garden of Gethsemane and say to Him, **"May He grant You according to Your heart's desire, and fulfill all Your purpose."**

ii. On a personal level, we also see that God gives each one a **purpose** to fulfill in His great plan of the ages. The key to a life of fulfilled **desire** and achieved **purpose** is to find our place in His great plan, instead of hoping to make God an actor in our plan.

- Jesus knew this fulfilled desire and purpose, shown by His prayer in John 17: *I have finished the work which You have given Me to do* (John 17:4).

- The Apostle Paul knew this fulfilled desire and purpose, shown by these words toward the end of his earthly life: *I have fought the good fight, I have finished the race, I have kept the faith* (2 Timothy 4:7).

4. (5) May the LORD answer prayer.

We will rejoice in your salvation,
And in the name of our God we will set up *our* **banners!**
May the LORD fulfill all your petitions.

a. **We will rejoice in your salvation**: This was the confidence the people had in King David's success. They had so much trust in God's deliverance that they had already planned to **set up our banners** of joyful celebration.

i. "Here the raising of the banners signifies God's victory over the enemies." (VanGemeren)

ii. The **banners** are "Our flags of defiance to the enemy, or our tokens of triumph to God's glory, who hath given us the victory." (Trapp)

b. **May the LORD fulfill all your petitions**: Once again the prayer demonstrates the confidence that God would hear and **fulfill** the prayers of His king.

i. This was true both of David and the Son of David (John 17:1-5); of the King of Israel and the King of Kings. Jesus prayed for success in His work on the cross, and it was unthinkable that the Father would not answer the prayers of the Son.

B. The triumph of the LORD's Anointed.

1. (6) The LORD saves His anointed.

Now I know that the LORD saves His anointed;
He will answer him from His holy heaven
With the saving strength of His right hand.

a. **Now I know that the LORD saves His anointed**: Here King David expressed the great confidence that God would answer the prayers of His people. God would save (rescue) the king (**His anointed**).

  i. **His anointed**: In a sense, all of the kings of Israel were God's **anointed** because they were all appointed to their office by a literal anointing of oil poured upon their head. This literal anointing with oil was a picture of the spiritual anointing with the Holy Spirit needed for their duty of leading the people of God as king. In saying "**His anointed**," David refers to himself as king.

  ii. **His anointed**: At the same time, it was also understood that there would come an ultimate Anointed One, the perfect King of Israel – the Meshiach, the Christ, the Messiah (as in Psalm 2 and others). It was true of David and Israel in his day that the Lord **saves His anointed** and his people; it is even more perfectly true of the ultimate and perfect Anointed One, Jesus Christ.

  iii. "The verb 'saves', from the same root as 'victorious,' could yield the translation 'the LORD gives victory to his anointed.'" (VanGemeren) Kidner also notes that **saves** (in Psalm 20:6 and 20:9) comes from the same root in Hebrew as the name of Jesus.

  iv. Indeed, **the LORD saves His anointed**:

  • The Father saved the Son from sin.

  • The Father saved the Son from pride.

  • The Father saved the Son from self-reliance.

  • The Father saved the Son from doubt.

  • The Father saved the Son from failure.

  • The Father saved the Son from death, by raising Him from the dead.

b. **He will answer him from His holy heaven with the saving strength of His right hand**: This confirms and strengthens the idea that the LORD **saves His anointed**.

  i. He is saved by an **answer**; God is not silent to His anointed.

  ii. He is saved from **heaven**; God hears and sends help from His throne.

  iii. He is saved with power, **with the saving strength**.

  iv. He is saved with skill and favor, with the **strength** that comes from **His right hand**.

  v. Each of these was true for King David, but even more perfectly true of the Son of David, the ultimate **anointed** of the LORD.

2. (7) Trusting in the name of the LORD.

Some *trust* in chariots, and some in horses;
But we will remember the name of the LORD our God.

a. **Some trust in chariots, and some in horses**: David knew what kings and their people usually trusted in – human strength and the ways it is often expressed (**in chariots** and **in horses**).

i. If writing today, David might say something like, "Some trust in nuclear weapons and some trust in tanks." It is part of human nature to put our **trust** in such things.

ii. "Chariots and horses are very terrible, especially to raw soldiers unaccustomed to their whirling onset; but the Name is mightier." (Maclaren)

iii. Part of the reason David refused to **trust in chariots** and **horses** was because God had commanded it so, commanding in the Law of Moses that the Kings of Israel would *not* multiply horses for themselves, either for use in cavalry or to pull war-chariots (Deuteronomy 17:16).

b. **But we will remember**: David drew a strong contrast. "They trust in those things, **but** our trust is in God."

i. "In the spiritual war, in which we are all engaged, the first and necessary step to victory is, to renounce all confidence in the wisdom and strength of nature and the world; and to remember, that we can do nothing, but in the name, by the merits, through the power, and for the sake of Jesus Christ, our Lord, and our God." (Horne)

ii. "Alas, how many in our day who profess to be the Lord's are as abjectly dependent upon their fellow-men or upon an arm of flesh in some shape or other, as if they had never known the name of Jehovah at all." (Spurgeon)

c. **But we will remember the name of the LORD our God**: David put his trust in the person, the character of God. He didn't carry the **name of the LORD** as a magical incantation; rather **the name** speaks of the comprehensive character of God and is an expression of His faithfulness to His covenant with Israel.

i. "By *the name of God* is generally understood, in Holy Writ, the various properties and attributes of God: these properties and attributes make up and constitute the *name* of God. As when Solomon says, 'The name of the Lord is a strong tower; the righteous runneth into it and is safe.'" (Melvill, cited in Spurgeon)

ii. *This* – the character and faithfulness of God – was stronger to David and Israel than thousands of **chariots** or **horses**.

iii. Therefore, we sense a triumphant defiance in David when he says, **"But we will remember."** He acknowledges how easy it is to forget, and how counter-intuitive to human nature it is to trust God instead of human strength and resources.

3. (8-9) The triumph of those who trust in the LORD.

They have bowed down and fallen;
But we have risen and stand upright.
Save, LORD!
May the King answer us when we call.

a. **They have bowed down and fallen; but we have risen and stand upright**: David's trust in God could be justified on many grounds, but one of those was the simple truth that David found that *trusting God works*, he learned that this faith leads to success. Those who trusted in chariots and horses **have bowed down and fallen**. Those who remembered the name of the LORD **have risen and stand upright**.

b. **Save, LORD! May the King answer us when we call**: The rescue David confidently sang of had not completely come. He still needed to cry out, **"Save, LORD!"** He still had his trust in the anticipated **answer** of the LORD.

i. "This is the language of faith, not after the battle, but before it." (Morgan)

ii. "The final phrase, literally 'in the day of our calling', has a telling echo of the opening verse." (Kidner)

Psalm 21 – The Joyful King

The title of this psalm is the same as several others: **To the Chief Musician. A Psalm of David.** *It logically connects with the previous one, Psalm 20. It would seem that the victory prayed for and trusted in has been realized, and now David thanks God for the victory given.*

"There the people prayed for the king; here they give thanks for him: there they asked that his desires might be fulfilled; here they bless Jehovah, who has fulfilled them; there the battle was impending; here it has been won, though foes are still in the field." (Alexander Maclaren)

A. A grateful, joyful king.

1. (1-2) The king's joy in God's strength.

The king shall have joy in Your strength, O Lord;
And in Your salvation how greatly shall he rejoice!
You have given him his heart's desire,
And have not withheld the request of his lips. Selah

   a. **The king shall have joy in Your strength, O Lord:** King David had many reasons to take **joy** in the **strength** of God. Perhaps this **joy** came from preservation and success in battle or some other deliverance.

      i. The *tone* of the opening of this psalm is passionate. "The shoutings of the early Methodists in the excitement of the joy were far more pardonable than our own lukewarmness. Our joy should have some sort of inexpressibleness in it." (Spurgeon)

      ii. **The king**: "The ancient Jewish Targum (the Chaldean paraphrase of the Old Testament) and Talmud render the word *king* in verse 1 by *melek mashiach* (King Messiah), which means that the Jews in an early period understood these words to be spoken of the Messiah. A change came in the Middle Ages as a result of a judgment by Rabbi Solomon Isaaci, known as Rashi (b. A.D. 1040). He endorsed the early view but suggested it be dropped, saying, 'Our old doctors interpreted this psalm of King Messiah, but in order to meet the Schismatics [that is, the Christians] it is better to understand it of David himself.'" (Boice)

b. **You have given him his heart's desire**: The **strength** and **salvation** of God came to David in response to both the **desire** of his heart and his spoken prayers (**the request of his lips**).

i. This speaks to the special place *answered prayer* has in the life of the believer. Every Christian should know the thrill of frequent, wonderful answers to prayer. When a Christian does not enjoy the blessing of answered prayer, it is because he is prayerless, he is praying wrongly, or he has some hindrance in prayer.

ii. There are many things that can hinder prayer in the life of the believer, things which would prevent him from saying with David, **"You have given him his heart's desire, and have not withheld the request of his lips."** Unanswered prayer should be regarded as a warning signal that there may be a problem in one or more of the following reasons for unanswered prayer:

- Not abiding in Jesus (John 15:7).
- Unbelief (Matthew 17:20-21).
- Failure to fast (Matthew 17:21).
- Husband not honoring his wife (1 Peter 3:7).
- Not asking (James 4:2).
- Selfish praying (James 4:3).
- Disobedience (1 John 3:22).
- Not praying in God's will (1 John 5:14-15).
- Unconfessed sin (James 5:16).
- Cold, passionless prayer (James 5:16-18; 2 Kings 20:5).
- Prayerlessness or a lack of persistence in prayer (Luke 18:1-7; Psalm 55:17).
- Sin against others (Matthew 5:23-24).
- Lack of unity (Matthew 18:19).
- Not praying in the name of Jesus (John 14:13-14).
- Pride (James 4:6, 1 Peter 5:5, Proverbs 3:34).
- Lying and deceitfulness (Psalm 17:1).
- Lack of Bible reading and Bible teaching (Proverbs 28:9).

- Trusting in the length or the form of prayer (Matthew 6:7).

iii. The avoidance of these things does not *earn* or *merit* God's response; He is not in debt to us if we avoid them. Yet they are clearly hindrances to answered prayer.

c. **Selah**: The idea in the Hebrew for this word (occurring 74 times in the Old Testament) is for a *pause*. Most scholars think it speaks of a reflective pause, a pause to meditate on the words just spoken. It may also be a musical instruction, or a musical interlude of some kind.

i. We take this **Selah** as an opportunity to thank God for the **strength** and **salvation** He has shown in our lives, and for the glorious way He answers prayer. We, like King David of old, take **joy** in such a great and loving God.

2. (3-7) Reasons for the king's joy.

For You meet him with the blessings of goodness;
You set a crown of pure gold upon his head.
He asked life from You, *and* You gave *it* to him—
Length of days forever and ever.
His glory *is* great in Your salvation;
Honor and majesty You have placed upon him.
For You have made him most blessed forever;
You have made him exceedingly glad with Your presence.
For the king trusts in the LORD,
And through the mercy of the Most High he shall not be moved.

a. **You meet him with the blessings of goodness**: King David could see that the **goodness** of God had come to **meet** him. God brought it to him, more than David chasing down these **blessings of goodness**.

i. It was certainly true that God went before David with blessings, and that David recognized and praised Him for it. Yet often it did not *seem* like that in the many long years between his anointing for the throne as a young man and when he finally took the throne of Israel.

ii. God's goodness and grace come to meet us all the time.

- The grace of His love loves us before we ever loved Him.

- The grace of restraint keeps us back from committing sins that would put us even more out of reach of the Gospel.

- The grace of salvation comes out to meet us, bringing us the goodness of God and making us able to receive the Gospel.

- The grace of ministry prepares us a thousand ways for what God has for us in the future.

- The grace of service prepares the ground where we will work before we ever get there.

b. **You set a crown of pure gold upon his head**: David wore the crown both of the throne of Israel – God's special nation – and the crown of victory. Its nature of **pure gold** shows how special the nation and the victory were.

> i. It was undeniably true of King David that he let *God* put the **crown** on his head. Though in some sense he had the right and the reasons to forcibly take the crown from Saul, he waited for God to place it **upon his head**.

c. **He asked life from You, and You gave it to him**: David went into battle praying that God would preserve his life, and now he celebrated the answer to that prayer. In the life-and-death danger of battle, David was given life and **length of days**.

> i. "While the gift of *life…for ever and ever* might have implied to an Old Testament reader either a hyperbole…or an allusion to the endless dynasty promised to David in 2 Samuel 7:16, the New Testament has filled in the picture firmly with the figure of the ultimate king, the Messiah, for whom the whole stanza is true without exaggeration." (Kidner)

d. **His glory is great in Your salvation**: David knew the exaltation that came to kings and victors in battle; but here he declared that this **glory**, this **honor**, this **majesty** he enjoyed came from God and not from himself.

e. **You have made him exceedingly glad with Your presence**: David proclaimed that he was **most blessed forever**, but it was the **presence** of God Himself that was his greatest blessing and gladness. David was more thrilled with the **presence** of God than with the crown of royalty or victory.

f. **The king trusts in the LORD, and through the mercy of the Most High he shall not be moved**: David declared his trust in the **mercy** of God, and that it would continue to preserve and bless him in the future.

> i. Each of these things was certainly true of King David, but they are also – or perhaps even more so – true of David's greater Son, the Messiah, Jesus Christ the Son of David. We can apply each line in Psalm 21:3-7 to Jesus, victorious after His great work on the cross.
>
> - Victorious Jesus was met with the **blessings of goodness** when He ascended to heaven.
>
> - Jesus wears the **crown**, both as King of Kings and glorious conqueror – and His crown is of **pure gold**.

- Jesus **asked life from** God the Father, and as God's Holy One was delivered from the grave.

- Jesus gloried in the **salvation** extended to Him from the Father – not a salvation from sin, but a victory over sin and death.

- Jesus rejoiced in the **presence** of His Father, even though there was a sense in which it was turned away from Him on the cross.

- Jesus continues to trust in His Father and will **not be moved**.

ii. "Napoleon crowned himself, but Jehovah crowned the Lord Jesus; the empire of the one melted in an hour, but the other has an abiding dominion." (Spurgeon)

iii. We think particularly of what Psalm 21:6 tells us of Jesus: **For You have made him most blessed forever; You have made him exceedingly glad with Your presence**. This verse tells us that even though Jesus was a man of sorrows and well acquainted with grief (Isaiah 53:3), yet at the same time He was a man who knew what it was to be **most blessed forever** and **exceedingly glad**.

iv. "He was the Prince of Peace, even when he was despised and rejected of men. Deep as were his griefs, we may reckon Jesus of Nazareth among the happiest of men." (Spurgeon)

v. We can think of many reasons why Jesus is so happy:

- He never sinned, and sin is the mother of sorrow.

- He never was pained by His conscience.

- He never endured in Himself hatred, envy, bitterness or unforgiveness.

- He had perfect peace in the wisdom and power of God the Father.

- He was a giving, generous man who knew the joy of giving.

- He completely finished His work and knew the satisfaction of that.

- He is the source of all blessing and knows the joy of blessing others.

- He rejoices over every sinner that comes to repentance.

- He rejoices in seeing His people at work for Him.

- He rejoices in the sufferings they endure for Him.

B. The judgments of God defend His people.

1. (8-10) What God will do to His enemies.

Your hand will find all Your enemies;
Your right hand will find those who hate You.
You shall make them as a fiery oven in the time of Your anger;
The Lord shall swallow them up in His wrath,
And the fire shall devour them.
Their offspring You shall destroy from the earth,
And their descendants from among the sons of men.

a. **Your hand will find all Your enemies**: David recognized that even though he was victorious in battle, God was not done finding and judging His **enemies**.

i. **The time of Your anger**: "The expression, 'the time of thine anger,' reminds us that as now is the time of his grace, so there will be a set time for his wrath…. There is a day of vengeance of our God; let those who despise the day of grace remember this day of wrath." (Spurgeon)

b. **The Lord shall swallow them up in His wrath**: David confidently expressed his confidence that God would judge His enemies, and he expressed that confidence in the strongest terms – even that God would also judge the posterity of those who fight against Him.

i. "We pity the lost for they are men, but we cannot pity them as enemies of Christ." (Spurgeon)

ii. **The fire shall devour them**: "Those that might have had Christ to rule and save them, but rejected him, and fought against him, even the remembrance of that will be enough to make them to eternity a fiery oven to themselves." (Henry, cited in Spurgeon)

2. (11-12) Why the enemies of God deserve judgment.

For they intended evil against You;
They devised a plot *which* they are not able *to perform.*
Therefore You will make them turn their back;
You will make ready *Your arrows* on Your string toward their faces.

a. **For they intended evil against You**: The strong statements of judgment in Psalm 21:8-10 seem to demand an explanation. Why such a severe judgment? Because they intentionally rebelled against God and His people, even though their plans were bigger than their ability to perform (**they devised a plot which they are not able to perform**).

i. "Intentional evil has a virus in it which is not found in sins of ignorance; now as ungodly men with malice aforethought attack the gospel of Christ, their crime is great, and their punishment will be proportionate." (Spurgeon)

ii. We find comfort in the truth that **they devised a plot which they are not able to perform**. Many threaten and confidently announce the demise of God's work in our day, but they most definitely are **not able to perform** it.

b. **You will make them turn their back**: David sees – and perhaps literally saw – the enemies of God running away on the field of battle, with their **back** turned against the advancing armies of God.

c. **You will make ready Your arrows on Your string toward their faces**: David saw the enemies of God as helpless before the **ready** arrows and taut bow **string** of the war-like, judging God. His **arrows** are aimed right at **their faces**.

i. "The judgments of God are called his 'arrows,' being sharp, swift, sure, and deadly." (Horne)

ii. This reminds us how *near* the judgment of God actually is against those who reject Him, and how it is only His *great mercy* that prevents the release of His arrow of judgment against them. It is a great (but rarely regarded or understood) sin that man ignores and presumes upon this great mercy.

3. (13) Praising the God of strength.

Be exalted, O LORD, in Your own strength!
We will sing and praise Your power.

a. **Be exalted, O LORD, in Your own strength**: David worshipped God directly here. He exalted the LORD who had this great strength within Himself, and never needed to rely on another for strength.

i. "*Exalt thyself, O Lord* – thy creatures cannot exalt thee." (Clarke)

b. **We will sing and praise Your power**: After the direct statement of praise, David expressed the determination that he and the people of God would *continue* to praise God, and to do so in song.

i. The psalm's end is consistent with the tone throughout. It is full of praise to God for the blessings of victory, deliverance, and answered prayer. This attitude should always be among the people of God.

Psalm 22 – The Servant of God Forsaken, Rescued, and Triumphant

This is another psalm with a title: **To the Chief Musician. Set to "The Deer of the Dawn." A Psalm of David**. *We can say that this is a Psalm sung to the Greatest Musician, to an unknown tune, by the Sweet Psalmist of Israel (2 Samuel 23:1). Here, David sings as more than an artist, but also as one of the greatest prophets ever to speak, pointing more to his Greater Son, Jesus the Messiah, than even to himself.*

"This is a kind of gem among the Psalms, and is peculiarly excellent and remarkable. It contains those deep, sublime, and heavy sufferings of Christ, when agonizing in the midst of the terrors and pangs of divine wrath and death which surpass all human thought and comprehension." (Martin Luther, cited in Charles Spurgeon)

A. The agony of the Forsaken One.

1. (1-2) The cry of the forsaken.

My God, My God, why have You forsaken Me?
***Why are You so* far from helping Me,**
***And from* the words of My groaning?**
O My God, I cry in the daytime, but You do not hear;
And in the night season, and am not silent.

a. **My God, My God, why have You forsaken Me**: This psalm begins abruptly, with a disturbing scene: someone who knows and trusts God is **forsaken**, and cries out to God in agony.

i. This is a *Psalm of David*, and there were many instances in the life of David where he might write such an agonized poem. Before and after taking the throne of Israel, David lived in seasons of great danger and deprivation.

ii. While this psalm was certainly true of King David in his life experience, it – like many psalms – is even truer of Jesus the Messiah than of David. Jesus deliberately chose these words to describe His agony on the cross (Matthew 27:46).

iii. "We can be fairly certain that Jesus was meditating on the Old Testament during the hours of his suffering and that he saw his crucifixion as a fulfillment of Psalm 22 particularly." (Boice)

iv. "I doubt not that David, though he had an eye to his own condition in diverse passages here used, yet was carried forth by the Spirit of prophecy beyond himself, and unto Christ, to whom alone it truly and fully agrees." (Poole)

b. **My God, My God**: This opening is powerful on at least two levels. The cry "**My God**" shows that the Forsaken One truly did have a relationship with God. He was a victim of the cruelty of men, but the cry and the complaint is to **God** – even **My God** – and not to or against man. Second, the repetition of the plea shows the intensity of the agony.

i. "Then it was that he felt in soul and body the horror of God's displeasure against sin, for which he had undertaken." (Trapp)

c. **Why have You forsaken Me?** There is a note of *surprise* in this cry and in the following lines. The Forsaken One seems bewildered; "Why would My God forsake Me? Others may deserve such, but I cannot figure out why He would forsake Me."

i. We may easily imagine a situation in the life of King David where he experienced this. Many times he found himself in seemingly impossible circumstances and wondered why God did not rescue him immediately.

ii. Yet beyond David and his life, this agonized cry and the intentional identification of Jesus with these words are some of the most intense and mysterious descriptions of what Jesus experienced on the cross. Jesus had known great pain and suffering (both physical and emotional) during His life. Yet He had never known separation or alienation from God His Father. At this moment He experienced what He had not yet ever experienced. There was a significant sense in which Jesus rightly felt **forsaken** by God the Father on the cross.

iii. On the cross, a holy transaction took place. God the Father regarded God the Son as if He were a sinner. As the Apostle Paul would later write, *God made Him who knew no sin to be sin for us, that we might become the righteousness of God in Him.* (2 Corinthians 5:21)

iv. Yet Jesus not only endured the *withdrawal* of the Father's fellowship, but also the actual outpouring of the Father's *wrath* upon Him as a substitute for sinful humanity. "This was the blackness and darkness of his horror; then it was that he penetrated the depths of the caverns of suffering." (Spurgeon)

v. "To be forsaken means to have the light of God's countenance and the sense of his presence eclipsed, which is what happened to Jesus as he bore the wrath of God against sin for us." (Boice)

vi. "It was necessary that he should feel the loss of his Father's smile, – for the condemned in hell must have tasted of that bitterness – and therefore the Father closed the eye of his love, put the hand of justice before the smile of his face, and left his Son to cry, 'My God, my God, why hast thou forsaken me?'" (Spurgeon)

vii. Horrible as this was, it fulfilled God's good and loving plan of redemption. Therefore Isaiah could say *Yet it pleased the Lord to bruise Him* (Isaiah 53:10).

viii. At the same time, we cannot say that the separation between the Father and the Son at the cross was complete. Paul made this clear in 2 Corinthians 5:19: *God was in Christ reconciling the world to Himself* at the cross.

d. **Why have You forsaken Me?** There is a definite *question* in these words of David, and as Jesus appropriated them to Himself on the cross. What Jesus endured on the cross was so complex, so dark, and so mysterious that it was, at the moment, beyond emotional comprehension.

i. Spurgeon considered this question with an emphasis on the word **You**. "'*Thou:*' I can understand why traitorous Judas and timid Peter should be gone, but *thou,* my God, my faithful friend, how canst thou leave me? This is worst of all, yea worse than all put together. Hell itself has for its fiercest flame the separation of the soul from God." (Spurgeon)

ii. We can imagine the answer to Jesus' question: **Why**? "Because, My Son, You have chosen to stand in the place of guilty sinners. You, who have never known sin, have made the infinite sacrifice to become sin and receive My just wrath upon sin and sinners. You do this because of Your great love, and because of My great love."

iii. Then the Father might give the Son a glimpse of His reward – the righteously-robed multitude of His people on heaven's golden streets, "all of them singing their redeemer's praise, all of them chanting the name of Jehovah and the Lamb; and this was a part of the answer to his question." (Spurgeon)

e. **Why are You so far from helping Me?** David knew what it was like to feel the presence and the deliverance of God and had experienced such many times before. Every prior time of help made this dramatic *absence* of God's help more devastating. Worse yet, there seemed to be *no explanation* for the lack of God's help; thus the question, "**Why?**"

i. No doubt David experienced this, but only as a shadow compared to how Jesus experienced this. Prior to the cross, Jesus lived every moment in conscious fellowship with God the Father, combined with a continual dependence upon the help of both the Father and the Spirit. At the cross, Jesus felt *helpless*, as it seemed that the Father was **so far from helping** Him.

f. **O My God, I cry in the daytime, but You do not hear**: A further dimension of David's agony was the fact that he made repeated, constant appeals to God and yet felt utterly unheard. His **groaning** was unanswered, his **cry** ignored.

i. David certainly experienced this; the greater Son of David experienced it in a far greater degree. On the cross Jesus felt abandoned by the Father, and felt that His groaning and cries went unanswered.

2. (3-5) Remembrance of God's nature and prior help.

But You *are* holy,
Enthroned in the praises of Israel.
Our fathers trusted in You;
They trusted, and You delivered them.
They cried to You, and were delivered;
They trusted in You, and were not ashamed.

a. **But You are holy**: The Forsaken One remembered God and His greatness, even when immersed in suffering. He did not curse or blaspheme God, and he knew that his present agony did not change God's holiness (**You are holy**) or greatness (**Enthroned in the praises of Israel**).

i. We have the sense that the present crisis filled David (and the greater Son of David) with doubt and confusion, yet he would not allow doubts as to the holiness or greatness of God. Whatever he did *not* know in his present situation, he did know that God was **holy**.

ii. "Here is the triumph of faith – the Saviour stood like a rock in the wide ocean of temptation. High as the billows rose, so did his faith, like the coral rock, wax greater and stronger till it became an island of salvation to our shipwrecked souls. It is as if he had said, 'It matters not what I endure. Storms may howl upon me; men despise; devils tempt; circumstances overpower; and God himself forsake me, still God is holy; there is no unrighteousness in him.'" (Stevenson, cited in Spurgeon)

iii. "We may not question the holiness of God, but we may argue from it, and use it as a plea in our petitions." (Spurgeon)

b. **Our fathers trusted in You…. They cried to You, and were delivered**: David also remembered how God had answered and **delivered** many times before. Strangely, this would add measures of both comfort and despair: *comfort*, knowing that he cried to the same God who had **delivered** before and who could deliver again; *despair*, knowing that the God who *had* **delivered** before now seemed so distant and silent.

i. We can almost hear the agony of the Forsaken One: "**They cried to You, and were delivered**; I cry to You and am ignored."

ii. **Our fathers**: "The use of the plural pronoun '*our*' shows how one with his people Jesus was even on the cross." (Spurgeon)

3. (6-8) Mocking the forsaken.

But I *am* a worm, and no man;
A reproach of men, and despised by the people.
All those who see Me ridicule Me;
They shoot out the lip, they shake the head, *saying,*
"He trusted in the LORD, let Him rescue Him;
Let Him deliver Him, since He delights in Him!"

a. **But I am a worm, and no man**: The intensity of the conflict made David feel not only ignored, but insignificant. God seems to help other men, but seems to give no help to worms. The low standing he had in his own eyes and in the eyes of others simply added to his agony.

i. It was dramatically fulfilled in the greater Son of David, that on the cross He was **a reproach of men, and despised by the people**. Cruel men mocked Jesus in His greatest agony (Matthew 27:39-44).

ii. "This verse is a miracle in language. How could the Lord of glory be brought to such abasement as to be not only lower than the angels, but even lower than men. What a contrast between 'I am' and '*I am a worm*'!" (Spurgeon)

iii. "He felt himself to be comparable to a helpless, powerless, downtrodden worm, passive while crushed, and unnoticed and despised by those who trod upon him. He selects the weakest of creatures, which is all flesh; and becomes, when trodden upon, writhing, quivering flesh, utterly devoid of any might except strength to suffer. This was a true likeness of himself when his body and soul had become a mass of misery – the very essence of agony – in the dying pangs of crucifixion." (Spurgeon)

b. **They shoot out the lip, they shake the head, saying, "He trusted in the LORD, let Him rescue Him"**: David's misery multiplied at those who mocked and misunderstood his agony. They used it as an excuse to call into question his relationship with God, even as the friends of Job did with him in his suffering.

i. It was as if they said, "It seemed that he **trusted in the LORD**, but we all know that the LORD rescues those who trust in Him. It seemed that he delighted in God, but that must be false because he is not delivered."

ii. **He trusted in the LORD, let Him rescue Him**: If Jesus identified with the opening words of Psalm 22 with His great cry from the cross (Matthew 27:46), then His enemies unwittingly identified with the scornful enemies of God and His Anointed in their mockery of Jesus on the cross (Matthew 27:43: *He trusted in God; let Him deliver Him now*).

iii. Spurgeon preached a sermon (*Faith Among Mockers*) in which he considered the implication of this word against the Forsaken One, "**He trusted in the LORD, let Him rescue Him.**"

- In a truly grace-filled man, his trust in God is known.
- This trust demonstrated by believing men is not understood by the world.
- This true faith will almost certainly be mocked at some time or another.
- The time shall come when the man of faith who has trusted in God shall be abundantly justified.

c. **Let Him deliver Him, since He delights in Him**: This statement reveals the frequent ignorance and cruelty of those who oppose God and His people. It claimed to see no deliverance, when it would indeed come soon. It also questioned the delight of God in the Forsaken One, when God did and does truly delight in that one.

i. "A most virulent irony, whereby they sought to cajole him out of his confidence, and so to drive him into utter desperation and destruction." (Trapp)

4. (9-11) A plea: "You are my God since the earliest days."

But You *are* He who took Me out of the womb;
You made Me trust *while* on My mother's breasts.
I was cast upon You from birth.
From My mother's womb

You *have been* My God.
Be not far from Me,
For trouble *is* near;
For *there is* none to help.

> a. **But You are He who took Me out of the womb**: David understood –
> both for himself and, prophetically speaking, for the later-to-come Messiah
> – that in the depth of agony and the sense of abandonment, one could still
> appeal to God in remembrance of better times.

> > i. The Forsaken One did not say, "Since I feel abandoned by God, I
> > will abandon Him." He remained steadfast through the dark night of
> > the soul, and still made appeal to the God who cared for Him since
> > birth.

> > ii. "That Child now fighting the great battle of his life, uses the
> > mercy of his nativity as an argument with God. Faith finds weapons
> > everywhere. He who wills to believe shall never lack reasons for
> > believing." (Spurgeon)

> b. **Out of the womb...while on My mother's breasts...from birth...You
> have been My God**: The Forsaken One argued on good, logical grounds.
> He reminded God of the care given since His very earliest days. That prior
> grace might seem to be wasted if the sufferer was not rescued in His present
> crisis.

> c. **Be not far from Me, for trouble is near; for there is none to help**: The
> plea for help is again eloquently and persuasively stated. God seems **far**
> away; but **trouble is near** – and **there is none to help**, so *You* must help
> me, God!

5. (12-18) The agony of the forsaken.

Many bulls have surrounded Me;
Strong *bulls* of Bashan have encircled Me.
They gape at Me *with* their mouths,
Like a raging and roaring lion.
I am poured out like water,
And all My bones are out of joint;
My heart is like wax;
It has melted within Me.
My strength is dried up like a potsherd,
And My tongue clings to My jaws;
You have brought Me to the dust of death.
For dogs have surrounded Me;
The congregation of the wicked has enclosed Me.

They pierced My hands and My feet;
I can count all My bones.
They look *and* **stare at Me.**
They divide My garments among them,
And for My clothing they cast lots.

a. **Many bulls have surrounded Me**: The Forsaken One again describes His crisis. He described the people tormenting Him as **strong bulls of Bashan**, large animals proverbial for their strength. They surround Him and threaten Him.

i. "The *bull* is the emblem of brutal strength, that gores and tramples down all before it." (Clarke)

ii. "The priests, elders, scribes, Pharisees, rulers, and captains bellowed round the cross like wild cattle, fed in the fat and solitary pastures of Bashan, full of strength and fury; they stamped and foamed around the innocent One, and longed to gore him to death with their cruelties." (Spurgeon)

b. **I am poured out like water**: The Forsaken One felt completely empty. He perceived no resource in Himself able to meet the crisis at hand. Whatever strength or resistance He had was **poured out like water** upon the ground.

i. "My heart faileth, my spirits are spent and gone like water, which once spilt can never be recovered; my very flesh is melted within me, and I am become as weak as water." (Poole)

c. **My bones are out of joint; My heart is like wax; it has melted within Me**: This described the physical extremity of David at the time, but it also is an amazingly specific prophecy of the future suffering of the Son of David on the cross.

i. The deliberately awkward and strained position of the crucified man meant that on the cross Jesus could say, "**My bones are out of joint**." David did not know the practice of crucifixion in his day, but he described the physical agony of it with the accuracy of a prophet of the LORD.

ii. There is also some reason to believe (based mainly on John 19:34) that on the cross Jesus suffered from a ruptured heart, making the words "**My heart is like wax; it has melted within Me**" also amazingly specific.

iii. **My tongue clings to My jaws**: As was normal for anyone under the agony of crucifixion, Jesus suffered great thirst on the cross (John 19:28).

d. **You have brought me to the dust of death**: David used this moving poetic phrase to describe the extent of his misery. He probably had in mind the curse God pronounced upon Adam after his sin: *For dust you are, and to dust you shall return* (Genesis 3:19). Since all humanity was contained in Adam, this curse extends to the entire human race, and David felt himself close **to the dust of death**.

i. Obviously, David did not die in the crisis described by this psalm; he lived to write it and others. He came to the edge of mortality when God **brought** him **to the dust of death**. Yet Jesus, the Son of David, did not merely come to the edge of death; He was plunged into **the dust of death** and into all of the cursedness implied by that. Jesus bore the sting of Adam's curse for us (Galatians 3:13) so that we would not have to bear it ourselves.

e. **For dogs have surrounded Me; the assembly of the wicked has enclosed Me**: David's crisis would be bad enough even if surrounded by sympathetic friends; his misery was multiplied because there were violent and wicked men on every side.

i. In His death, the Son of David had few sympathizers. Haters, scoffers, and mockers surrounded Jesus on the cross and sought to make His suffering *worse* (Matthew 27:39-44, Mark 15:29-32).

f. **They pierced My hands and My feet**: Perhaps here David referred to wounds he received in struggling against these determined enemies; perhaps he wrote purely prophetically. In any regard, hundreds of years before the Romans adopted the Persian practice of crucifixion, the prophet David described the wounds of crucifixion that his Greater Son would bear.

i. The Masoretic Hebrew text of Psalm 22:16 doesn't say *pierced*; it says "as a lion." Yet the Septuagint (Greek) translation of the Old Testament – long before the Christian era – renders the Hebrew text as saying *pierced*. While the Masoretic text shouldn't be casually disregarded, there is good reason to side with the Septuagint and almost every other translation here. "It may even suggest that the Masoretic text was deliberately pointed in the way it was by later Jewish scholars to avoid what otherwise would be a nearly inescapable prophecy of Jesus' crucifixion." (Boice)

g. **I can count all My bones**: David examined his wounds and understood that he had no broken bones. The Son of David also, despite his great suffering on the cross, suffered no broken bones. John carefully noted this (John 19:31-37). This fact fulfilled this prophecy, as well as Psalm 34:20

and the pattern of the Passover lamb as described in Exodus 12:46 and Numbers 9:12.

h. **They look and stare at Me**: In his crisis, David was the focus of unwanted attention. His tormentors did not allow him the dignity of private suffering, but exposed all things to their **stare**. David's Great Son also found no place to hide from the unwanted stares of cruel, mocking men at the cross.

i. On the cross Jesus was the focus not only of mocking and humiliation (Matthew 27:39-44, Mark 15:29-32), but also of simple astonishment, as when the centurion said, "*Truly this was the Son of God!*" (Matthew 27:54). Luke also noted, *the whole crowd who came together to that sight, seeing what had been done, beat their breasts and returned* (Luke 23:48).

ii. "'*They look and stare upon me.*' Oh, how different is that look which the awakened sinner directs to Calvary, when faith lifts up her eye to him who agonised, and bled, and died, for the guilty!" (Morison, cited in Spurgeon)

i. **They divide My garments among them, and for My clothing they cast lots**: David was so humbled before his adversaries, so powerless against them, that they took even his clothing and used it for themselves.

i. As with other aspects of Psalm 22, this was fulfilled even *more* literally in the experience of Jesus than in the life of David. As was the custom of that time, Jesus was stripped naked or nearly naked for the cross, and soldiers gambled (**cast lots**) for his clothing at the very foot of the cross. John 19:23-24 and Matthew 27:35 quote this line of Psalm 22 as being fulfilled.

ii. "Unholy eyes gazed insultingly upon the Saviour's nakedness, and shocked the sacred delicacy of his holy soul. The sight of the agonizing body ought to have ensured sympathy from the throng, but it only increased their savage mirth, as they gloated their cruel eyes upon his miseries." (Spurgeon)

6. (19-21a) A plea for help and deliverance.

But You, O Lord, do not be far from Me;
O My Strength, hasten to help Me!
Deliver Me from the sword,
My precious *life* from the power of the dog.
Save Me from the lion's mouth
And from the horns of the wild oxen!

a. **But You, O Lord, do not be far from Me**: The request of Psalm 22:11 is here repeated. David seemed to believe that he could endure *anything* if he enjoyed the conscious presence of God. His plea is not focused on the change of his situation, but on the presence of God in the crisis.

b. **Hasten to help Me…. Deliver Me…. Save Me**: Picturing his adversaries as vicious animals (**the dog…the lion's mouth…the horns of the wild oxen**), David pled for the help and deliverance the presence of God brings.

i. These lines reflect not only the great danger and misery of both David and his Greater Son, but especially their trust in the Lord God as their deliverer. He and He alone is their hope.

ii. **Deliver Me from the sword**: "The wrath of God was the 'sword,' which took vengeance on all men…it was the 'flaming sword,' which kept men out of paradise." (Horne)

B. The answer to the Forsaken One.

1. (21b-23) The Forsaken One praises God among His people.

You have answered Me.
I will declare Your name to My brethren;
In the midst of the assembly I will praise You.
You who fear the Lord, praise Him!
All you descendants of Jacob, glorify Him,
And fear Him, all you offspring of Israel!

a. **You have answered Me**: After pouring out His soul in agony, now the Forsaken One has a glorious sense that God has **answered** Him. The crisis became bearable in the knowledge that God is not removed from His suffering nor silent in it.

i. The answer of God to the Forsaken One instantly meant that He no longer felt forsaken. The deliverance from the crisis itself may be yet to come, but the deliverance from the sense of being forsaken by God in the midst of the crisis was His. There is immense relief, joy, and peace in the words, "**You have answered Me**."

ii. "As he thus cries, the conviction that he is heard floods his soul…. It is like a parting burst of sunshine at the end of a day of tempest." (Maclaren)

iii. It is easy to see these words fulfilled in the experience of David; but they were perfectly completed in Jesus. This was also the resolution that another forsaken one – Job – fought so hard for. Even without an immediate deliverance from difficulty, there is immense comfort in knowing that God is there and that He is not silent in the midst of our crises.

iv. Knowing that Jesus fulfilled this prophetic psalm, it is fair to wonder just when He could speak or live the fulfillment of these words, "**You have answered Me**." Perhaps – though it is impossible to say with certainty – it was while He still hung on the cross, yet after the mysterious, glorious transaction of bearing the sin of mankind. Perhaps it was after the triumphant announcement, *It is finished!* (John 19:30), yet before (or even in) the warm words, *Father, into Your hands I commend My Spirit* (Luke 23:46). Those words point to a re-established sense of fellowship replacing the prior sense of forsakenness.

b. **I will declare Your name to My brethren**: Having been delivered – if not from the crisis itself, certainly from the sense of being forsaken in the crisis – now the promise is made to glorify and **praise** the God of deliverance. *Others* needed to know of God's greatness in such extremity.

i. Hebrews 2:12 quotes the *second half* of Psalm 22 (specifically, Psalm 22:22), proving clearly that the *entire* psalm points to Jesus, not just the agony of the first half.

ii. On the night before His crucifixion, Jesus prayed a glorious prayer, and one line of that prayer reads: *I have declared to them Your name, and will declare it* (John 17:26). Those words, prayed in the shadow of the cross, can be understood as a deliberate desire to fulfill this word in Psalm 22, **I will declare Your name to My brethren**. Jesus understood that His obedient work on the cross would bring great glory to His God and Father, declaring the greatness of His **name**.

iii. We may say that this section of Psalm 22 reflects the *primary* reason Jesus went to the cross: to glorify and obey His God and Father.

c. **You who fear the LORD, praise Him**: The command is given to **praise**, to **glorify**, and to **fear** the LORD. The God of such great deliverance deserves all three things from all humanity.

i. We prophetically see in this section Jesus doing two great things in the aftermath of His great work on the cross:

- Jesus declares God's name (**I will declare Your name to My brethren**).
- Jesus leads the redeemed in praise (**In the midst of the assembly I will praise You**).

ii. Of this second point, Spurgeon observed: "I like to think that when we pray on earth our prayers are not alone, but our great High Priest is there to offer our petitions with his own. When we sing on earth it is the same. Is not Jesus Christ in the midst of the congregation, gathering up all the notes which come from sincere lips, to put them into the golden censer, and to make them rise as precious incense before the throne of the infinite majesty?" (Spurgeon)

2. (24-25) Praising the God who answers the forsaken.

For He has not despised nor abhorred the affliction of the afflicted;
Nor has He hidden His face from Him;
But when He cried to Him, He heard.
My praise *shall be* of You in the great assembly;
I will pay My vows before those who fear Him.

a. **For He has not despised nor abhorred the affliction of the afflicted**: David's triumphant words – again, perfectly fulfilled in his greater son Jesus – reflect a profound spiritual wisdom and depth. The God who answers the Forsaken One allowed **the affliction of the afflicted**; yet **He has not despised or abhorred it**. God has used and would use that **affliction** to good and great purpose.

i. Some of God's people automatically associate all **affliction** with the disfavor of God. It is true that sometimes **affliction** may come as punishment (for the unbeliever) or as discipline (for the believer). Yet sometimes **affliction** is something God does not despise, and uses to good effect in the lives of His people.

ii. It is in this sense that the words of Isaiah 53:10 were fulfilled: *Yet it pleased the Lord to bruise Him.* The **affliction** was not **despised**.

b. **Nor has He hidden His face from Him**: Certainly David (and the greater Son of David) *felt* that the Father hid His face (*Why have You forsaken Me? Why are You so far from helping Me?.... You do not hear*, Psalm 22:1-2). Yet now, after God's answer has come (Psalm 22:21b), it is clear that He never did leave the **afflicted**, even in the midst of **the affliction**.

c. **But when He cried to Him, He heard**: The answer seemed an intolerably long time in coming, but it came. David and the Son of David could both say, "He heard My cry."

d. **My praise shall be of You in the great assembly; I will pay my vows**: There are two aspects to a right response to such a wonderful deliverance. The first is *public praise*, and the second is *keeping promises*.

3. (26-27) Others who rejoice in the God who answers.

The poor shall eat and be satisfied;
Those who seek Him will praise the LORD.

Let your heart live forever!
All the ends of the world
Shall remember and turn to the LORD,
And all the families of the nations
Shall worship before You.

a. **The poor shall eat and be satisfied**: If God shows such faithfulness to the afflicted, there is hope for **the poor**. The good God will take care of the **poor** who trust Him and **seek Him**. They will **praise the LORD** also.

i. The faithfulness of God to the Forsaken One becomes a foundation for His faithfulness to others in need, such as **the poor**. His satisfaction in the work of the Son of David means grace and blessing and *joy* (**Let your heart live forever!**) for others.

b. **Those who seek Him will praise the LORD**: There is a *promise* in this, that **those who seek Him** will in fact find the LORD, and thus they will **praise** Him.

i. "There are souls now weeping for sin and longing for a Savior who will soon find them, and then will become most hearty singers of the new song. They are coming, coming in their thousands even now. The music of praise shall be continued as long as the sun, and the glory of the Lord shall cover the earth as the waters cover the sea. From generation to generation shall the name of the Lord be praised." (Spurgeon)

c. **All the ends of the world shall remember and turn to the LORD**: The faithfulness of God to the Forsaken One even becomes the base for bringing **all the ends of the world** to the LORD. Not only is it true that the LORD has *not despised nor abhorred the affliction of the afflicted* (Psalm 22:24), but He uses that affliction to reach **all the ends of the world** for the knowledge of God, for repentance unto Him, and for His worship (**all the families of the nations shall worship before You**).

i. We may say that this section of Psalm 22 shows the *second* great reason why Jesus went to the cross: out of simple love for those who would believe on Him and His saving work, and therefore **remember and turn to the LORD**. It is not an overly-sentimental exaggeration to say that Jesus thought of His redeemed and loved them up to the cross and on the cross.

ii. Hebrews 12:2 says of Jesus: *who for the joy that was set before Him endured the cross, despising the shame.* Psalm 22 powerfully displays that joy, both in His obedience to and glorifying of His God and Father, and the joy of rescuing and loving those who would trust on Him;

that there would be *brethren* that He declared the name of God unto (Psalm 22:22).

iii. "In that last happy interval, before he actually gave up his soul into his Father's hands, his thoughts rushed forward and found a blessed place of rest in the prospect that, as the result of his death, all the kindreds of the nations would worship before the Lord, and that by a chosen seed the Most High should be honored." (Spurgeon)

iv. "I think it is an absolutely wonderful thought and one that should move us to the most intent love for and devotion to Jesus Christ. You and I were in Jesus' thoughts at the very moment of his death. It was for you and me explicitly and for our salvation from sin that he was dying." (Boice)

4. (28-31) Enduring praise for a faithful God.

For the kingdom *is* the Lord's,
And He rules over the nations.
All the prosperous of the earth
Shall eat and worship;
All those who go down to the dust
Shall bow before Him,
Even he who cannot keep himself alive.
A posterity shall serve Him.
It will be recounted of the Lord to the *next* generation,
They will come and declare His righteousness to a people who will be born,
That He has done *this*.

a. **For the kingdom is the Lord's, and He rules over the nations**: The experience of affliction and crisis did not make the formerly Forsaken One lose any sense of confidence in God's power and authority. The Lord's reign over the nations makes sense of both His prior crisis and the call to all nations to worship before the Lord (Psalm 22:27).

i. This reminds us that one day Jesus *will* reign over all nations. It would be unthinkable otherwise. "Is Christ, the great King, satisfied to settle down in a corner of the world as ruler over one scanty province?" (Spurgeon)

ii. "Our new-born nature craves for the spread of the Redeemer's kingdom, and prays for it instinctively." (Spurgeon)

b. **All the prosperous of the earth shall eat and worship; all those who go down to the dust shall bow before Him**: The Lord God is *so* highly exalted that all honor Him, both **the prosperous of the earth** and **those who go down to the dust.**

i. It is of note that though all honor the LORD, they honor Him in different ways. **The prosperous of the earth** enjoy a fellowship meal and **worship** God. In contrast, **those who go down to the dust** simply **bow before** the LORD in humble reverence.

ii. This has much the same idea as the later passage of the Apostle Paul, when he wrote: *that at the name of Jesus every knee should bow, of those in heaven, and of those on earth, and of those under the earth, and that every tongue should confess that Jesus Christ is Lord, to the glory of God the Father* (Philippians 2:10-11).

iii. **Those who go down to the dust** suggests those who are rightly humbled, but it can also be understood in a broader sense. Earlier in the psalm, **dust** suggested the mortality of man and his place under the curse (Psalm 22:15). David may here use **those who go down to the dust** as a simple representation of all humanity.

iv. If this is true, then the phrase **even he who cannot keep himself alive** follows the same thought. It is a suggestive phrase, especially considering the connection in this psalm with Jesus the Messiah, the greater Son of David. Of all humanity, Jesus was singular as One who *could* **keep himself alive.** Jesus Himself said of His life, *No one takes it from Me, but I lay it down of Myself. I have power to lay it down, and I have power to take it again* (John 10:18).

c. **A posterity shall serve Him. It will be recounted of the LORD to the next generation:** The faithfulness of God unto the formerly Forsaken One is told throughout the generations, bringing great glory to the LORD. They will all look at what has been accomplished in and through the formerly Forsaken One and hear, "**That He has done this.**"

- This results in *service* through the generations (**a posterity shall serve Him**).
- This results in *God's fame* through the generations (**It will be recounted of the LORD to the next generation**).
- This results in the *spread of the message of God's righteousness* through the generations (**They will come and declare His righteousness to a people who will be born**).

i. We can say that Jesus thought of His Jewish brothers on the cross (*My brethren*, Psalm 22:22). He thought of the Gentiles who come into the assembly of the redeemed (*in the great congregation*, Psalm 22:25). He even thought of future generations whom He would rescue and who would trust Him (**to the next generation...to a people who will be born**, Psalm 22:30-31).

ii. "Finally the vision extends to unborn generations (30f.), in terms which anticipate the preaching of the cross, recounting God's righteousness (or *deliverance*, a secondary meaning of the word) revealed in the action He has taken." (Kidner)

iii. This all adds to the wonderful truth – true for King David of Israel, but far more gloriously fulfilled in Jesus Christ – that *none of the Forsaken One's sufferings were wasted*. Every drop of that cup of agony was and is used to the great glory of God.

iv. In the fullest measure, Jesus appropriated the victory of the second half of this psalm just as much as He did the agony of the first half. "Just before He died, Jesus cried out, 'It is finished' (John 19:30). This is a quotation from the last verse of Psalm 22. In our text that verse reads, 'he has done it,' referring to God as subject. But there is no object for the verb in Hebrew, and it can equally well be translated, 'It is finished.'" (Boice)

v. "The psalm which began with the cry of dereliction ends with the word *he has wrought it*, and announcement not far removed from our Lord's great cry, 'It is finished.'" (Kidner)

Psalm 23 – The LORD Is My Shepherd and My Host

Like many others, this beloved psalm bears the simple title **A Psalm of David**. *Most account it to be a psalm of David's maturity, but with vivid remembrance of his youth as a shepherd. Charles Spurgeon wrote, "I like to recall the fact that this psalm was written by David, probably when he was a king. He had been a shepherd, and he was not ashamed of his former occupation."*

"It [Psalm 23] has charmed more griefs to rest than all the philosophy of the world. It has remanded to their dungeon more felon thoughts, more black doubts, more thieving sorrows, than there are sands on the sea-shore. It has comforted the noble host of the poor. It has sung courage to the army of the disappointed. It has poured balm and consolation into the heart of the sick, of captives in dungeons, of widows in their pinching griefs, of orphans in their loneliness. Dying soldiers have died easier as it was read to them; ghastly hospitals have been illuminated; it has visited the prisoner, and broken his chains, and, like Peter's angel, led him forth in imagination, and sung him back to his home again. It has made the dying Christian slave freer than his master, and consoled those whom, dying, he left behind mourning, not so much that he was gone, as because they were left behind, and could not go, too." (Henry Ward Beecher, cited in Charles Spurgeon)

"Millions of people have memorized this psalm, even those who have learned few other Scripture portions. Ministers have used it to comfort people who are going through severe personal trials, suffering illness, or dying. For some, the words of this psalm have been the last they have ever uttered in life." (James Montgomery Boice)

A. The LORD as Shepherd sustains.

1. (1) A declaration and its immediate result.

The LORD is my shepherd;
I shall not want.

> a. **The LORD is my shepherd**: David thought about God, the God of Israel; as he thought about his relationship with God, he made the analogy of a

177

shepherd and his sheep. God was like a **shepherd** to David, and David was like a sheep to God.

i. In one sense, this was not unusual. There are other references to this analogy between the deity and his followers in ancient Middle Eastern cultures. "In all Eastern thought, and very definitely in Biblical literature, a king is a shepherd." (Morgan)

ii. It is also a familiar idea throughout the Bible that the LORD is a shepherd to His people. The idea begins as early as the Book of Genesis, where Moses called the LORD *the Shepherd, the Stone of Israel* (Genesis 49:24).

- In Psalm 28:9 David invited the LORD to shepherd the people of Israel, and to *bear them up forever.* Psalm 80:1 also looks to the LORD as the *Shepherd of Israel, who would lead Joseph like a flock.*

- Ecclesiastes 12:11 speaks of the words of the wise, which *are like well-driven nails, given by one Shepherd.*

- Isaiah 40:11 tells us that the LORD *will feed His flock like a shepherd; He will gather the lambs with His arm.* Micah 7:14 invites the LORD to *Shepherd Your people with Your staff...As in days of old.*

- Zechariah 13:7 speaks of the Messiah as the Shepherd who will be struck, and the sheep scattered (quoted in Matthew 26:31).

- In John 10:11 and 10:14, Jesus clearly spoke of Himself as the good shepherd, who gives His life for the sheep and who can say, *"I know My sheep, and am known by My own."* Hebrews 13:20 speaks of Jesus as *that great Shepherd of the sheep,* 1 Peter 2:25 calls Jesus *the Shepherd and Overseer of your souls,* and 1 Peter 5:4 calls Jesus *the Chief Shepherd.*

- The idea of Jesus as the Good Shepherd was precious to early Christians. One of the more common motifs in catacomb paintings was Jesus as a shepherd, with a lamb carried across His shoulders.

iii. It's remarkable that the LORD would call Himself our shepherd. "In Israel, as in other ancient societies, a shepherd's work was considered the lowest of all works. If a family needed a shepherd, it was always the youngest son, like David, who got this unpleasant assignment... Jehovah has chosen to be our shepherd, David says. The great God of the universe has stooped to take just such care of you and me." (Boice)

iv. "Saith Rabbi Joseph Bar Hamna, there is not a more contemptible office than that of a shepherd.... But God disdaineth not to feed his flock, to guide, to govern, to defend them, to handle and heal them, to tend and take care of them." (Trapp)

v. David knew this metaphor in a unique way, having been a shepherd himself. "David uses the most comprehensive and intimate metaphor yet encountered in the Psalms, preferring usually the more distant 'king' or 'deliverer', or the impersonal 'rock', 'shield', *etc.*; whereas the shepherd lives with his flock and is everything to it: guide, physician and protector." (Kidner)

b. **The LORD is my shepherd**: David knew this in a personal sense. He could say, "**my shepherd**." It wasn't just that the LORD was a shepherd for others in a theoretical sense; He was a real, personal **shepherd** for David himself.

i. "A sheep is an object of property, not a wild animal; its owner sets great store by it, and frequently it is bought with a great price. It is well to know, as certainly as David did, that we belong to the Lord. There is a noble tone of confidence about this sentence. There is no 'if' nor 'but,' nor even 'I hope so;' but he says, 'The Lord *is* my shepherd.'" (Spurgeon)

ii. "The sweetest word of the whole is that monosyllable, '*My.*' He does not say, 'The Lord is the shepherd of the world at large, and leadeth forth the multitude as his flock,' but 'The Lord is *my* shepherd;' if he be a Shepherd to no one else, he is a Shepherd to *me; he cares for me,* watches over *me,* and preserves *me.*" (Spurgeon)

iii. Overwhelmingly, the idea behind God's role as **shepherd** is of *loving care and concern*. David found comfort and security in the thought that God cared for him like a shepherd cares for his sheep.

iv. David felt that he *needed* a shepherd. The heart of this psalm doesn't connect with the self-sufficient. But those who acutely sense their need – the *poor in spirit* Jesus described in the Sermon on the Mount (Matthew 5:3) – find great comfort in the idea that God can be a shepherd to them in a personal sense.

v. Spurgeon said that before a man can truly say, "**the LORD is my shepherd**," he must first feel himself to be a sheep by nature, "for he cannot know that God is his Shepherd unless he feels in himself that he has the nature of a sheep." He must relate to a sheep in its foolishness, its dependency, and in the warped nature of its will.

vi. "A sheep, saith Aristotle, is a foolish and sluggish creature...aptest of anything to wander, though it feel no want, and unablest to return...a sheep can make no shift to save itself from tempests or inundation; there it stands and will perish, if not driven away by the shepherd." (Trapp)

c. **I shall not want**: For David, the fact of God's shepherd-like care was the end of dissatisfied need. He said, "**I shall not want**" both as a declaration and as a decision.

i. "**I shall not want**" means, "All my needs are supplied by the Lord, my shepherd."

ii. "**I shall not want**" means, "I decide to not desire more than what the Lord, my shepherd gives.

2. (2) How the Shepherd sustains.

He makes me to lie down in green pastures;
He leads me beside the still waters.

a. **He makes me to lie down**: The Lord as a shepherd knew how to make David rest when he needed it, just as a literal shepherd would care for his sheep. The implication is that a sheep doesn't always know what it needs and what is best for itself, and so needs help from the shepherd.

i. "The loveliest image afforded by the natural world, is here represented to the imagination; that of a flock, feeding in verdant meadows, and reposing, in quietness, by the rivers of water, running gently through them." (Horne)

b. **To lie down in green pastures**: The shepherd also knew the good places to make his sheep rest. He faithfully guides the sheep to **green pastures**.

i. Philip Keller (in *A Shepherd Looks at Psalm 23*) writes that sheep do not lie down easily and will not unless four conditions are met. Because they are timid, they will not lie down if they are afraid. Because they are social animals, they will not lie down if there is friction among the sheep. If flies or parasites trouble them, they will not lie down. Finally, if sheep are anxious about food or hungry, they will not lie down. Rest comes because the shepherd has dealt with fear, friction, flies, and famine.

c. **He leads me beside the still waters**: The shepherd knows when the sheep needs **green pastures**, and knows when the sheep needs **the still waters**. The images are rich with the sense of comfort, care, and rest.

B. The Lord as Shepherd leads.

1. (3) Where the Shepherd leads and why.

He restores my soul;
He leads me in the paths of righteousness
For His name's sake.

a. **He restores my soul**: The tender care of the shepherd described in the previous verse had its intended effect. David's soul was restored by the figurative *green pastures* and *still waters* the shepherd brought him to.

i. **Restores** has the idea of the rescue of a lost one. "It may picture the straying sheep brought back." (Kidner)

ii. "In Hebrew the words 'restores my soul' can mean 'brings me to repentance' (or conversion)." (Boice)

iii. "'*He restoreth my soul.*' He restores it to its original purity, that was now grown foul and black with sin; for also, what good were it to have '*green*' pastures and a *black* soul!" (Baker, cited in Spurgeon)

b. **He leads me**: The shepherd was a *guide*. The sheep didn't need to know where the green pastures or still waters were; all it needed to know was where the shepherd was. Likewise, the LORD would guide David to what he needed.

c. **In the paths of righteousness**: The leadership of the shepherd did not only comfort and restore David; He also guides His sheep into **righteousness**. God's guidance of David had a *moral* aspect.

i. "They are thenceforth led in 'the path of righteousness'; in the way of holy obedience. Obstructions are removed; they are strengthened, to walk and run in the paths of God's commandments." (Horne)

d. **For His name's sake**: The shepherd guides the sheep with an overarching view to the credit and glory of the shepherd's own **name**.

i. **For His name's sake**: "To display the glory of his grace, and not on account of any *merit* in me. God's motives of conduct towards the children of men are derived from the perfections and goodness of his own nature." (Clarke)

2. (4) The gift of the Shepherd's presence.

Yea, though I walk through the valley of the shadow of death,
I will fear no evil;
For You are with me;
Your rod and Your staff, they comfort me.

a. **Yea, though I walk through the valley of the shadow of death**: This is the first dark note in this beautiful psalm. Previously David wrote of *green* *pastures* and *still waters* and *paths of righteousness*. Yet when following the LORD as shepherd, one may still **walk through the valley of the shadow of death**.

> i. David used this powerful phrase to speak of some kind of dark, fearful experience. It is an imprecise phrase, yet its poetry makes perfect sense.
>
> - It is a **valley**, not a mountaintop or broad meadow. A **valley** suggests being hedged in and surrounded.
> - It is a valley of **the shadow** of death – not facing the substance of death itself, but **the shadow of death**, casting its dark, fearful outline across David's path.
> - It is a valley of the shadow **of death**, facing what seemed to David as the ultimate defeat and evil.
>
> ii. Notably, David recognized that under the shepherd's leading, he may **walk through** the valley of the shadow of death. It isn't his destination or dwelling place. Like the Preacher in Ecclesiastes, David might say that *all of life* is lived under **the shadow of death**, and it is the conscious presence of the LORD as shepherd that makes it bearable.
>
> iii. This line is especially suggestive when we read this psalm with an eye towards Jesus, the Great Shepherd. We understand that a shadow is not tangible but is cast by something that is. One can rightly say that we face only **the shadow of death** because Jesus took the *full reality* of death in our place.

b. Yea, though I walk through the valley of the shadow of death: This line from the psalm – and the psalm as a whole – has proven itself precious to many a dying saint through the ages. They have been comforted, strengthened, and warmed by the thought that the LORD would shepherd them **through the valley of the shadow of death**.

> i. Near death, the saint still calmly walks – he does not need to quicken his pace in alarm or panic. Near death, the saint does not walk *in* the valley, but **through** the valley.
>
> ii. "Death in its substance has been removed, and only the shadow of it remains.... Nobody is afraid of a shadow, for a shadow cannot stop a man's pathway even for a moment. The shadow of a dog cannot bite; the shadow of a sword cannot kill; the shadow of death cannot destroy us." (Spurgeon)
>
> iii. "It has an inexpressibly delightful application to the dying; but it is for the living, too.... The words are not in the future tense, and therefore are not reserved for a distant moment." (Spurgeon)

c. **I will fear no evil**: Despite every dark association with the idea of **the valley of the shadow of death**, David could resolutely say this because he was under the care of the LORD his shepherd,. Even in a fearful place, the presence of the shepherd banished the **fear** of evil.

i. We might say that the shepherd's presence did not eliminate the *presence* of evil, but certainly the **fear of evil**.

d. **For You are with me**: This emphasizes that it is the *presence* of the shepherd that eliminated the **fear of evil** for the sheep. No matter his present environment, David could look to the fact of God's shepherd-like presence and know, "**You are with me**" and "**I will fear no evil.**"

i. Significantly, it is at the dangerous moment pictured in the psalm that the "He" of Psalm 23:1-3 changes to "**You**." The LORD as Shepherd is now in the second person.

e. **Your rod and Your staff, they comfort me**: The **rod** and the **staff** were instruments used by a shepherd. The idea is of a sturdy walking stick, used to gently (as much as possible) guide the sheep and protect them from potential predators.

i. There is some debate among commentators as to whether David had the idea of two separate instruments (the **rod** and the **staff**) or one instrument used two ways. The Hebrew word for **rod** (*shaybet*) here seems to simply mean "a stick" with a variety of applications. The Hebrew word for **staff** (*mishaynaw*) seems to speak of "a support" in the sense of a walking stick.

ii. Kidner notes: "The *rod* (a cudgel worn at the belt) and *staff* (to walk with, and to round up the flock) were the shepherd's weapon and implement: the former for defence (*cf.* 1 Samuel 17:35), and the latter for control – since discipline is security."

iii. Maclaren writes: "The rod and the staff seem to be two names for one instrument, which was used both to beat off predatory animals and to direct the sheep."

iv. These instruments (or instrument) of guidance were a **comfort** to David. It helped him – even in **the valley of the shadow of death** – to know that God guided him, even through correction. It is a great **comfort** to know that God will correct us when we need it.

C. The LORD as Host.

1. (5) Blessing in the presence of danger.

You prepare a table before me in the presence of my enemies;
You anoint my head with oil;
My cup runs over.

a. **You prepare a table before me**: Without departing from the previous picture of *the valley of the shadow of death*, David envisioned the provision and goodness given by the LORD as a host, inviting David to a rich **table** prepared for him.

i. "Here the *second allegory* begins. A magnificent banquet is provided by a most liberal and benevolent host; who has not only the *bounty* to feed me, but power to protect me; and, though surrounded by *enemies*, I sit down to this table with confidence, knowing that I shall feast in perfect security." (Clarke)

ii. David gives a beautiful picture: **table** suggests *bounty*; **prepare** suggests *foresight and care*; **before me** suggests the personal connection.

b. **In the presence of my enemies**: This is a striking phrase. The goodness and care suggested by the prepared **table** is set right in the midst of **the presence of my enemies**. The host's care and concern doesn't eliminate **the presence of my enemies** but enables the experience of God's goodness and bounty even in their midst.

i. "This is the condition of God's servant – always conflict, but always a spread table." (Maclaren)

ii. "When a soldier is in the presence of his enemies, if he eats at all he snatches a hasty meal, and away he hastens to the fight. But observe: 'Thou *preparest* a table,' just as a servant does when she unfolds the damask cloth and displays the ornaments of the feast on an ordinary peaceful occasion. Nothing is hurried, there is no confusion, no disturbance, the enemy is at the door and yet God prepares a table, and the Christian sits down and eats as if everything were in perfect peace." (Spurgeon)

c. **You anoint my head with oil; my cup runs over**: Despite the dangers about and the **presence** of **enemies**, David enjoyed the richness of his host's goodness. He was refreshed by a **head** anointed **with oil**; his **cup** was over-filled.

i. "Beloved, I will ask you now a question. How would it be with you if God had filled your cup in proportion to your faith? How much would you have had in your cup?" (Spurgeon)

ii. "Those that have this happiness must carry their cup upright, and see that it overflows into their poor brethren's emptier vessels." (Trapp)

2. (6) Blessing for the future.

Surely goodness and mercy shall follow me
All the days of my life;
And I will dwell in the house of the LORD
Forever.

    a. **Surely goodness and mercy shall follow me all the days of my life**:
The host's care brought the **goodness and mercy** of God to David, and he
lived in the faithful expectation of it continuing **all the days of** his **life**.

        i. "*Mercy* is the covenant-word rendered 'steadfast love' elsewhere....
Together with *goodness* it suggests the steady kindness and support that
one can count on in the family or between firm friends." (Kidner)

        ii. "We are well escorted, with a Shepherd in front and these twin
angels behind!" (Meyer)

        iii. "These twin guardian angels will always be with me at my back
and my beck. Just as when great princes go abroad they must not go
unattended, so it is with the believer." (Spurgeon)

    b. **And I will dwell in the house of the L**ORD **forever**: The psalm ends
with the calmest assurance that he would enjoy the presence of the LORD
forever – both in his days on this earth and beyond.

        i. "In the Old Testament world, to eat and drink at someone's table
created a bond of mutual loyalty, and could be the culminated token of
a covenant.... So to be God's guest is to be more than an acquaintance,
invited for a day. It is to live with Him." (Kidner)

        ii. "While I am here I will be a child at home with my God; the whole
world shall be his house to me; and when I ascend into the upper
chamber I shall not change my company, nor even change the house;
I shall only go to dwell in the upper story of the house of the Lord for
ever." (Spurgeon)

Psalm 24 – The Great and Sovereign God

This psalm is simply titled **A Psalm of David**. *Many think this psalm was written upon the occasion of the entrance of the Ark of the Covenant into Jerusalem during the reign of David (2 Samuel 6). Yet Charles Spurgeon correctly wrote, "The eye of the Psalmist looked, however, beyond the typical upgoing of the ark to the sublime ascension of the King of glory."*

A. The great and sovereign God.

1. (1) The declaration: The whole world belongs to the LORD God.

The earth *is* the LORD's, and all its fullness,
The world and those who dwell therein.

> a. **The earth is the LORD's**: David was a noble, successful king – but of a relatively small and insignificant kingdom. One might easily think that the gods of the Egyptians or Assyrians were greater because those kingdoms were greater. Yet David rightly knew that the **LORD**, Yahweh, the covenant God of Israel, was God of all the **earth**.

> b. **The earth is the LORD's, and all its fullness**: It wasn't enough for David to say that the entire earth belonged to the **LORD**; he added that **all its fullness** also belonged to Him. It's difficult to think of a more sweeping statement of God's ownership.

> > i. "The '*fulness*' of the earth may mean its harvests, its wealth, its life, or its worship; in all these senses the Most High God is Possessor of all. The earth is full of God; he made it full and he keeps it full." (Spurgeon)

> > ii. There is a sense in which the "world" belongs to Satan. Satan is called *the god of this age* (2 Corinthians 4:4), and when he tempted Jesus with the promise of giving Him the kingdoms of this world, Jesus did not question the devil's ability to do so. Yet Satan can only do anything at God's allowance, so God's ultimate ownership is true.

iii. Paul quoted **the earth is the LORD's, and all its fullness** twice (1 Corinthians 10:26 and 10:28) to establish the principle that no food is in itself unclean, and that there is in fact nothing that actually belongs to the false gods the pagans made offerings unto.

c. **The world and those who dwell therein**: God's ownership of the earth extends to the *people* who live upon it. Through the rights of *creation* and *continuing provision*, God has a claim upon every person who has ever lived.

2. (2) The reason: God is creator.

For He has founded it upon the seas,
And established it upon the waters.

a. **For He has founded it upon the seas**: God has the right to the earth and all who dwell upon it because He created both it and them. Specifically, David looks back to the creation account of Genesis 1 and remembers the creation of land in the midst of earth's waters on the third day of creation.

b. **And established it upon the waters**: To the best of our knowledge, David had never ventured more than a few hundred miles beyond Israel, and had never seen a large sea other than the Mediterranean (perhaps also the Red Sea). David never saw a modern globe or earth projection. Yet he knew that the waters of the earth dominated the globe, so much so that it could be said that the earth is in the midst of the waters instead of the waters in the midst of the earth's land.

i. To David, this may have seemed to be a wonderful engineering marvel – that God could establish the earth **upon the waters**.

ii. "*Upon* could be translated 'above', as in Psalm 8:1." (Kidner)

B. Received by the great and sovereign God.

1. (3) The question asked – whom does God receive?

Who may ascend into the hill of the LORD?
Or who may stand in His holy place?

a. **Who may ascend into the hill of the LORD?** In light of God's sovereign ownership of the earth and all who live upon it, David wondered exactly who had the right to stand before God. This wasn't about mountain climbing or hill ascending ability, but about the *right* to come before God.

b. **Who may stand in His holy place?** David here clarified his previous question. David asked, "Who has the right to stand before God at His holy temple, in the holy place?"

i. This is a question that used to concern mankind much more than it does in our present day. There was a time when men and women genuinely wondered what was required of them to make them right with God. Today, it seems the most-asked question is something like, "How can I be happy?"

ii. Personal happiness is important; but it isn't more important than being in right relationship with our Creator and Provider. David not only asked an important question, but the *most* important question.

2. (4) The answer to the question: the moral character of the one whom God receives.

He who has clean hands and a pure heart,
Who has not lifted up his soul to an idol,
Nor sworn deceitfully.

a. **He who has clean hands and a pure heart**: This speaks of a man or woman who is pure in both their actions (**hands**) and intentions (**heart**). This one can *ascend the hill of the* LORD and *stand in His holy place*.

i. David already established that God ruled the earth; now he declared that God rules the earth on a *moral* foundation. He is concerned with the moral behavior of mankind.

ii. **Clean hands** are important for good hygiene, but this speaks of much more than washing with water. Pontius Pilate washed his hands, but they were not clean.

iii. "But '*clean hands*' would not suffice, unless they were connected with '*a pure heart*.' True religion is heart-work." (Spurgeon)

b. **Who has not lifted up his soul to an idol**: The one accepted by God also rejects idolatry, in his actions but especially in his **soul**.

i. "The meaning of *lift up his soul* is illuminated by Psalm 25:1, where it is parallel to 'trust'." (Kidner)

c. **Nor sworn deceitfully**: The words we speak are a good indication of the state of our heart, the inner man or woman (Matthew 12:34). One who makes deceptive promises finds no welcome from God.

i. David understood all this under the general principles of the Old Covenant, in which God promised to bless and receive obedient Israel, and also promised to curse and afflict a disobedient Israel (Deuteronomy 27-28).

ii. Outside the terms of the Old Covenant that God made with Israel, these answers of David may cause one to despair. It's easy to look at this list and see that my hands are not always clean; my heart is not always pure. Idolatry can be both subtle and stubborn in my heart. I also find it too easy to make promises with at least a tinge of deceit.

iii. Fortunately, God established a better covenant, a new covenant through the person and work of Jesus. Under the new covenant, we see that Jesus is the one **who has clean hands and a pure heart**, perfectly so. Jesus has *never* **lifted up his soul to an idol**, and has *never* **sworn deceitfully**. In *His* righteousness, given to all who believe (Romans 3:22), we can ascend His holy hill and stand in His holy place.

iv. "Our Lord Jesus Christ could ascend into the hill of the Lord because his hands were clean and his heart was pure, and if we by faith in him are conformed to his image we shall enter too." (Spurgeon)

v. Nevertheless, David's principle is also accurate under the New Covenant in this sense: the conduct of one's life is a reflection of his fellowship with God. As John wrote: *If we say that we have fellowship with Him, and walk in darkness, we lie and do not practice the truth* (1 John 1:6). We might say that under the Old Covenant a righteous walk was the *precondition* for fellowship with God; under the New Covenant a righteous walk is the *result* of fellowship with God, founded on faith. Yet under both covenants, God cares very much about the moral conduct of mankind, especially those who identify themselves as His people.

3. (5) The promise of blessing to the righteous man.

He shall receive blessing from the LORD,
And righteousness from the God of his salvation.

a. **He shall receive blessing from the LORD**: God knows and cares about the moral behavior of men and women. He rewards those who honor Him with their lives.

i. This blessing may be understood sometimes in *rewards* that God grants to the obedient; other times it may be understood as the *natural result* of living according to God's wise order.

ii. "It is here very observable, that the character of a right and acceptable worshipper of God is not taken from his nation and relation to Abraham, or from all those costly and laborious rites and ceremonies of the law, in which the generality of the Israelites pleased themselves, but in moral and spiritual duties, which most of them grossly neglected." (Poole)

iii. **He shall receive blessing**: "Perhaps alluding to Obed-edom, at whose house the ark had been lodged, and on whom God had poured out especial blessings." (Clarke)

b. **And righteousness from the God of his salvation**: David here spoke in the idiom of the Old Covenant, where right standing with God might be assumed from the life of the obedient. At the same time, David wrote of a *received* righteousness that came **from the God of his salvation**.

i. We might say that the obedient life spoken of in Psalm 24:4 is the *product* of the received righteousness obtained by faith, the **righteousness from the God of his salvation**.

ii. Even with the important distinctions between the Old and New Covenants, it is a mistake to say that salvation was by works under the Old Covenant. One might say that in some sense *blessing* was by works of obedience, but **righteousness** was always and is always **from the God of his salvation**.

iii. Under the Old Covenant, that faith was often expressed by the trust in the work of sacrifice, looking forward to the ultimate, perfect sacrifice promised by God and fulfilled in the work of Jesus at the cross.

4. (6) A description of the blessed and righteous ones.

This *is* Jacob, the generation of those who seek Him,
Who seek Your face. Selah

a. **This is Jacob**: This was David's way of identifying *God's covenant people*. The blessed and righteous ones have entered into covenant with God.

b. **The generation of those who seek Him**: The blessed and righteous ones do more than enter into covenant with God; they also *pursue* Him with a continual seeking. This is something each **generation** must do afresh.

i. "Heaven is a generation of finders, of possessors, of enjoyers, seekers of God. But here we are a generation of seekers." (Sibbes, cited in Spurgeon)

c. **Who seek Your face**: The idea is intensified by repetition, by description (to **seek Your face** is even closer than seeking **Him**), and by the use of a contemplative pause (**Selah**).

C. Receiving the great King.

1. (7-8) A call to welcome the God who reigns over all the earth.

Lift up your heads, O you gates!
And be lifted up, you everlasting doors!
And the King of glory shall come in.
Who *is* this King of glory?
The Lord strong and mighty,
The Lord mighty in battle.

a. **Lift up your heads, O you gates**: The first section of this psalm declared the greatness of God. The second section spoke of how man can come into relationship with this great God. Now the third section welcomes God unto His people by the opening of the **gates**.

i. "When the King of England wishes to enter the city of London, through the Temple Bar, the gate being closed against him, the herald demands entrance. 'Open the gate.' From within a voice is heard, 'Who is there?' The herald answers, 'The King of England!' The gate is at once opened, and the king passes, amidst the joyful acclamations of his people." (Evans, cited in Spurgeon)

b. **And the King of glory shall come in**: If we assume that King David wrote this psalm either for the arrival of the Ark of the Covenant into Jerusalem or in commemoration of it, we can also see that "the singer saw in that ceremony the symbol of greater things." (Morgan)

i. "Ancient rabbinical sources tell us that, in the Jewish liturgy, Psalm 24 was always used in worship on the first day of the week. The first day of the week is our Sunday. So, putting these facts together, we may assume that these were the words being recited by the temple priests at the very time the Lord Jesus Christ mounted a donkey and ascended the rocky approach to Jerusalem." (Boice)

ii. Therefore we can make several connections to this idea that **the King of glory shall come in**.

- This was fulfilled when the ark of the covenant came to Jerusalem (2 Samuel 6:11-18).

- This was fulfilled when the ascended Jesus entered into heaven (Acts 1:9-10; Ephesians 1:20).

- This is fulfilled when an individual heart opens to Jesus as King.

c. **And the King of glory shall come in**: The idea is plain; it is *assumed* that when God is welcomed with open **gates** and **doors**, He is pleased to **come in**. The **King of glory** will meet with His people when approached correctly and the doors are opened unto Him.

i. The idea that the doors or gates might be opened unto God, but He would not come unto man, isn't even considered. When we draw near to Him, He draws near to us (James 4:8).

ii. "For the Church is Christ's temple; and every faithful soul is a gate thereof to let him in, as in Revelation 3:20." (Trapp)

iii. In Revelation 3:20 this idea is presented as a plea from Jesus unto His people: *Behold, I stand at the door and knock. If anyone hears My voice and opens the door, I will come in to him and dine with him, and he with Me.* Jesus promised: open the door, and I will come in.

iv. "Surely, if there were doors and gates that needed to be lifted up before Christ could enter into heaven, much more are there doors and gates that must be opened to receive him into our hearts." (Spurgeon)

v. "We must have the King of Glory *within*. To have Him without, even though He be on the Throne, will not avail." (Meyer)

c. **Who is the King of glory? The Lord strong and mighty**: Perhaps with a touch of amazement, David notes that the same God who responds to man's welcome is still the **King of glory**; He is **mighty in battle**. His openness to man doesn't diminish His glory or might.

i. "The expression *mighty in battle* is but a stronger form of God's title of 'warrior' first heard in the song of victory at the Red Sea (Exodus 15:3)." (Kidner)

2. (9-10) Repetition for the sake of emphasis.

Lift up your heads, O you gates!
Lift up, you everlasting doors!
And the King of glory shall come in.
Who is this King of glory?
The Lord of hosts,
He *is* the King of glory. Selah

a. **Lift up your heads, O you gates**: As is common in Hebrew poetry, *repetition* communicates *emphasis*. The ideas of Psalm 24:7-8 were important and glorious enough to repeat.

i. When Jesus entered Jerusalem at the Triumphal Entry, Matthew tells us that the city asked, "Who is this?" (Matthew 21:10). If they had known who He was, the response should have been, "**The Lord of hosts, He is the King of glory!**"

ii. **Lord of hosts**: "Under whose command are all the hosts of heaven and earth, angels and men, and all other creatures." (Poole)

iii. **Lord of hosts**: "In fact, the conception underlying the name is that of the universe as an ordered whole, a disciplined army, a cosmos obedient to His voice." (Maclaren)

b. **He is the King of glory. Selah**: This psalm rightly ends on a reflective pause. It is no small thing that this **King of glory** stoops down to receive men and even to be received by men.

i. G. Campbell Morgan connected these three psalms of David (22, 23, and 24) in an interesting way. "By our calendars, yesterday He passed through Psalm 22. Today He is exercising the office of Psalm 23. Tomorrow, He will exercise finally the authority of Psalm 24." (Morgan)

Psalm 25 – A Plea for Help from the Humble and Reverent

Like several other psalms, Psalm 25 is an acrostic, or nearly so; there are a few irregularities in the acrostic pattern. James Montgomery Boice suggested three reasons why there are nine acrostic psalms (9, 10, 25, 34, 37, 111, 112, 119, and 145). First, the acrostic pattern is a literary device used to add beauty and form to the psalm. Second, it gives the sense that the subject is being covered completely, as if from A to Z. Third, the acrostic pattern may be a device used to encourage learning and memorization.

This psalm is merely titled **A Psalm of David**. *We do not know the precise time period it came from; David was so often in trouble that it could have been from several different points. It is a wonderful display of the heart of a well-taught believer in a season of crisis.*

"David is pictured in this Psalm as in a faithful miniature. His holy trust, his many conflicts, his great transgressions, his bitter repentance, and his deep distresses are all here; so that we see the very heart of 'the man after God's own heart.'" (Charles Spurgeon)

A. Troubled by enemies, David lifts his soul to God.

1. (1-2) David casts his trust upon God.

To You, O LORD, I lift up my soul.
O my God, I trust in You;
Let me not be ashamed;
Let not my enemies triumph over me.

> a. **To You, O LORD, I lift up my soul**: This is an expressive figure of speech speaking of the surrender, submission, and waiting upon God that David directed toward Yahweh (the **LORD**), the covenant God of Israel. It was as if David held his **soul** in outstretched hands up to heaven saying, "Here I am LORD, completely surrendered unto you."

i. "The very nature of such aspiration after God demands that it shall be exclusive. 'All in all or not at all' is the requirement of true devotion." (Maclaren)

ii. "Cares and pleasures are the weights which press the soul down to earth, and fasten here thereto; and it is the spirit of prayer, which must enable her to throw off those weights, to break these cords, and to 'lift up' herself to heaven." (Horne)

b. **O my God, I trust in You; let me not be ashamed**: As David declared his trust in God, he seemed to speak more to *himself* than to God. He assured himself of not only his trust in the LORD, but also the expected reward of that trust – to not be **ashamed** before either the LORD or his enemies.

c. **Let not my enemies triumph over me**: This gives some context to this psalm. Like many others, it was written from a time of trouble. David faced enemies who wanted the worst for him.

2. (3-5) A plea to the God who helps.

Indeed, let no one who waits on You be ashamed;
Let those be ashamed who deal treacherously without cause.
Show me Your ways, O LORD;
Teach me Your paths.
Lead me in Your truth and teach me,
For You *are* the God of my salvation;
On You I wait all the day.

a. **Let no one who waits on You be ashamed**: The idea of **waits on You** isn't of passively doing nothing; rather, it is of an active service. The idea isn't of a waiting room, but of a waiter attending to every desire and need of the one being served. David included himself among those **who wait** upon the LORD, but also knew that others did – and wanted all of them to be vindicated publically and unashamed.

i. "This is not a petition, as the King James' version rendered it, but an affirmation of confidence." (Morgan)

ii. The Biblical idea of **ashamed** is not primarily embarrassment (though sometimes it is used that way). The primary idea "is that of being let down or disappointed or of having trusted in something that in the end proves unworthy of our trust." (Boice) This is especially reflected in passages such as Romans 5:5 and Isaiah 49:23.

b. **Let those be ashamed who deal treacherously without cause**: Instead of the servants of the LORD being publically embarrassed, David prayed that his enemies would suffer this shame.

c. **Show me Your ways...teach me Your paths...Lead me in Your truth**: This shows that though David longed for public vindication, he was not haughty and proud. If he needed guidance or correction, he wanted God to give it, and to give it *before* any public humiliation, to *prevent* public humiliation.

> i. "The petitioner reveals an earnest desire to do God's will by praying to know 'your ways,' 'your paths,' and 'your truth.'" (VanGemeren)

> ii. We can be sure that no man or woman who has been shown the way by God, or taught in His paths, or led in His truth, has been led into sin or compromise that led to public disgrace and dishonor.

d. **For You are the God of my salvation; on You I wait all the day**: Because David had received **salvation** from God, it made him want to **wait** upon the LORD all the more. It was an appropriate demonstration of commitment and gratitude to the God who had done so much for him.

> i. We should regard the **salvation** David received here as being rescued in a broad sense. Spiritually speaking, he was rescued from despair and sin, both for now and in the life to come. Yet God also rescued his life and health again and again in the present age.

3. (6-7) A plea for God to remember and to not remember.

Remember, O LORD, Your tender mercies and Your lovingkindnesses,
For they *are* from of old.
Do not remember the sins of my youth, nor my transgressions;
According to Your mercy remember me,
For Your goodness' sake, O LORD.

a. **Remember, O LORD**: David asked God to **remember** His grace and goodness. First, he described them as **tender mercies**: *compassionate compassions* (*racham racham*, with the repetition indicating intensity). Then, he used the plural of the wonderful word *lovingkindness* (*hesed*), which speaks of God's deep, covenant love.

> i. "*Steadfast love*, or 'true love' (NEB) is that faithfulness to a covenant, to which marital devotion gives some analogy." (Kidner)

> ii. "This is the love by which he enters into a favorable relationship with his people, promising to be their God." (Boice)

> iii. David thought of this love in the plural – **lovingkindnesses** – as if God's covenant love was so great that it could not be thought of in the singular.

b. **For they are from of old**: David pressed his request to God on the basis of His prior work. "LORD, you have shown me great mercy and covenant love in the past; remember it now and do it again at my point of present need."

    i. "A more correct translation would be 'from eternity.' David was a sound believer in the doctrine of God's eternal love. The Lord's loving-kindnesses are no novelties." (Spurgeon)

c. **Do not remember the sins of my youth**: Immediately after asking God to remember (Psalm 25:6), David then asked God to *forget*. He wanted God to forget his own youthful sins (in the sense of forgiving them), and he wanted God to remember God's own faithfulness in prior times.

    i. **Sins of my youth**: "Which, though long since committed, must not be remembered without remorse." (Trapp)

    ii. "When God remembers his mercy, he forgets our sins." (Horne)

d. **According to Your mercy remember me, for Your goodness' sake, O LORD**: These are strong expressions of David's humility and even repentance. He asked to be remembered not on the basis of merit, but on the basis of **mercy**. He wanted God to do all this remembering and forgetting for the sake of God's own **goodness**, not David's supposed goodness.

    i. "Never did prisoner at the bar beg more earnestly for his life than David did for pardon of his great offence, especially in the matter of Uriah; for that lay heaviest." (Trapp)

B. Declaring the goodness of God.

1. (8-11) God's goodness to the humble.

Good and upright *is* the LORD;
Therefore He teaches sinners in the way.
The humble He guides in justice,
And the humble He teaches His way.
All the paths of the LORD are mercy and truth,
To such as keep His covenant and His testimonies.
For Your name's sake, O LORD,
Pardon my iniquity, for it *is* great.

a. **Good and upright is the LORD; therefore He teaches sinners**: David's observation here was not learned through simple logic. It is just as logical for God to *judge* or *destroy* sinners as it is for Him to teach them. Yet David had learned this through love more than logic, that God is **good and upright**, and this goodness can be for the benefit of sinners instead of for their destruction.

b. **The humble He guides...the humble He teaches**: David knew there was a particular *kind* of sinner that received this instruction and guidance from the good God – the **humble** man or woman. Not every sinner receives these good things from God, but those who will humble themselves before Him do.

i. "Meek spirits are in high favour with the Father of the meek and lowly Jesus, for he sees in them the image of his only-begotten Son." (Spurgeon)

c. **All the paths of the LORD are mercy and truth, to such as keep His covenant and His testimonies**: This is a remarkable promise. The conditions are that one stay in God's covenant and in His word (**His testimony**), both in the sense of knowing them and obeying them. The promise is that God will continually reveal His **mercy and truth** in all that we live and experience.

i. We imagine a discouraged believer who says, "God's path for me is severe and terrible, at least at the present moment." David answers from both his knowledge and experience, "**All the paths of the LORD are mercy and truth**, for those who stay in His covenant and in His word. Focus yourself once again on His covenant and His testimonies, and you will see this for yourself."

ii. **Paths of the LORD**: "In the Hebrew I find the word here used is 'wheel tracks,' such ruts as wagons make when they go down our green roads in wet weather and sink in up to the axles. God's ways are at times like heavy wagon-tracks, and they cut deep into our souls; yet they are all of them mercy." (Spurgeon)

iii. "*Mercy* and *truth* are the *paths* in which God *constantly walks* in reference to the children of men; and so *frequently* does he show them *mercy*, and so frequently does he fulfil his *truth*, that his paths are earnestly discerned. How frequent, how deeply indented, and how multiplied are those *tracks* to every *family* and *individual*!" (Clarke)

iv. **All the paths of the LORD**: "They say there is no rule without an exception, but there is an exception to that rule. All God's dealings with his people are gracious and faithful." (Spurgeon)

d. **For Your name's sake, O LORD, pardon my iniquity, for it is great**: Once again we see a strong expression of David's humility. He expected **pardon** for God's sake, not his own. He humbly recognized the greatness of his own **iniquity**.

i. Our sin is **great**:

• Our sin is great when we consider against whom it is committed.

• Our sin is great when we consider it is against a just and fair law.

- Our sin is great when we consider it is committed by those made in the image of God.

- Our sin is great when we consider the amount of our sin.

ii. It is strange (but true) spiritual logic: **pardon my iniquity, for it is great**. We can only imagine a criminal in a court of law appealing to the judge on this basis. "Your honor, find me not guilty, because my crimes have been many and large."

iii. David seemed to know the freedom and peace that comes from saying, "LORD, I know that I am a great sinner; but You are an even greater Savior. I humbly submit myself to You and ask you to **pardon my iniquity**."

2. (12-14) God's goodness to the reverent man.

Who *is* the man that fears the LORD?
Him shall He teach in the way He chooses.
He himself shall dwell in prosperity,
And his descendants shall inherit the earth.
The secret of the LORD is with those who fear Him,
And He will show them His covenant.

a. **Who is the man that fears the LORD? Him shall He teach**: Using the Hebrew poetic tool of repetition, David set the idea of *humility* (Psalm 25:9) next to the idea of a reverent fear of God. The two concepts are closely connected, and this humble, reverent person can expect the gift of God's guidance and instruction.

b. **He himself shall dwell in prosperity**: David described the earthly, material blessings that often come to the humble and reverent. We sense that perhaps David said this in faith; though his present situation was bad, he trusted that **prosperity** and blessing for his descendants would come in time.

c. **The secret of the LORD is with those who fear Him, and He will show them His covenant**: After touching on the material blessings that may come to the humble and reverent man, David then spoke of the greatest blessing that one may receive – the **secret of the LORD**, and a greater understanding of **His covenant**.

i. "The Hebrew idiom for 'the LORD confides' is 'the secret of Yahweh,' which may here be translated by 'intimate circle' (cf. Job 19:19; 29:4; Proverbs 3:32). Those who do his will are his confidants, as was Abraham (Genesis 18:17)." (VanGemeren)

ii. "Some read it 'the friendship:' it signifies familiar intercourse, confidential intimacy, and select fellowship. This is a great secret. Carnal minds cannot guess what is intended by it, and even believers cannot explain it in words, for it must be felt to be known." (Spurgeon)

iii. "Whether we translate the first word 'secret' or 'friendship,' the sense is substantially the same. Obedience and the true fear of Jehovah directly tend to discernment of His purposes, and will besides be rewarded by whispers from heaven." (Maclaren)

iv. **The secret of the LORD is with those who fear Him** reminds us that there are realities of Christian knowledge and experience known only by those who have new life by the Spirit of God; *the natural man does not receive the things of the Spirit of God, for they are foolishness to him; nor can he know them, because they are spiritually discerned* (1 Corinthians 2:14). To explain such secrets to those who do not have the Spirit of God is like explaining colors to a blind man or musical harmonies to a deaf man.

v. "There are secret passages of love between Christ and the believing soul, which it would not be lawful to utter. High fellowship: deep blessedness." (Meyer)

C. Eyes toward the God of help.

1. (15) Eyes toward God, even from trouble.

My eyes *are* ever toward the LORD,
For He shall pluck my feet out of the net.

a. **My eyes are ever toward the LORD**: David said this both as a statement of fact and as a prayer for the future. He knew the importance of keeping the attention of his mind and soul **toward the LORD**.

i. "He looks in confidence and waits in hope. We may add to this look of faith and hope the obedient look of service, the humble look of reverence, the admiring look of wonder, the studious look of meditation and the tender look of affection." (Spurgeon)

b. **For He shall pluck my feet out of the net**: This reminds us that this psalm was written from a season of trouble, in which David still felt himself caught. His **feet** were still in the **net** his enemies set against him.

2. (16-21) The plea for help presented again.

Turn Yourself to me, and have mercy on me,
For I *am* desolate and afflicted.
The troubles of my heart have enlarged;
Bring me out of my distresses!

Look on my affliction and my pain,
And forgive all my sins.
Consider my enemies, for they are many;
And they hate me with cruel hatred.
Keep my soul, and deliver me;
Let me not be ashamed, for I put my trust in You.
Let integrity and uprightness preserve me,
For I wait for You.

a. **Turn Yourself to me, and have mercy on me**: We see David did not hesitate to repeat his request to God, and he did so with a clever turn of thought. In Psalm 25:15 he spoke of how he had turned his attention toward the Lord; here he asked God to **turn** His attention towards His needy servant.

b. **Desolate and afflicted...troubles...distresses...affliction...pain**: This sweet, comforting psalm came from a season of agony for David. Much of the agony came from **enemies**, for **many** were set against him.

i. Some thousand years before Paul, David lived what the Apostle would later write at 2 Corinthians 4:8-10: *We are hard pressed on every side, yet not crushed; we are perplexed, but not in despair; persecuted, but not forsaken; struck down, but not destroyed – always carrying about in the body the dying of the Lord Jesus, that the life of Jesus also may be manifested in our body.*

c. **And forgive all my sins**: It was as if David recognized, "I have many enemies and troubles, but none greater than my own **sins**. Please God, deal also with **all my sins**."

d. **I put my trust in You...I wait for You**: The present difficulty David endured would not prevent him from trusting and serving God. This was a deep relationship with God, not one easily damaged or separated by disappointment.

3. (22) A closing request.

Redeem Israel, O God,
Out of all their troubles!

a. **Redeem Israel, O God**: We don't know if this psalm came from the time *before* David was king, or after. Whether it was before or after, David had a deep concern for the blessing and welfare of God's people as a whole, not merely himself.

i. "If thou will not pity and help me, yet spare thy people, who suffer for my sake, and in my sufferings." (Poole)

b. **Out of all their troubles**: It is remarkable that David could spare a care and a prayer for the **troubles** of others when he was in a season of such difficulty. This shows a life that was indeed instructed in God's ways, even as David prayed (Psalm 25:8-14).

i. One of the worst aspects of difficulty and trial in the life of the believer is that it can lead one to become terribly self-focused and concerned only with one's own problems. David, in his humility and reverence to God, was guided in a better way.

Psalm 26 – Standing in an Even Place

Psalm 26 is simply titled **A Psalm of David**. *Attempts to place it at a specific time in David's life are unsure. It shares themes with many psalms, but we note that despite the danger of evil associates, David remained confident that he would not slip, and that he would securely stand in an even place.*

A. Innocence proclaimed.

1. (1-3) A plea for vindication and the reason for it.

Vindicate me, O Lord,
For I have walked in my integrity.
I have also trusted in the Lord;
I shall not slip.
Examine me, O Lord, and prove me;
Try my mind and my heart.
For Your lovingkindness *is* before my eyes,
And I have walked in Your truth.

a. **Vindicate me, O Lord**: Like many of David's psalms, this song was written from a time of great trouble. He here pleaded for God to **vindicate** him, presumably by his enemies. The request carries with it the implication that David himself was unable to vindicate himself or had chosen not to.

i. "It is not David's reputation in the eyes of other people that concerns him but rather God's reputation that he covets." (Boice)

b. **For I have walked in my integrity. I have also trusted in the Lord; I shall not slip**: David had confidence that God would answer his prayer and **vindicate** him, because he had faith in God (**trusted in the Lord**) which he demonstrated by a faithful life (**I have walked in my integrity**). Therefore, despite his present difficulty, he could say, "**I shall not slip.**"

c. **Examine me, O Lord, and prove me**: David was confident enough in his demonstrated life of faith that he asked God to **examine** and **try** him. If

David were not in fact trusting in God or walking rightly, he wanted God to show him and teach him.

i. The request to **examine**, **prove**, and **try** refers mainly to the *inward* working of a man or woman – the **mind** and the **heart**.

d. **For Your lovingkindess is before my eyes, and I have walked in Your truth**: David here again combined the ideas of trusting in God and His mercy (God's **lovingkindness**), and in his demonstrated life of faith (**I have walked in Your truth**).

i. **Your lovingkindess is before my eyes**: David knew the value of sustained examination and meditation upon the **lovingkindess** of God. "Brethren, depend upon it that you shall find, each of you when you get dull and flagging in the practical part of your religion, that the proper way to revive it is to think more than you have done upon the lovingkindness of God." (Spurgeon)

- His lovingkindness is a good subject.
- His lovingkindness is a wide subject.
- His lovingkindness is a pleasing subject.
- His lovingkindness is a plain and simple subject.
- His lovingkindness is an always suitable and seasonable subject.
- His lovingkindness begins in eternity.
- His lovingkindness is given freely.
- His lovingkindness is certain.
- His lovingkindness is faithful.
- His lovingkindness goes into the smallest details.

e. **And I have walked in Your truth**: The idea of **walked** speaks of action, of manner of living. David knew the importance of both a right *inward* life (**mind** and **heart**) and right *actions* and deeds.

i. "We need people who have been taught and who then also walk in that way so that they demonstrate to unbelievers that the path of faith and morality is the happy and successful way to live." (Boice)

ii. "If our actions are evil, it is vain to take comfort from our thoughts. If actions speak louder than words, they may well speak louder than thoughts." (Spurgeon)

2. (4-8) Innocence proclaimed.

I have not sat with idolatrous mortals,
Nor will I go in with hypocrites.

I have hated the assembly of evildoers,
And will not sit with the wicked.
I will wash my hands in innocence;
So I will go about Your altar, O Lord,
That I may proclaim with the voice of thanksgiving,
And tell of all Your wondrous works.
Lord, I have loved the habitation of Your house,
And the place where Your glory dwells.

a. **I have not sat with idolatrous mortals**: Having stated the fact of his faithful life to God, David then described several specific ways that his life demonstrated a living faith. He did not associate with idolaters, **hypocrites, evildoers**, or the **wicked**.

i. "*I have not sat*, i.e. chosen or used to converse with them; for *sitting* is a posture of ease and continuance." (Poole)

ii. David described idol worshippers as **mortals** because it was helpful for him to remember and for them to know that their lives were short, and they would soon enough have to answer to the *true* and living God, instead of idols of their own making.

iii. David did this under the assumption that at least some kind of association with these people was morally wrong. One might say that he took 1 Corinthians 15:33 to heart a thousand years before Paul wrote the words by inspiration of the Holy Spirit: *Evil company corrupts good habits.*

iv. **Hypocrites**: "The *hidden ones*, the *dark designers*, the *secret plotters*." (Clarke)

b. **And will not sit with the wicked**: David had in mind the people he chose to associate with. We have little or no control over many contacts and associations in life; but of those we do, we are obligated to choose and value our associations with a heavenly perspective, not an earthly one.

i. In the modern world this idea takes on an entirely different dimension, in many ways unknown to King David. We choose associations in our entertainment, and we often choose very poorly. We allow the wicked to amuse us, then to be our examples, then our models, and finally our idols. David's statement here also applies to these kind of contacts and associations.

ii. "Many Christians can trace a lost youth or fruitless middle years to the bad influence of evil persons, whom they looked up to and even envied at one time." (Boice)

iii. "Many people have a very strong desire to meet celebrated or 'important' people, including those whom they disapprove…. But I am inclined to think a Christian would be wise to avoid, where he decently can, any meeting with people who are bullies, or lascivious, cruel, dishonest, spiteful and so forth. Not because we are 'too good' for them. In a sense we are not good enough. We are not good enough to cope with all the temptations, nor clever enough to cope with all the problems, which an evening spent in such society produces." (C.S. Lewis, cited in Boice)

c. **I will wash my hands in innocence; so will I go about Your altar, O LORD**: David did not believe he was sinless or perfect. He did need to **wash** his hands, but he could do so in the **innocence** of a clear conscience before God. He availed himself of God's **altar**, both for atonement and for offerings of **thanksgiving**.

i. Probably people wash or cleanse their hands more today than ever before in history. Perhaps every time we do, we should remind ourselves to *receive* the cleansing that comes from Jesus and His work on the cross, and our *responsibility* to cleanse our hands from wicked actions, our mouth from wicked words, and our heart from wicked desires. Outward cleanliness is good, but worth little for eternity if our life and heart are filthy before God.

ii. **So will I go about Your altar**: To the best of our knowledge, there was no ritual practice of walking around or dancing around God's **altar** among the ancient Hebrews. It may be that David had in mind the spiritual sacrifices of praise, and he joined a happy circle of worshippers (as Maclaren thought). Or, if David meant literal sacrifice, he probably had in mind the idea of offering so many animals to God at one time that the sacrifices themselves circled the altar in a sense. "He implies that he would offer many sacrifices together, which would employ the priests about the altar." (Poole)

d. **I have loved the habitation of Your house**: For David, a right walk with God was more than the avoidance of evil. It was also a simple yet deep love for God and His presence. He loved the tabernacle because it represented the **house** of God; it was the **place** of God's **glory**.

i. Obedience cannot be sustained without the sweetness of God's presence and glory.

ii. "The *habitation* must mean the *holy of holies*, where the Divine Presence was manifest; and the *place of the tabernacle* must refer to the *mercy-seat*, or the place where the *glory of the Lord* appeared between the cherubim, upon the lid or cover of the ark of the covenant." (Clarke)

B. What David wants from God.

1. (9-10) What David does not want God to do.

**Do not gather my soul with sinners,
Nor my life with bloodthirsty men,
In whose hands *is* a sinister scheme,
And whose right hand is full of bribes.**

a. **Do not gather my soul with sinners**: In light of David's great need and his great trust in God, he asked God to *preserve his life*. He refused to associate with the wicked in life; he asked God to keep him from **sinners** in death.

i. "The worst and most abandoned wretch on earth agrees with David in this. Sinners do not wish to be gathered with sinners. Balaam's prayer is, 'Let me die the death of the righteous, and let my last end be like his,' which only differs in words from David's petition, 'Gather not my soul with sinners.'" (Spurgeon)

b. **In whose hands is a sinister scheme**: David knew of many wicked men with evil plots who were **full** of greedy **bribes**; he considered it a curse to be associated with them either in the present age or in death.

i. Many who would never think of taking **bribes** from a businessman still take bribes of a sort; they take bribes from sin. A bribe simply is a reward for doing something morally wrong. Sin may bribe us with momentary pleasure, attention, fame of a sort, excitement, comfort of life, or whatever. We should never be willing to do something morally wrong because it is rewarded in some way.

ii. "A soul walking in its integrity will take bribes neither from men, nor sin itself." (William Gurnall, cited in Spurgeon)

2. (11-12) What David wants God to do.

**But as for me, I will walk in my integrity;
Redeem me and be merciful to me.
My foot stands in an even place;
In the congregations I will bless the LORD.**

a. **But as for me, I will walk in my integrity**: We note David's confident proclamation. Despite the danger to his life, despite the presence of the wicked, he – God helping him – would **walk** in his **integrity**.

b. **Redeem me and be merciful to me**: David had appropriate resolve, but even more appropriate trust in God. He could only **walk** in **integrity** *if* God would **redeem** him and **be merciful** to him.

c. **My foot stands in an even place**: With this combination of appropriate resolve and trust in God, David – despite the dangers all around – could be confident of his position (**my foot stands**). He stood on level ground, **in an even place** – a repeat of his confidence in the first verse, *I shall not slip*.

> i. "He seems to say to them all, 'Hoot at me if you will: seek to trip me up as you please: God is high above you all, and in him I shall still stand my ground, for, blessed be his name, notwithstanding every attempt of the enemy to throw me down, my foot standeth in an even place, and in the congregation will I bless the Lord.'" (Spurgeon)

d. **In the congregations I will bless the LORD**: He was so confident that he said that he would **bless** and praise God publicly, among others (**in the congregations**), not as an outcast or castaway.

> i. "The song began in the minor, but it has now reached the major key. Saints often sing themselves into happiness. The *even place* upon which our foot stands is the sure, covenant faithfulness, eternal promise and immutable oath of the Lord of Hosts; there is no fear of falling from this solid basis, or of its being removed from under us." (Spurgeon)

Psalm 27 – The Seeking, Waiting Life Rewarded

This psalm is simply titled **A Psalm of David**. *As with many of David's psalms, it is impossible to confidently state which period of his life it comes from. It speaks of trouble from enemies, adversaries, false witnesses, and violent men, but this was true of many periods of King David's life. There is such a marked change between the first half and the second half of this psalm that many suggest that it was two different psalms stitched together. Alexander Maclaren said this idea "has much in its favour"; but it neglects how the experience of the man or woman of God can change so much even within a day or a song.*

A. David's confidence in and desire for God.

1. (1-3) A proven confidence.

The LORD is my light and my salvation;
Whom shall I fear?
The LORD is the strength of my life;
Of whom shall I be afraid?
When the wicked came against me
To eat up my flesh,
My enemies and foes,
They stumbled and fell.
Though an army may encamp against me,
My heart shall not fear;
Though war may rise against me,
In this I *will be* **confident.**

a. **The LORD is my light and my salvation**: Like many psalms, King David wrote this from a season of trouble. Yet it is a song of confidence and triumph: because David was not in *darkness* or *ultimate peril* because **the LORD** was his **light** and **salvation**.

i. God Himself brought **light** to David's life. He did not despair in darkness and all that it represented. His life was filled with the LORD, and his life was filled with **light**.

ii. God Himself brought **salvation** to David. He probably meant this as rescue both in the immediate and the ultimate senses. God had rescued him time and again, and would do so into eternity. "The Hebrew word for salvation means 'deliverance' explicitly, and again this probably has to do with deliverance from the king's immediate enemies." (Boice)

iii. "Although God is often associated with light in the Bible, this verse is the only direct application of the name *light* to God in the Old Testament." (Boice) John 1:5 and 1:9 say this specifically of Jesus.

iv. **Light** and **salvation** were also wonderfully promised to the Gentiles through the person and work of the Messiah (Isaiah 49:6; repeated in Acts 13:47).

b. **The LORD is the strength of my life**: David was a skilled, experienced warrior and must have been a man of impressive physical strength. Nevertheless, he looked to the LORD as the **strength** of his **life**. David knew something of what the Apostle Paul would write many years later: *Be strong in the Lord and in the power of His might* (Ephesians 6:10).

i. "The very names of Jehovah as 'Light,' 'Salvation,' 'the Stronghold of my life,' imply darkness, danger, and besetting foes." (Maclaren)

ii. If we rarely know what it is to have God be the **strength** of our life, perhaps it is because we trust in so many other things for strength. We find it easy to trust in our wisdom, our experience, our friends, and our resources. David knew a strength greater than all of those.

c. **Whom shall I fear?...Of whom shall I be afraid?** David used the poetic tool of repetition to make his point and bring together parallel ideas. Because God was his **light**, his **salvation**, and his **strength**, there was really no reason to **fear** or **be afraid**.

d. **When the wicked came against me...they stumbled and fell**: David remembered how God had proven Himself reliable in the past. There were times when **the wicked** or even **an army** came against him, yet God still showed that He was David's **light**, his **salvation**, and his **strength**.

i. David's confidence in God was battle-tested. He did not have fair-weather faith that lived in always-easy circumstances. This isn't the joy of a man in a comfortable monastery; this is the song of a man who knew God's goodness even in danger and despair.

ii. 1 Samuel 17:44 relates that Goliath told the young David, *Come to me, and I will give your flesh to the birds of the air and the beasts of the field!* Perhaps David remembered that when he wrote, **When the wicked came against me to eat up my flesh, my enemies and foes, they stumbled and fell.**

iii. **They stumbled and fell**: "God's breath blew them off their legs.... This was literally true in the case of our Lord in Gethsemane, when those who came to take him went backward and fell to the ground; and herein he was a prophetic representative of all wrestling believers who, rising from their knees shall, by the power of faith, throw their foes upon their faces." (Spurgeon)

v. **In this will I be confident**: "Because of his confidence in the Lord, the psalmist is not afraid. In his inner being there is no fear. This confident confession in God's saving love is similar to Paul's confession in Romans 8:31-39." (VanGemeren)

2. (4) David's desire for God's presence.

One *thing* I have desired of the LORD,
That will I seek:
That I may dwell in the house of the LORD
All the days of my life,
To behold the beauty of the LORD,
And to inquire in His temple.

a. **One thing I have desired of the LORD**: The tone of the song suddenly changes from celebration to contemplation. The experience of the goodness and greatness of God made David think about how wonderful it is to seek Him and to experience His presence.

i. "One purpose dominated his prayer and life. It was never long absent from the Psalmist's thought. The men of one idea are irresistible." (Meyer)

b. **That I may dwell in the house of the LORD**: David wished he could live in the tabernacle itself, surrounded every day by the presence and beauty of God.

i. In these few verses we note the many ways David referred to the **house of the LORD**. "David seems to be ransacking the Hebrew language for nouns to describe it: 'the house of the Lord' (v. 4) 'his temple' (v. 4), 'his dwelling' (v. 5), 'his tabernacle' (vv.5-6)." (Boice)

c. **To behold the beauty of the LORD**: David knew there was **beauty** in the nature and presence of God, beauty that could be perceived by the seeking eye of faith. He could think of no greater occupation than to fill his mind and heart with the goodness and greatness of God.

i. There is richness in God, revealed to the seeking heart, that many people never know. It is a shame that David knew this under the Old Covenant, and so many of us – with a greater covenant and greater promises – never know it.

ii. "The character of God is attractive, and fitted to inspire us with love for him, and to make us, as it were, run after him." (Gray, cited in Spurgeon)

iii. Alexander Pope, a famous writer, once wrote: "Know then thyself, presume not God to scan; the proper study of mankind is man." He thought it was more important for us to learn about ourselves than about God.

iv. An even more famous writer, Charles Spurgeon, responded to Pope's statement: "It has been said by someone that 'the proper study of mankind is man.' I will not oppose the idea, but I believe it is equally true that the proper study of God's elect is God; the proper study of a Christian is the Godhead. The highest science, the loftiest speculation, the mightiest philosophy, which can ever engage the attention of a child of God, is the name, the nature, the person, the work, the doings, and the existence of the great God whom he calls his Father." (This came from Spurgeon's first published sermon, titled *The Immutability of God*, delivered on January 7, 1855 – when he was 20 years old.)

d. **And to inquire in His temple**: In God's presence, David wished to go from contemplation to inquiry. He wanted to know more of God and more of His ways.

i. It wasn't that the earthly structure so fascinated David; he wrote this when the tabernacle tent served as a rather humble **temple** for Israel, before the wonderful building that Solomon built. "It was not the earthly temple itself that charmed David but rather the beauty of the Lord that was to be found at the temple in a special way." (Boice)

ii. "The two acts complete the joyful employment of a soul communing with God: first perceiving and then reflecting upon His uncreated beauty of goodness." (Maclaren)

3. (5-6) The blessings of God's presence.

For in the time of trouble
He shall hide me in His pavilion;
In the secret place of His tabernacle

He shall hide me;
He shall set me high upon a rock.
And now my head shall be lifted up above my enemies all around me;
Therefore I will offer sacrifices of joy in His tabernacle;
I will sing, yes, I will sing praises to the LORD.

a. **For in the time of trouble He shall hide me in His pavilion**: David knew that there was special blessing and protection for the one who earnestly sought God. It wasn't a promise to prevent all trouble, but to give security and blessing even in the midst of it.

i. "God's dwelling is a 'tent,' where He will shelter His guests. The privilege of asylum is theirs." (Maclaren)

b. **He shall set me high upon a rock**: David believed that a life spent seeking God would know a measure of safety and security, even in the presence of **enemies all around**.

i. **My head shall be lifted up**: "Two things make the head hang down – fear and shame; hope easeth the Christian's heart of both these, and so forbids him to give any sign of a desponding mind by a dejected countenance." (Gurnall, cited in Spurgeon)

c. **Therefore I will offer sacrifices of joy**: David's life was filled with celebration and gratitude for all God had done. He would **sing praises to the LORD** who blessed him with His presence and rescued him so often.

i. "*Sacrifices of joy,* or *of shouting and resounding,* i.e. of thanksgiving; which were accomplished with the sound of trumpets and other instruments, Numbers 10:10; 1 Chronicles 16:41, 42; Psalm 33:3." (Poole)

B. A prayer.

1. (7-10) Seeking the faithful God.

Hear, O LORD, *when* I cry with my voice!
Have mercy also upon me, and answer me.
When You said, "Seek My face,"
My heart said to You, "Your face, LORD, I will seek."
Do not hide Your face from me;
Do not turn Your servant away in anger;
You have been my help;
Do not leave me nor forsake me,
O God of my salvation.
When my father and my mother forsake me,
Then the LORD will take care of me.

a. **Hear, O LORD, when I cry with my voice**: The celebration of the first half of this psalm might make us think that it was all easy for David. One might think that when trouble came there was no struggle, either with self or God. Yet David showed us that even he – the one who sought God with such passion – sometimes felt that God did not hear him immediately.

i. "Note his anxiety to be heard. Pharisees care not a fig for the Lord's hearing them, so long as they are heard of men, or charm their own pride with their sounding devotions; but with a genuine man, the Lord's ear is everything." (Spurgeon)

b. **When You said, "Seek My face"**: God invited David to seek Him; yet there was a sense in which David felt that God was *hiding* from him (**Do not hide Your face from me**). David didn't become angry with God or turn against Him; in his disappointment he sought God all the more diligently and desperately (**Do not leave me nor forsake me**).

c. **You have been my help; do not leave me nor forsake me**: David used God's *past* **help** as a reason to ask and expect *future* help.

d. **When my father and mother forsake me, then the LORD will take care of me**: David knew that the love and care of God could go beyond even the closest human bonds. David probably did not expect his parents to **forsake** him; yet even if they did, God would not.

i. David sent his parents to Moab for protection in 1 Samuel 22:3-4. Perhaps, without their ever intending it, this made David feel forsaken by his parents.

ii. Boice points out that from a parent, we want acceptance, to be heard, guidance, and protection. God can fulfill each of these for all, including someone who never received these from a parent.

2. (11-13) A believing prayer for guidance.

Teach me Your way, O LORD,
And lead me in a smooth path, because of my enemies.
Do not deliver me to the will of my adversaries;
For false witnesses have risen against me,
And such as breathe out violence.
***I would have lost heart,* unless I had believed**
That I would see the goodness of the LORD
In the land of the living.

a. **Teach me Your way, O LORD**: This was a simple prayer for a life of true discipleship. David didn't want to live *his* way, but the LORD's **way**.

b. **And lead me in a smooth path, because of my enemies**: David didn't ask for an *easy* path, but instead a *level* or *even* place, a place of secure standing. It's the same word used in Psalm 26:12 to describe *an even place*.

i. "The simplest meaning of the word rendered *plain* [**smooth**], is level, or even." (Morgan)

ii. David had many **adversaries**, **false witnesses** against him, and violent men opposing him. In asking for a **smooth path**, he wasn't asking for an easy life but for a stable and secure place to stand against the storms of this life.

iii. **My enemies**: "The word *enemies* is rendered by Thirtle 'watchful foes,' and that exactly conveys the idea. It is that of enemies lying in ambush, waiting to catch him unawares, to attack him treacherously. The plain path for which he asks is one, traveling along which there shall be no pitfalls or lurking places for these foes." (Morgan)

c. **I would have lost heart, unless I had believed that I would see the goodness of the LORD in the land of the living**: David's seeking after God, and his knowledge of the Lord, led him to this triumphant statement. He would have given up (**lost heart**), but he knew that the good God would find a way to show His goodness in this life (as well as the next).

i. Some speculate that David meant *the life to come* when he wrote of **the land of the living**. One can fairly say that this is the land of the dying, "in which there are more dead than living, more under ground than above it; where the earth is fuller of graves than houses; where life lies trembling under the hand of death; and where death hath power to tyrannise over life! No, my soul, *there* only is the *land of the living* where there are none but the living; where there is a church, not militant, but triumphant; a church indeed, but no church-yard, because none dead, nor none that can die; where life is not passive, nor death active; where life sits crowned, and where death is swallowed up in victory." (Baxter, cited in Spurgeon)

3. (14) An encouragement to others.

Wait on the LORD;
Be of good courage,
And He shall strengthen your heart;
Wait, I say, on the LORD!

a. **Wait on the LORD; be of good courage**: Here King David spoke to you and to me, to his readers. From the reservoir of his experience he can encourage us to seek after God (**Wait on the LORD**) and to take courage in Him (**be of good courage**).

i. "Wait at his door with prayer; wait at his foot with humility; wait at his table with service; wait at his window with expectancy." (Spurgeon)

ii. "To wait for Jehovah is ever to find the plain path, however rough that path may be." (Morgan)

b. **And He shall strengthen your heart**: This profound promise is *for us*. Across the centuries David spoke to us, telling us to be confident that there is strength in the LORD for those who seek Him and trust Him.

c. **Wait, I say, on the LORD**: As in Isaiah 40:31, the idea behind **wait...on the LORD** is not a passive sitting around until the LORD does something. Yes, God gives us strength; but we don't expect it to come as if He were pouring it into us as we sit passively. He brings it to us as we seek Him, and rely on Him, instead of relying on our own strength. If we are weak, it is because we do not **wait...on the LORD**.

i. We should wait **on the LORD**:

- As a beggar waits for handouts at the rich man's door.
- As a student waits to be taught.
- As a servant waits on his master.
- As a traveler waits for the directions of the guide.
- As a child waits upon his parent.

ii. "Many of his promises bear a long date; but they are sure and infallible. Wait, therefore." (Trapp)

Psalm 28 – Praise from Prayer Heard and Answered

*This psalm is again simply titled "**A Psalm of David**." It shows David the son of Jesse once again crying out to God, and praising Him for the hearing and answering of his prayer. In this psalm we see the heart in a few different aspects: the evil heart (Psalm 28:3), the trusting heart (Psalm 28:7), and the rejoicing heart (Psalm 28:7).*

A. The prayer of petition, making requests of God.

1. (1-2) Asking to be heard by God.

To You I will cry, O LORD my Rock:
Do not be silent to me,
Lest, if You *are* silent to me,
I become like those who go down to the pit.
Hear the voice of my supplications
When I cry to You,
When I lift up my hands toward Your holy sanctuary.

a. **To You will I cry, O LORD my Rock: do not be silent to me**: With this opening to the psalm, David was both trusting and hopeful. In faith he gave God the title he longed for Him to fulfill: to be David's **Rock** in the present season of difficulty. David said this also in hope, because at the moment he felt God to be **silent to** him.

   i. David said that the **LORD** was his **Rock** – his foundation, his stability, his security. "It is a remarkable fact that in all the Old Testament literature, 'rock' is reserved as a figure of Deity...never for man." (Morgan)

b. **Lest, if You are silent to me, I become like those who go down to the pit**: In his trouble, David felt the grave was near – and if God did not intervene he would not live long. The response and intervention of God (opposite of being **silent**) was what David needed and longed for.

i. "The situation is probably illness or deep despair, and the fear is not a dread of death as such, but of death with unmerited disgrace." (Kidner)

ii. To avoid this disgrace, David needed God to hear him, to no longer be **silent**. "Jehovah seems deaf when prayer is unanswered, and is silent when He does not speak in deliverance" (Maclaren).

iii. "Mere formalists may be content without answers to their prayers, but genuine suppliants cannot; they are not satisfied with the results of prayer itself in calming the mind and subduing the will – they must go further and obtain actual replies from heaven, or they cannot rest." (Spurgeon)

c. **When I cry to You, when I lift up my hands toward Your holy sanctuary**: David used the poetic techniques of repetition and parallelism to say essentially the same thing in two ways. His prayer was a cry to God, and his body was set in the traditional posture of prayer (**I lift up my hands**).

i. "An ordinary gesture in prayer, expressing faith (for they held out their open hands, as craving beggars)." (Trapp)

ii. Some (like Clarke and others) believe the line **Your holy sanctuary** proves that David did not write this psalm, and that it was actually composed at a later time when the temple stood. This is not necessary, because the tabernacle (which was certainly present in King David's day) was also a **holy sanctuary**.

iii. "This need not mean that the psalm is later than David; only that the word had become the standard term for the ark's abode by Solomon's time, which suggests that it was in use well before this." (Kidner)

2. (3-5) Asking to be spared the fate of the wicked.

Do not take me away with the wicked
And with the workers of iniquity,
Who speak peace to their neighbors,
But evil *is* in their hearts.
Give them according to their deeds,
And according to the wickedness of their endeavors;
Give them according to the work of their hands;
Render to them what they deserve.
Because they do not regard the works of the LORD,

Nor the operation of His hands,
He shall destroy them
And not build them up.

a. **Do not take me away with the wicked**: David happily knew that his life was different than **the workers of iniquity**, and he asked that God would treat him differently than the **wicked**.

i. "Even worse than consignment to the will of the wicked, which was the fear of Psalm 27:12, is consignment *with* them to the disgrace they have earned." (Kidner)

b. **Who speak peace to their neighbors, but evil is in their hearts**: When David thought to describe the wicked, he began noting that they were false in their words, hiding the **evil** in **their hearts**.

i. "Soft words, oily with pretended love, are the deceitful meshes of the infernal net in which Satan catches the precious life; many of his children are learned in his abominable craft, and fish with their father's nets, almost as cunningly as he himself could do it." (Spurgeon)

c. **Give them according to their deeds**: In his own seasons of sin, David cast himself upon the mercy of God and asked to be forgiven for his sinful deeds. Here, he prayed for a harsh judgment to be applied to the wicked, that God would deal with them according to their wicked **deeds**.

i. To emphasize the point, David repeated the same idea in four different phrases:

- **According to their deeds.**
- **The wickedness of their endeavors.**
- **The work of their hands.**
- **What they deserve.**

ii. "These verses are not simply vindictive, but put into words the protest of any healthy conscience at the wrongs of the present order, and the conviction that a day of judgment is a moral necessity." (Kidner)

d. **Because they do not regard the works of the Lord, nor the operation of His hands**: When David considered the wicked deeds of the ungodly, he also considered that they ignored the creative work of God. To David, this was evidence of one being sinful and ripe for judgment.

i. Paul expressed the same idea in Romans 1:20-21: *For since the creation of the world His invisible attributes are clearly seen, being understood by the things that are made, even His eternal power and Godhead, so that they are without excuse, because, although they knew God, they did not glorify*

Him as God, nor were thankful, but became futile in their thoughts, and their foolish hearts were darkened.

ii. "The acts of the Lord in creation, redemption, and Yahweh's rule through David reveal the wonder of God's purpose. The history of redemption condemns the wicked." (VanGemeren)

e. **He shall destroy them and not build them up**: The wicked forget about God, but He does not forget about them. God promises to give those who reject Him what they deserve.

B. The prayer of praise, happy in the answer to prayer.

1. (6-7) Praising the LORD who hears prayer.

Blessed *be* the LORD,
Because He has heard the voice of my supplications!
The LORD is my strength and my shield;
My heart trusted in Him, and I am helped;
Therefore my heart greatly rejoices,
And with my song I will praise Him.

a. **Blessed be the LORD, because He has heard**: In his trouble, David cried out to God. Now he praises the God who heard and answered his prayer, becoming David's **strength** and **shield**.

i. "Suddenly the prayer becomes a song of praise, an act of adoration." (Morgan)

ii. This praise was founded on a reason, indicated by the word **because**. "Real praise is established upon sufficient and constraining reasons; it is not irrational emotion, but rises, like a pure spring, from the deeps of experience." (Spurgeon)

iii. It's a beautiful thing to say, "**my strength**" and "**my shield**." Some have a theoretical knowledge of God as a strength or shield, without knowing the goodness of it in their individual lives.

iv. "My dear friend, if you can say, 'The Lord is my strength,' you can bear anything and everything. You could bear a martyr's death if the Lord should be your strength. He could make a stalk of wheat to bear up the whole world if he strengthened it." (Spurgeon)

b. **My heart trusted in Him, and I am helped**: David here adds his voice to the testimony of countless others who have found help as their **heart trusted** in God. This brought great rejoicing and singing to David.

i. David *knew* that God answered his prayer, perhaps even before the answer was in hand. "It is a modern refinement in theology which teaches that no man *can know* when God hears and answers his prayers…. True religion knows nothing of these abominations; it teaches its votaries to pray to God, to expect an answer from him, and to look for the Holy Spirit to bear witness with their spirits that they are the sons and daughters of God." (Clarke)

2. (8-9) Praising the LORD who is the strength of His people.

The LORD is their strength,
And He *is* the saving refuge of His anointed.
Save Your people,
And bless Your inheritance;
Shepherd them also,
And bear them up forever.

a. **The LORD is their strength, and He is the saving refuge of His anointed**: This is the blessing given to the heart that trusts God; God *becomes* their strength. He doesn't merely *give* strength; He **is their strength**, and the **refuge of His anointed**.

i. The word **anointed** (*mashiach*) reminds us of the ultimate Anointed One, Jesus the Messiah. **His anointed** ones are secure in the Messiah, and therefore strong and safe.

b. **Save Your people, and bless Your inheritance; shepherd them also, and bear them up forever**: David concludes this psalm with a series of short prayers asking God to bring His people what they need and long for.

i. The psalm started with a plea for *personal* help and rescue, but by the end of the psalm, David's concern is for the LORD's **people** as a whole. "Whatever is dear to the loved one is dear to the lover. You cannot love the pastor without taking a keen interest in all that interests him, and especially in the sheep of his pasture, and the people of his hand. Hence when you are nearest the Lord, you are almost certain to begin pleading for his inheritance, and saying: 'Save thy people; bless them, feed them, and lift them up forever.'" (Meyer)

- **Save**: God's people need to be rescued and they look to God for it.

- **Bless**: God's people need His blessing and favor, and they receive it by being His **inheritance**.

- **Shepherd**: God's people need His care and guidance as a shepherd guides his flock. "*Raah* [**shepherd**] signifies both to *feed* and to *govern*. *Feed them*, as a *shepherd* does his *flock; rule them*, as a *father* does his *children*." (Clarke)

- **Bear them up**: God's people need God's constant, sustaining presence – and they need it **forever**.

ii. "Jesus does not simply lead us to green pastures and still waters…He bears us up, and He does so for ever. Never tiring, though He imparts infinite rest; never ceasing for a moment his shepherd-care." (Meyer)

Psalm 29 – *The Voice of the* LORD *in the Storm*

This wonderful song is simply titled **A Psalm of David**. *In poetic beauty it describes the strength of a storm and understands it as the voice and power God. In so doing it repeats the name of the* LORD *eighteen times and uses the phrase "the voice of the* LORD*" seven times. "This psalm has no other elements. It is pure praise. It does not call upon us to do anything because the psalm itself is doing the only thing it is concerned about. It is praising God." (James Montgomery Boice)*

A. The command to worship the LORD.

1. (1) A word to the mighty ones.

Give unto the LORD**, O you mighty ones,**
Give unto the LORD **glory and strength.**

> a. **Give unto the** LORD**, O you mighty ones**: David speaks to the **mighty ones** of this earth, and warns them to look away from themselves and unto the LORD God of Israel. Though they may consider themselves to be **mighty ones,** and be so considered by others, they still should recognize their obligation to the LORD God.

> > i. This psalm is notable in its emphasis on the name, "**The** LORD" (Yahweh), using it some 18 times in these 11 verses. This is the name taken by the covenant God of Israel, rendered by the Jews with the replacement word *LORD* out of reverence to the holy name.

> > ii. As God says in Isaiah 42:8: *I am the* LORD*, that is My name.* It is perhaps best to think of Yahweh as representing the Triune God. We may say it this way:

> > *There is one God, Creator of all and the covenant God of Israel – His name is Yahweh. There are three persons who claim to be Yahweh: the Father, the Son, and the Holy Spirit. In some way, therefore, there is One God in Three Persons.*

iii. "This is the famous tetragrammaton, or name of *four letters*, which we write *Jehovah, Yehovah, Yehveh, Yeveh, Jhuh, Javah,* etc. The letters are Y H V H. The Jews never pronounce it, and the true pronunciation is utterly unknown." (Clarke, commentary on Isaiah)

iv. Some take these **mighty ones** to be those regarded as great on the earth; others take them as angelic beings. "The phrase is used elsewhere to denote 'heavenly beings' or angels (cf. Genesis 6:2, 4; Job 1:6; 2:1; 38:7; Psalms 82:6; 89:6). In this context the phrase may be used as a technical term for the divine assembly of heavenly beings who surround the throne of God." (VanGemeren)

b. **Give unto the Lord glory and strength**: David called upon these **mighty ones** of the earth to recognize that the Lord has a **glory and strength** that far exceeds their own.

i. When they **give unto the Lord** these things, they are not giving or attributing things to Him that He did not have before. They are recognizing things as they really are, because God is full of **glory and strength**.

ii. "Neither men nor angels can confer anything upon Jehovah, but they should recognise his glory and might, and ascribe it to him in their songs and in their hearts." (Spurgeon)

2. (2) A call to worship the worthy God.

Give unto the Lord the glory due to His name;
Worship the Lord in the beauty of holiness.

a. **Give unto the Lord the glory due His name**: His **name** being Yahweh, this is a call to recognize the character and nature of the covenant God of Israel. God's **name** is **due** a lot of **glory**; therefore it is right to call men (even the *mighty ones*) to worship Him.

i. **Give**: This is the third time this word is used in three lines. "Give, give, give. This showeth how unwilling such are usually to give God his right, or to suffer a word of exhortation to this purpose." (Trapp)

b. **Worship the Lord in the beauty of holiness**: The idea is that man should bow in humble recognition of the greatness, the **beauty**, and the surpassing **holiness** of God.

i. "The appeal describes the praising of God as consisting of two things: *ascribing* glory to him, that is, acknowledging his supreme worth with our minds, and *worshipping* or bowing down to him (the Hebrew word means 'to bow down'), which means a subordination of our wills and minds to him." (Boice)

c. **In the beauty of holiness**: **Beauty** and **holiness** are not often connected ideas in our popular culture. Yet in reality, there is surpassing allure and attractiveness in true holiness. If a purported type of holiness has little beauty, it may be questioned whether if it is true holiness.

i. There are four Biblical passages presenting the idea of the beauty of holiness (1 Chronicles 16:29, 2 Chronicles 20:21, Psalm 29:2, and Psalm 96:9), and each of them associates worship or praise with the concept. Perceiving the **beauty of holiness** should compel us to true **worship** and praise.

ii. God's holiness – His "set-apart-ness" – has a wonderful and distinct **beauty** about it. It is *beautiful* that God is God and not man; He is more than the greatest man or a superman. His holy love, grace, justice, and majesty are *beautiful*.

B. The awesome voice of the LORD.

1. (3-4) The voice of the LORD over the waters.

The voice of the LORD is over the waters;
The God of glory thunders;
The LORD is over many waters.
The voice of the LORD is powerful;
The voice of the LORD is full of majesty.

a. **The voice of the LORD is over the waters**: The *mighty ones* mentioned in the first verse of this psalm may have a high regard for their own power, but their power is nothing compared to the power of God. His authoritative **voice** proclaims His dominion **over the waters**.

i. This is the first of seven descriptions of the **voice of the LORD** in this psalm. Each one emphasizes the idea of the strength and authority of God expressed through His **voice**.

ii. The strength and authority of God's voice is also connected to His *word*. If the voice of God has such power, then the words uttered with that voice have the same strength and authority.

b. **The God of glory thunders**: The association of thunder and the voice of the LORD suggests this psalm was prompted by David witnessing a great storm, hearing the power of thunder, and associating it with the voice of God.

i. "The thunder is not only poetically but instructively called 'the voice of God,' since it peals from on high; it surpasses all other sounds, it inspires awe, it is entirely independent of man, and has been used on some occasions as the grand accompaniment of God's speech to Adam's sons." (Spurgeon)

ii. David saw a mighty thunderstorm and thought, "This shows me something of the power and the voice of God." The spiritual man or woman can see something of the hand of God, or the shadow of God, in almost every event of life. "The thunder is only a poetic image for a reality, the actual voice of God, which is infinitely beyond it." (Boice)

iii. Exodus 9:28 (in the Hebrew text) also associates the voice of God with thunder, as does Exodus 19:16, when Israel heard from God at Mount Sinai. Additionally, two passages from Job clearly make this connection:

He thunders with His majestic voice, and He does not restrain them when His voice is heard. God thunders marvelously with His voice. (Job 37:4-5)

God asked Job in Job 40:9, *Or can you thunder with a voice like His?*

c. **The LORD is over many waters**: Generally, the ancient Hebrews were not a seafaring people, and they saw the **many waters** of the sea as dangerous and foreboding. Yet David knew that the **powerful** voice of God, **full of majesty**, set Him **over many waters**.

i. The ancient Canaanites recognized deities over the sea (the god *Yam*) and the god of fertility and thunder (*Baal*). Here David recognized that Yahweh, the covenant God of Israel, was the real Master **over many waters** and the **God of glory** who **thunders**.

ii. Scientists calculate that a typical thunderstorm (not even the kind of great or major storm described here by David) releases around 10,000,000 kilowatt-hours of energy – the equivalent of a 20-kiloton nuclear warhead. Storms *still* are examples of the massive power of God.

2. (5-9) The voice of the LORD over creation.

The voice of the LORD breaks the cedars,
Yes, the LORD splinters the cedars of Lebanon.
He makes them also skip like a calf,
Lebanon and Sirion like a young wild ox.
The voice of the LORD divides the flames of fire.
The voice of the LORD shakes the wilderness;
The LORD shakes the Wilderness of Kadesh.
The voice of the LORD makes the deer give birth,
And strips the forests bare;
And in His temple everyone says, "Glory!"

a. **The voice of the LORD breaks the cedars**: The **cedars of Lebanon** were well-known for their size and strength. Yet the LORD's **voice** is so strong that He splinters these mighty trees and sends their wood in flight.

i. Again, we can imagine a mighty thunderbolt striking and shattering a strong cedar tree. David saw this and thought: "The voice of the LORD is like this, though even more powerful!"

ii. **Lebanon and Sirion like a young wild ox**: **Sirion** is "A Sidonian name for [Mount] Hermon." (Maclaren)

iii. In an archaic translation, the old King James has *unicorn* for **young wild ox**.

b. **The voice of the LORD divides...shakes...makes the deer give birth**: David could see the effect of lightning bolts, and understood that they were an illustration of the power and effect of God's word.

c. **In His temple everyone says, "Glory"**: David thought of how thunder and lightning attract attention and give a sense of awe. This sense of **glory** is even more appropriately given to the LORD at **His temple**. There, the people of God do not tremble in fear of the storm, but in awe of their great God – to whom they say, **"Glory!"**

i. "Is not this a noble Psalm to be sung in stormy weather? Can you sing amid the thunder? Will you be able to sing when the last thunders are let loose, and Jesus judges the quick and the dead?" (Spurgeon)

ii. It is also worthwhile for each believer to ask himself or herself if he or she are among those who say, **"Glory!"** – if the Word of God, the voice of God, still feels like thunder. If not (and for many this would be an honest assessment), he or she should humbly come to God and confess that His voice, His Word, sounds more like the drop of a paper clip than a thunderbolt – and ask for a fresh filling of the Holy Spirit to make a cold heart warm once again, and dull hearing sharp once more.

iii. "The commentators tell us that in the early church this psalm was often read to children or to an entire congregation during storms." (Boice)

C. The LORD as the reigning, blessing King.

1. (10) The enthroned LORD.

The LORD sat *enthroned* at the Flood,
And the LORD sits as King forever.

a. **The LORD sat enthroned at the Flood**: David saw the storm bring a deluge of rain, and it made him think of the Genesis account of the **Flood**, remembering it as a remarkable demonstration of the power and authority of the voice of God.

> i. "The word rendered 'flood' is only used elsewhere in reference to the Noachic deluge, and here has the definite article, which is most naturally explained as fixing the reference to that event." (Maclaren)

> ii. "Psalm 29:10 is the only place in the Old Testament where this particular Hebrew word for flood occurs except in the classic flood narrative of Genesis 6-9." (Boice)

> iii. David's reflection on **the Flood** reminds us of what a staggering expression it was of God's power and justice. "Even as in the days of the Flood, when he destroyed creation with his power but saved his own, so it is at any time that God's glory is expressed in the severity of judgment." (VanGemeren)

b. **The LORD sits as King forever**: The Flood was a radical expression of God's authority; yet His authority did not end those many generations ago. The LORD God continues to sit **as King forever**.

> i. Matthew Poole considered the connection between **the LORD sat enthroned at the flood** and **the LORD sits as King forever**: "As God showed himself to be the King and the Judge of the world at that time, so he doth still *sit*, and will sit, as *King forever*, sending such tempests when it pleaseth him." (Poole)

2. (11) The King as a Shepherd to His people.

The LORD will give strength to His people;
The LORD will bless His people with peace.

a. **The LORD will give strength to His people**: As David considered the earth-shattering strength and authority of God, he recognized that God brought that same strength **to His people**.

b. **The LORD will bless His people with peace**: The power of God may come as a destructive storm upon creation and upon those who rebel against God. Yet God's **people** can be confident that He **will bless** them with **peace**, and the strength of God comes to them as a comfort, not a storm.

> i. "During the storm He will give strength to His people. Following it He will give them peace." (Morgan)

Psalm 30 – Remembering the Greatness of God at a Great Event

This psalm has a unique title: **A Psalm. A Song at the dedication of the house of David**. *Though the title of the psalm (as it is in the English translation) indicates it was written for the dedication of David's palace, Charle Spurgeon (and Adam Clarke) thought that it was actually written prophetically for the dedication of the temple – which David prepared for, but Solomon built. Nevertheless, we take this psalm as being written for the dedication of David's palace. It says nothing about the house itself; rather the focus is on God and the greatness of His deliverance. At the dedication of David's house, David wanted God to be praised, not himself.*

Matthew Poole on **A Song***: "This Hebrew word schir may be here taken not simply for a song, but for a joyful song, as it is in Genesis 31:27; Exodus 15:1; Psalm 33:3."*

A. David gives thanks to the LORD.

1. (1) Thanks for victory over enemies.

I will extol You, O LORD, for You have lifted me up,
And have not let my foes rejoice over me.

> a. **I will extol You, O LORD**: At the dedication of his own house, David did not extol himself – rather, the LORD. What might have been understood as the achievement of a man was instead the occasion for praising God.

> > i. 2 Samuel 5:11-12 (and 1 Chronicles 14:1-2) describe the completion of King David's palace: *Then Hiram king of Tyre sent messengers to David, and cedar trees, and carpenters and masons. And they built David a house. So David knew that the LORD had established him as king over Israel, and that He had exalted His kingdom for the sake of His people Israel.*

> > ii. In this, we see that King David knew three things that made his reign great. Every godly leader should know these three things well.

229

- *David knew that the LORD had established him as king over Israel*: David knew that God called him and established him over Israel.

- *He had exalted His kingdom*: David knew that the kingdom belonged to God – it was *His kingdom*.

- *For the sake of His people Israel*: David knew God wanted to use him as a channel to bless His people. It was not for David's sake that he was lifted up, but for the *sake of His people Israel*.

b. **For You have lifted me up**: This explains the core reason for David's praise. He knew that his security and status were the work of God. It wasn't as if God did it all as David sat passively; he was a man of energy and action. Nevertheless, it was God's work far more than his own.

i. "The verbal phrase 'you lifted me' is a metaphorical usage of a verb meaning 'to draw up out of the water' (cf. Exodus 2:16, 19). Like a bucket that was lowered down in a well and then raised to draw water up, so the Lord pulled the psalmist out of the grips of Sheol." (VanGemeren)

ii. "Grace has uplifted us from the pit of hell, from the ditch of sin, from the Slough of Despond, from the bed of sickness, from the bondage of doubts and fears: have we no song to offer for all this?" (Spurgeon)

c. **And have not let my foes rejoice over me**: For David, this was a significant part of God's victory on his behalf. He was constantly confronted by **foes**, and God protected him and made him the winner in regard to them.

2. (2) Thanks for healing.

O LORD my God, I cried out to You,
And You healed me.

a. **I cried out to You**: David lived a prayerful dependence upon God. God helped, but David **cried out** and prayed unto Him.

b. **And You healed me**: No doubt there were many times when David received healing from God from both illness and injury. Yet the idea of *healing* is also broad enough to include the sense of God's help and rescue from any great need.

i. Many commentators believe that David remembered when God saved his life from a life-threatening illness. "It has similarities to Hezekiah's psalm of praise after his sickness (Isaiah 38:10-20)." (VanGemeren)

3. (3) Thanks for preservation of life.

O Lord, You brought my soul up from the grave;
You have kept me alive, that I should not go down to the pit.

a. **You have brought my soul up from the grave**: We don't know if David here described what we might call a near-death experience or if it would be more like a narrow escape from death. Either way, in his life as a soldier and leader, he had more than one time when death was near, and God rescued his **soul** from death.

b. **You have kept me alive, that I should not go down to the pit**: David wasn't immortal: one day his body would die and he would pass from this life to the next. Yet there were many occasions when God delayed his eventual death, not allowing him to **go down to the pit**.

i. "*To the pit*, i.e. into the grave, which is oft called *the pit*, as in Psalm 28:1; Psalm 69:15; Psalm 88:4; Isaiah 38:17." (Poole)

ii. As we think of this psalm as being sung at a dedication ceremony for David's palace, it was instructive for David to say to all, "You see the strength of my kingdom and the splendor of this palace. All seems good and secure on a day like today. Yet no one should forget that there were many times my life was in great danger and I was close to death. Praise the God who delivered me."

B. The testimony of a tested man.

1. (4) The exhortation to praise.

Sing praise to the Lord, you saints of His,
And give thanks at the remembrance of His holy name.

a. **Sing praise to the Lord, you saints of His**: Remembering the great works of God did not only cause David to praise, but also caused him to compel *others* to praise Him. It was fitting, because they also were **saints of His**, His special people.

i. "He felt that he could not praise God enough himself, and therefore he would enlist the hearts of others." (Spurgeon)

b. **Give thanks at the remembrance of His holy name**: Giving **thanks** is another way to praise God for His goodness, and is also good manners.

2. (5) The reason for praise.

For His anger *is but for* a moment,
His favor *is for* life;
Weeping may endure for a night,
But joy *comes* in the morning.

a. **His anger is but for a moment, His favor is for life**: After calling God's people to praise, King David then gave them more reasons for it. Here he rejoiced that the **anger** of God may be real but momentary, while His **favor** (acceptance, pleasure) is lasting, even **for life**.

> i. This is a contrast between the *momentary* nature of God's **anger** with His people and the *lasting* **favor** He holds them in. In New Testament vocabulary we might say that the correction or discipline of God is for a moment, but His grace abides forever.

> ii. "This description of God's slowness to anger, and readiness to save, is given by a man long and deeply acquainted with God as his *Judge* and as his *Father*." (Clarke)

b. **Weeping may endure for a night, but joy comes in the morning**: Almost certainly, David said this as a testimony from his own life. There were may tearful nights, followed by joyful mornings – perhaps with the recognition that the mercies of God to His people are new every morning (Lamentations 3:22-23).

> i. **Weeping may endure for a night**: "…(literally, 'will spend the night') is a poetic expression of how weeping personified may spend the night with him, only to be gone by morning." (VanGemeren)

> ii. "By itself, this passage could mean, merely, 'into each life a little rain must fall' or 'every cloud has a silver lining' or 'you've got to take the bad with the good' or 'cheer up, things will get better'…. But what David is talking about is God's disfavor versus his favor, expressed in the experiences of life. His conviction is that the favor always outweighs the disfavor for God's people." (Boice)

> iii. "Night and morning are contrasted, as are weeping and joy; and the latter contrast is more striking, if it be observed that 'joy' is literally 'a joyful shout,' raised by the voice that had been breaking into audible weeping." (Maclaren)

> iv. This is an emphasis on the *certainty* of God's comfort and joy to His people. **Morning** always follows **night**, and the weeping believer may be confident that as he keeps his focus on God, He will bring him once again to **joy**. "'*Weeping may endure for a night*': but nights are not for ever." (Spurgeon)

> v. "This is a most beautiful and affecting image of the sufferings and exaltation of Christ…of the night of death, and the morning of the resurrection." (Horne)

3. (6-7) David's troubled testimony.

Now in my prosperity I said,
"I shall never be moved."
Lord, by Your favor You have made my mountain stand strong;
You hid Your face, *and* I was troubled.

a. **In my prosperity I said, "I shall never be moved"**: One may wonder if David said (or sung) this to an assembly at the dedication of his palace and smiled at this line. It seems to communicate an overconfident assurance born of a season of **prosperity**.

i. "We are never in greater danger than in the sunshine of prosperity. To be always indulged of God, and never to taste of trouble, is rather a token of God's neglect than of his tender love." (Struther, cited in Spurgeon)

ii. "Self-satisfaction cannot praise Jehovah. Therefore it must be corrected by discipline. The final note of praise shows that through affliction and by deliverance the lesson has been learned." (Morgan)

b. **Lord, by Your favor You have made my mountain stand strong**: King David confessed that the strength of his life and kingdom was not due to his **prosperity**, but to the **favor** of God.

i. The palace of King David in Jerusalem (discovered by archaeologists) is situated in the great hills of Jerusalem. We almost see King David making a gesture towards these mountains and telling everyone that it was God's **favor** that **made my mountain stand strong**.

c. **You hid Your face, and I was troubled**: Without the constant sustaining work of God, David was deeply **troubled**. This isn't to imply that God played a hiding game with David, constantly hiding and then revealing Himself to him. The idea is that David was completely dependent upon the presence of God, fellowship with Him, and His favor.

i. "The Hebrew word *bahal* signifies to be greatly troubled, to be sorely terrified, as you may see in 1 Samuel 28:21, 'And the woman came unto Saul, and saw that he was sore troubled.' Here is the same Hebrew word *bahal*." (Brooks, cited in Spurgeon)

C. A prayer and its answer.

1. (8-10) The prayer from a time of trouble.

I cried out to You, O Lord;
And to the Lord I made supplication:
"What profit *is there* in my blood,
When I go down to the pit?
Will the dust praise You?

Will it declare Your truth?
Hear, O LORD, and have mercy on me;
LORD, be my helper!"

a. **I cried out to You, O LORD**: In Psalm 30:2 King David first said that he **cried out** to God. This is perhaps the content of his prayer on one of those occasions.

b. **What profit is there in my blood, when I go down to the pit? Will the dust praise You?** This was David's prayer in a life-threatening situation. He made rational arguments to God, knowing that he would *certainly* praise God if he escaped death, but he was *uncertain* if he could praise God from the **pit** or the **dust** of the grave.

i. These words of King David sound strange to someone familiar with the New Testament. It seems very different from the triumphant confidence of Paul who said, *to live is Christ and to die is gain* (Philippians 1:21). David seemed to see no *gain* in death, and therefore he pleaded that God would preserve his life.

ii. Only a shadowy understanding of the afterlife is present in the Old Testament. There are certainly moments of triumphant faith, such as when Job said, *For I know that my Redeemer lives, and He shall stand at last on the earth; and after my skin is destroyed, this I know, that in my flesh I shall see God* (Job 19:25-26). Yet there are also moments of uncertainty, such as here in Psalm 30:8-9.

iii. It wasn't until the New Testament that God revealed more clearly the fate of those who trust God from this life to the next. In 2 Timothy 1:10, Paul says these things have *now been revealed by the appearing of our Savior Jesus Christ, who has abolished death and brought life and immortality to light through the gospel.*

iv. Therefore David logically – and rightly, according to the revelation he had – only knew with certainty that he could praise God on this side of death. It was a valid question to bring before God in prayer. "It was an argument with God, an urging of reasons, a pleading of his cause. It was not a statement of doctrinal opinions, nor a narration of experience." (Spurgeon)

c. **Hear, O LORD, and have mercy on me**: Even though David prayed with rational reason, in an even greater sense he simply relied on the **mercy** of God. It was as if he said, "LORD, here are many good reasons for You to answer my prayer. Yet beyond all these, I simply ask for Your **mercy**, and ask You to be **my helper**."

i. **Lord, be my helper**: "Another compact, expressive, ever fitting prayer. It is suitable to hundreds of the cases of the Lord's people; it is well becoming in the minister when he is going to preach, to the sufferer upon the bed of pain, to the toiler in the field of service, to the believer under temptation, to the man of God under adversity; when God helps, difficulties vanish." (Spurgeon)

2. (11) The joyful answer to prayer.

You have turned for me my mourning into dancing;
You have put off my sackcloth and clothed me with gladness,

a. **You have turned for me my mourning into dancing**: The dedication of David's palace was a happy event. Without specifically mentioning the dedication of the house, David used it as a reason to remember all the times God brought him from sadness to joy, from **mourning** to **dancing**.

b. **You have put off my sackcloth and clothed me with gladness**: Using the Hebrew literary tool of repetition for the sake of emphasis, David repeats the idea of the transition from sadness to **gladness**. It was a happy day, but God had also been faithful to David in more difficult times.

i. "This might be true of David, delivered from his calamity; it was true of Christ, arising from the tomb, to die no more; it is true of the penitent, exchanging his sackcloth for the garments of salvation; and it will be verified in us all, at the last day, when we shall put off the dishonours of the grave, to shine in glory everlasting." (Horne)

ii. "My 'sackcloth' was but a loose garment about me, which might easily be put off at pleasure, but my *'gladness'* is *girt* about me, to be fast and sure, and cannot leave me though it would; at least none shall be able to take it from me." (Baker, cited in Spurgeon)

3. (12) God glorified and thanked for answered prayer.

To the end that *my* glory may sing praise to You and not be silent.
O Lord my God, I will give thanks to You forever.

a. **To the end that my glory may sing praise to You**: King David revealed the primary reason for God's transforming work in his life. It wasn't primarily to give him palaces; it was so that David could **praise** the Lord and **not be silent**.

i. God worked in David's life so that He would bring Himself glory and appropriate praise. Though it clearly benefited David, it was primarily for God's own glory that He did this. This principle means that God has a special reason to bring His transforming work to lives that will give Him praise.

ii. As it says, **that my glory may sing praise**, indicating that King David sang those praises with passion and exuberance, welling forth from whatever **glory** was associated with him as a man, a soldier, and a king.

iii. **Sing praise** indicates that David knew that in some special way, God regards and receives praise that is presented to Him in song. We sense that to David, it would be a sin to **be silent**.

b. **O Lord my God, I will give thanks to You forever**: King David closed this song for the dedication of his house with a determination to thank God **forever**. Palaces seem to be permanent things, but they eventually crumble. Yet God will rightly be thanked and praised **forever**.

i. "He concludeth as he began, engaging his heart to everlasting thankfulness; and therein becoming a worthy pattern to all posterity." (Trapp)

Psalm 31 – Shelter from Trouble in the Secret Place of God's Presence

This psalm is simply titled **To the Chief Musician. A Psalm of David.** *Charles Spurgeon rightly said regarding the title of this psalm, "The dedication to the chief musician proves that this song of mingled measures and alternate strains of grief and woe was intended for public singing, and thus a deathblow is given to the notion that nothing but praise should be sung." We have no definite marking place in David's life for this psalm because he was so often in trouble. It resonates with deep and personal trust in God in the depths of difficulty.*

An interesting feature of this psalm is that it is often quoted in other passages of Scripture.

- The author of Psalm 71 (possibly David himself) quotes the first three verses of Psalm 31 to start Psalm 71.

- Jonah seems to quote Psalm 31:6 in Jonah 2:8, his prayer from the belly of the great fish.

- Jeremiah quoted Psalm 31:13 six times, in Jeremiah 6:25; 20:3; 20:10; 46:5; 49:29, and Lamentations 2:22.

- Paul quoted Psalm 31:24 in 1 Corinthians 16:13 (according to Adam Clarke, this is more clear in the Septuagint – the early Greek translation of the Old Testament).

- Most significantly, Psalm 31:5 was quoted by Jesus Christ on the cross as His final words before yielding His life (Luke 23:46). Stephen, the first martyr of the church, also alluded to Psalm 31:5 (Acts 7:59).

A. A plea for rescue, and confidence in God's answer.

1. (1) Trusting the God who delivers His people.

In You, O Lord, I put my trust;
Let me never be ashamed;
Deliver me in Your righteousness.

a. **In You, O Lord, I put my trust**: This psalm of David begins in a similar way to many of his other psalms – with a declaration of trust in God in a time of trouble. We do not know the precise nature or time of the trouble, other than it severely afflicted David (Psalm 31:9-13) and made him despair of life. Nevertheless, David proclaimed his trust in the Lord.

b. **Let me never be ashamed**: David's bold declaration of trust showed that he was not ashamed to call upon the Lord. He considered it appropriate that God answered by **never** allowing His servant to **never be ashamed** before his enemies and adversaries.

c. **Deliver me in Your righteousness**: Because David trusted in God, he asked God to act righteously on his behalf, and to **deliver** him. He asked that the **righteousness** of God work on his behalf.

i. Early in the 16ᵗʰ Century, a German monk and seminary professor named Martin Luther taught through Psalms, verse-by-verse, at the University of Wittenberg. In his teaching he came upon this statement in Psalm 31:1 (31:2 in German). The passage confused him; how could God's **righteousness** deliver him? The righteousness of God – His great justice – could only condemn him to hell as a righteous punishment for his sins.

ii. One night up in a tower in the monastery, Luther thought about this passage in Psalms and also read Romans 1:17: *For in it [the gospel] the righteousness of God is revealed.* Luther said he thought about this day and night, until he finally understood what the **righteousness** of God revealed by the gospel is. It is not speaking of the holy righteousness of God that *condemns* the guilty sinner, but of the God-kind of **righteousness** that is *given to* the sinner who puts his trust in Jesus Christ.

iii. Luther said of this experience: "I grasped the truth that the righteousness of God is that righteousness whereby, through grace and sheer mercy, he justifies us by faith. Therefore I felt myself to be reborn and to have gone through open doors into paradise.… This passage of Paul became to me a gateway into heaven." Martin Luther was born again, and the reformation began in his heart. One great Lutheran scholar said this was "the happiest day in Luther's life."

2. (2-4) A plea for rescue based on relationship.

Bow down Your ear to me,
Deliver me speedily;
Be my rock of refuge,
A fortress of defense to save me.
For You *are* my rock and my fortress;
Therefore, for Your name's sake,
Lead me and guide me.
Pull me out of the net which they have secretly laid for me,
For You *are* my strength.

a. **Bow down...deliver me...be my rock**: In the previous verse David established the basis of God's rescue: *deliver me in Your righteousness*. David then called on God to act righteously on behalf of His needy servant, to rescue and protect him.

i. Clarke on **bow down Your ear to me**: "Put thy ear to my lips, that thou mayest hear all that my *feebleness* is capable of uttering. We generally put our ear near to the lips of the sick and dying, that we may hear what they say. To this the text appears to allude."

ii. David asked, **be my rock of refuge, a fortress of defense to save me**; then he said, **for You are my rock and my fortress**. Maclaren suggested that David's thougt was, "Be what Thou art; manifest Thyself in act to be what Thou art in nature: be what I, Thy poor servant, have taken Thee to be. My heart has clasped Thy revelation of Thyself and fled to this strong tower."

iii. "'You are...then be...,' should be the prayer of every Christian." (Boice)

b. **Therefore, for Your name's sake, lead me and guide me**: David did not ask for rescue because *he* was so good, but **for Your name's sake**. David believed that if God would **lead** and **guide** him, it would bring honor to God and His name.

c. **Pull me out of the net which they have secretly laid for me**: David knew his enemies wanted to trap and destroy him, but he also knew that God could rescue him even from clever and determined enemies.

3. (5-8) David's confidence in the LORD.

"In this turn of the stream, faith does not so much supplicate as meditate." (Maclaren)

Into Your hand I commit my spirit;
You have redeemed me, O LORD God of truth.
I have hated those who regard useless idols;
But I trust in the LORD.
I will be glad and rejoice in Your mercy,

For You have considered my trouble;
You have known my soul in adversities,
And have not shut me up into the hand of the enemy;
You have set my feet in a wide place.

a. **Into Your hand I commit my spirit**: David asked to be delivered from his enemies and their snares, but not so he could live unto himself. He utterly cast himself upon God, committing the deepest part of himself to God.

i. Jesus expressed His total surrender and submission to God on the cross when He quoted this line from Psalm 31. Luke 23:46 records that Jesus said, *Father, into Your hands I commit My spirit* – and then Jesus gave His last breath on the cross. "Thus he does not surrender his life despondingly to death for destruction, but with triumphant consciousness to the Father for resurrection." (Lange, cited in Spurgeon)

ii. Yet this committal of the soul unto God the Father is not reserved for David and the Son of David alone. Stephen, the first martyr of the church had the idea of this text in mind with his final words (Acts 7:59).

iii. **Into Your hand I commit my spirit**: "These words, as they stand in the *Vulgate*, were in the highest credit among our ancestors; by whom they were used in all dangers, difficulties, and in the article of death. *In manus tuas, Domine, commendo spiritum meum*, was used by the sick when about to expire, if they were sensible; and if not, the priest said it in their behalf." (Clarke)

iv. "These were the last words of Polycarp, of Bernard, of Huss, of Jerome of Prague, of Luther, of Melancthon, and many others." (Perowne, cited in Spurgeon)

v. "When John Huss was condemned to be burned at the stake, the bishop who conducted the ceremony ended with the chilling words, 'And now we commit thy soul to the devil.' Huss replied calmly, 'I commit my spirit into thy hands, Lord Jesus Christ; unto thee I commend my spirit, which thou hast redeemed.'" (Boice)

b. **You have redeemed me**: David understood that his surrender to God was appropriate because it was God who had **redeemed** him. He belonged to God both in *gratitude* for rescue, and in recognition that God had *purchased* him.

i. "In the Old Testament the word 'redeem' (*pada*) is seldom used of atonement: it mostly means to rescue or ransom out of trouble." (Kidner)

ii. "Redemption is a solid basis for confidence. David had not known Calvary as we have done, but temporal redemption cheered him; and shall not eternal redemption yet more sweetly console us? Past deliverances are strong pleas for present assistance." (Spurgeon)

c. **O LORD God of truth**: This is a second reason why it was good and appropriate for David to surrender his life to God – because God is the **God of truth**, and the **truth** demanded David's service and allegiance. David cared about what was true.

d. **I have hated those who regard useless idols**: David's surrender to God meant that he also had to *resist* the recognition or worship of idols – which are **useless idols**, having no power to speak or save. In contrast David could say, "**But I trust in the LORD.**"

e. **I will be glad and rejoice in Your mercy**: David's surrender and submission to God didn't produce misery – he was happy and joyful. Much of this was because his heart overflowed with gratitude, thinking of all God had done for him.

- **You have considered my trouble**: David was happy because he knew God did not ignore him in his time of **trouble**.

- **You have known my soul in adversities**: David was happy because he knew God had deep, substantial knowledge of David – even to the **soul** – in his seasons of **adversities**.

- **And have not shut me up into the hand of the enemy**: David was happy because he knew that God answered (or would answer) his prayer to be delivered from the snares of his enemies.

- **You have set my feet in a wide place**: David was happy because God did not only preserve him from enemies, but He also **set** David in a place of safety and security.

    i. **You have considered my trouble; You have known my soul in adversities**: "When we are so bewildered as not to know our own state, he knows us altogether. He has known us and will know us: O for grace to know more of him! 'Man, know thyself,' is a good philosophic precept, but 'Man, thou art known of God,' is a superlative consolation." (Spurgeon)

B. Trouble and trust.

1. (9-13) David describes the depths of his trouble.

Have mercy on me, O Lᴏʀᴅ, for I am in trouble;
My eye wastes away with grief,
Yes, my soul and my body!
For my life is spent with grief,
And my years with sighing;
My strength fails because of my iniquity,
And my bones waste away.
I am a reproach among all my enemies,
But especially among my neighbors,
And *am* repulsive to my acquaintances;
Those who see me outside flee from me.
I am forgotten like a dead man, out of mind;
I am like a broken vessel.
For I hear the slander of many;
Fear *is* on every side;
While they take counsel together against me,
They scheme to take away my life.

a. **Have mercy on me, O Lᴏʀᴅ, for I am in trouble**: The previous section of this psalm ended with calm trust and gratitude to God. Here David once again took up the lament, showing that both rest and adversity come to God's people in seasons. Yet in his trouble, David looks again to the Lᴏʀᴅ.

i. "It is as if David is riding an emotional roller coaster. Or, as if he is riding a wave from one high crest to a trough and then back to another high crest in closing." (Boice)

ii. **My soul and my body**: Literally, **body** is *belly*. "…i.e. my bowels contained in my belly; which was the seat of the affections, and fountains of support and nourishment to the whole body. Thus the whole man, both soul and body, inside and outside, are consumed." (Poole)

b. **My eye wastes away with grief**: David described his pitiful condition in terms that seem to be taken from the Book of Job. His affliction was

- Physical (**my strength fails...my bones waste away**). "The poetical expression need not imply that he is physically sick but could mean that his mental anguish has sapped his physical strength, to a point approaching death." (VanGemeren)

- Emotional (**my life is spent with grief, and my years with sighing... fear is on every side**).

- Social (**a reproach among all my enemies...repulsive to my acquaintances**).

- Mortal (**they take counsel together against me, they scheme to take away my life**).

- Spiritual (**because of my iniquity**).

  i. "Here the feelings of confidence ebb away in a flood of tears." (VanGemeren)

c. **I am forgotten like a dead man, out of mind; I am like a broken vessel**: With poetry and power, David expressed how complete his difficulty was.

  i. **I am a reproach among all my enemies**: "If anyone strives after patience and humility, he is a hypocrite. If he allows himself in the pleasures of this world, he is a glutton. If he seeks justice, he is impatient; if he seeks it not, he is a fool. If he would be prudent, he is stingy; if he would make others happy, he is dissolute. If he gives himself up to prayer, he is vainglorious. And this is the great loss of the church, that by means like these many are held back from goodness in which the Psalmist lamenting says, '*I became a reproof among all mine enemies.*'" (Chrysostom, cited in Spurgeon)

  ii. **Those who see me outside flee from me**: "Either loathing me as a monster of men, and an unlucky spectacle, and such a villain as mine enemies represented me, and they believed me to be; or to prevent their own danger and ruin, which might be occasioned by it." (Poole)

  iii. **I hear the slander of many**: "A man had better be dead than be smothered in slander. Of the dead we say nothing but good, but in the Psalmist's case they said nothing but evil." (Spurgeon)

d. **Fear is on every side; while they take counsel together against me, they scheme to take away my life**: David seemed almost overwhelmed by the dangers around him, but only *almost* and not completely.

  i. "This was literally true during much of David's reign. The kingdom was surrounded by hostile neighbors, just as the present nation of Israel is surrounded by hostile Arab neighbors. But David may also be thinking of plots within his kingdom by Jewish enemies or of the days he had to flee from King Saul." (Boice)

2. (14-18) In the midst of all his trouble, David declares his trust in God.

But as for me, I trust in You, O LORD;
I say, "You *are* my God."
My times *are* in Your hand;
Deliver me from the hand of my enemies,

And from those who persecute me.
Make Your face shine upon Your servant;
Save me for Your mercies' sake.
Do not let me be ashamed, O LORD, for I have called upon You;
Let the wicked be ashamed;
Let them be silent in the grave.
Let the lying lips be put to silence,
Which speak insolent things proudly and contemptuously against the righteous.

a. **But as for me, I trust in You, O LORD**: However great David's troubles were, his **trust** in God was even greater. He took careful inventory of his crisis but would not dwell on it. He understood that Yahweh was his God (**You are my God**) and therefore greater than all his trouble.

b. **My times are in Your hand**: David could not bear the thought of being given over to the **hand of** his **enemies**, but he was completely at peace (and even happy) with the knowledge, "**My times are in Your hand.**"

i. David could say **my times are in Your hand** because He understood that God was in control and ruled from heaven. Yet he also said this because in faith he had committed all things into God's hand.

ii. Late in David's life. he sinned by taking an unauthorized census of Israel. God presented him with the option of three punishments. David chose the punishment that would most completely set them in the hands of the Lord, explaining: *Please let us fall into the hand of the LORD, for His mercies are great; but do not let me fall into the hand of man* (2 Samuel 24:14).

iii. Boice saw in all this an application to the seasons of life for the Christian.

- The times of our *youth* are in God's hand, times when often we are subject to the decisions others make for us.

- The times of our *maturity* are in God's hand, times when we should be about our Father's business and face both apparent success and failure in it.

- The times of our *old age* are in God's hand, when God will care for us and bless those days as much as the others.

iv. G. Campbell Morgan saw in the words "**my times**" and in the entire psalm an allusion to the seasons of Christian experience. Morgan added the thought, "We need them all to complete our year!"

- Autumn (Psalm 31:1-8): "With its winds and gathering clouds, yet having sunlight and a golden fruitage even though the breath of death is everywhere."
- Winter (Psalm 31:9-13): "Chill and lifeless, full of sobs and sighing."
- Spring (Psalm 31:14-18): "With its hope and expectation and its sweeping rains and bursting sun gleams."
- Summer (Psalm 31:19-24): "At last the bright and golden summer."

v. "If we believe that all our times are in God's hand, we shall be expecting great things from our heavenly Father. When we get into a difficulty we shall say, 'I am now going to see the wonders of God, and to learn again how surely he delivers them that trust in him.'" (Spurgeon)

c. **Make Your face to shine upon Your servant**: David borrowed from the priestly blessing described in Numbers 6:23-27, asking for the goodness and the favor of God to be showered upon him.

d. **Let the wicked be ashamed; let them be silent in the grave**: David asked God to do to his enemies that which his enemies wished to do unto David.

i. **Do not let me be ashamed**: "…i.e. Disappointed of my hopes." (Trapp)

C. Praise, both personal and public.

1. (19-22) David praises God on a personal level.

Oh, how great *is* Your goodness,
Which You have laid up for those who fear You,
***Which* You have prepared for those who trust in You**
In the presence of the sons of men!
You shall hide them in the secret place of Your presence
From the plots of man;
You shall keep them secretly in a pavilion
From the strife of tongues.
Blessed *be* the LORD,
For He has shown me His marvelous kindness in a strong city!
For I said in my haste,
"I am cut off from before Your eyes";
Nevertheless You heard the voice of my supplications
When I cried out to You.

a. **Oh, how great is Your goodness, which You have laid up for those who fear You**: The same David who knew such trouble in Psalm 31:9-13 praised God so completely at the end of the song. This is because David had a deep trust in God (as reflected in Psalm 31:14-18), and that trust was rewarded with joy.

b. **You shall hide them in the secret place of Your presence**: Attacked by so many enemies and so many troubles, David found security in **the secret place of** God's **presence**. There was comfort and strength in the hidden place of God's **presence**, of true fellowship with Him.

i. There are many followers of Jesus Christ who seem to know very little of **the secret place of** God's **presence**. They regard it as only a thing for mystics or the super-spiritual. Yet David was a warrior and man well acquainted with the realities of life. It is true that the life of the spirit seems to come more easily for some than others, but there is an aspect of **the secret place of** God's **presence** that is for everyone who puts his trust in Him.

ii. **In the secret place of Your presence**: "'With the covering of thy countenance.' Their life shall be so hidden with Christ in God, that their enemies shall not be able to find them out. To such a hiding-place Satan himself dare not approach. There *the pride of man* cannot come." (Clarke)

c. **From the plots of man; you shall keep them secretly in a pavilion from the strife of tongues**: The presence of God was so secure for David that he found refuge from not only the **plots** of his enemies, but even from the attacks of their words (**the strife of tongues**).

d. **For I said in my haste, "I am cut off from before Your eyes"**: Earlier in his time of trouble, David hastily said and felt that God had forgotten him and no longer saw him with favor. Yet when David **cried out to** God, He **heard the voice of** David's **supplication**.

2. (23-24) A call for all God's people to praise Him.

Oh, love the LORD, all you His saints!
For the LORD preserves the faithful,
And fully repays the proud person.
Be of good courage,
And He shall strengthen your heart,
All you who hope in the LORD.

a. **Oh, love the LORD, all you His saints**: David's experience with God could not be kept to himself. He had to use what God had done in his life as the motivation and lesson to exhort all God's **saints** to **love the LORD**.

i. "The psalmist has been absorbed with his own troubles till now, but thankfulness expands his vision, and suddenly there is with him a multitude of fellow-dependents on God's goodness. He hungers alone, but he feasts in company." (Maclaren)

ii. "Do we, if we are called the saints of the Lord, need to be exhorted to love him? If we do, shame upon us! And we do, I am quite sure; so let us be ashamed and confounded that it should ever be needful to urge us to love our Lord." (Spurgeon)

iii. A soul that truly loves God does not lack any reasons for loving Him. God gives us many reasons to love Him. Spurgeon said of the call to **love the LORD**, "it has a thousand arguments to enforce it."

- Love God because of the excellence of His character.
- Love God because it is such a pleasant and profitable exercise.
- Love God because it is so beneficial to do so.
- Love God because it is the way to be cleansed from sin.
- Love God because it will strengthen you in times of trial.
- Love God because it will strengthen you for service.
- Love God because it is most ennobling.

iv. "You may pull up the sluices of your being, and let all your life-floods flow forth in this saved stream, for you cannot love God too much. Some passions of our nature may be exaggerated; and, towards certain objects, they may be carried too far; but the heart, when it is turned towards God, can never be too warm, nor too excited, nor too firmly fixed on the divine object: 'O love the Lord, all ye his saints.'" (Spurgeon)

b. **The LORD preserves the faithful, and fully repays the proud person**: Both aspects are true. God resists the proud, but gives grace to the humble. This encouragement to praise God has a warning to those who refuse to do so.

c. **Be of good courage, and He shall strengthen your heart, all you who hope in the LORD**: David closed this psalm as a true leader and friend, encouraging others to find what he had found in God. God's people have reason for **good courage**, because God does **strengthen** the trusting, hoping **heart**.

i. **Be of good courage**: "Dear friends, if you want to get out of diffidence, and timidity, and despondency, you must *rouse yourselves up*. This is incumbent upon you, for the text puts it so: 'Be of good courage.' Do not sit still, and rub your eyes, and say, 'I cannot help it, I must always be dull like this.' You must not be so; in the name of God, you are commanded in the text to 'be of good courage.' If you are indolent, like that, you must not expect the grace of God to operate upon you as though you were a block of wood, and could be made into something against your will. Oh, no! You must determine to be of good courage." (Spurgeon)

Psalm 32 – The Blessings of Forgiveness, Protection, and Guidance

This psalm is simply titled **A Psalm of David. A Contemplation.** *According to James Montgomery Boice, the Hebrew word for* **Contemplation** *(maskil) might be better understood as "instruction." This is the first of twelve psalms with this title. It is full of instruction and contemplation, and it is worthy of meditation, as indicated by the frequent repetition of Selah, three times in only eleven verses.*

The psalm itself does not tell us the specific occasion in David's life which prompted this song. In Psalm 51 – which was clearly written after David's sin with Bathsheba and against Uriah – David promised to "teach transgressors Your ways" (Psalm 51:13), and this psalm may be the fulfillment of that vow. John Trapp said that Psalm 32 and 51 are "tuned together."

"It is a Psalm of penitence, but it is also the song of a ransomed soul rejoicing in the wonders of the grace of God. Sin is dealt with; sorrow is comforted; ignorance is instructed." (G. Campbell Morgan)

"This was Saint Augustine's favorite psalm. Augustine had it inscribed on the wall next to his bed before he died in order to meditate on it better." (James Montgomery Boice)

A. The great blessing of sin forgiven.

1. (1-2) The blessing of forgiven sin described.

Blessed *is he whose* transgression *is* forgiven,
Whose sin *is* covered.
Blessed *is* the man to whom the LORD does not impute iniquity,
And in whose spirit *there is* no deceit.

> a. **Blessed is he whose transgression is forgiven**: David spoke of the great blessing there is for the man or woman who knows the forgiveness of God. His sin is no longer exposed; it **is covered**.

249

i. "The word blessed is in the plural, *oh, the blessednesses!* The double joys, the bundles of happiness, the mountains of delight!" (Spurgeon)

ii. Psalm 1 tells the way to be blessed: Don't walk in the counsel of the ungodly, don't stand in the path of sinners, but delight in God's word – thinking deeply on it all the time. Yet if one has failed to do this and fallen into sin, Psalm 32 shows another way to be blessed – to make full confession and repentance of sin.

iii. David had great opportunity to know this blessedness in his own life. This great man of God – a man after God's heart – nevertheless had some significant seasons of sin and what may be called backsliding or spiritual decline. Notable among these were David's time at Ziklag (1 Samuel 27, 29-30) and David's sin regarding Bathsheba and Uriah (2 Samuel 11). After both occasions, David came to confession, repentance, and forgiveness.

iv. Therefore, David knew what it was like to be a guilty sinner. He knew the seriousness of sin and how good it is to be truly **forgiven**. He knew – as Paul would later state in Romans 4:6-8 – *the blessedness of the man to whom God imputes righteousness apart from works.* If David were judged on works alone, the righteous God must condemn him; nevertheless he knew by experience, **blessed is he whose transgression is forgiven, whose sin is covered**.

v. "Sin is an odious thing, the devil's drivel or vomit, the corruption of a dead soul, the filthiness of flesh and spirit. Get a cover for it, therefore." (Trapp)

b. **Blessed is the man to whom the LORD does not impute iniquity**: David spoke of *real* forgiveness by the declaration of God, not merely the quieting of a noisy conscience or an imagined peace with God. This was a standing with God declared and given, not earned.

i. In these first two verses, David used three words to describe sin.

- The idea behind **transgression** is crossing a line, defying authority.

- The idea behind **sin** is falling short of or missing a mark.

- The idea behind **iniquity** is of crookedness and distortion.

ii. In the first two verses, David used three terms to describe what God does to put away sin.

- The idea behind **forgiven** is the lifting of a burden or a debt.

- The idea behind **covered** is that of sacrificial blood covering sin.

- The idea behind **does not impute** is bookkeeping; it does not count against a person.

iii. "The psalmist declares that the forgiveness of sin, of whatever kind – whether against God or man, whether great or small, whether conscientious or inadvertent, or whether by omission or commission – is to be found in God." (VanGemeren)

c. **And in whose spirit there is no deceit**: The prior life of sin and double-living was over for David, the repentant and forgiven sinner. The forgiven life needs no more **deceit** to cover one's ways.

i. "You must all have noticed in David's case that after he had fallen into his foul sin with Bathsheba he ceased to exhibit that transparent truth-speaking character which had charmed us so much before." (Spurgeon)

ii. "The lesson from the whole is this: be honest. Sinner, may God make you honest. Do not deceive yourself. Make a clean breast of it before God. Have an honest religion, or have none at all. Have a religion of the heart, or else have none. Put aside the mere vestment and garment of piety, and let your soul be right within. Be honest." (Spurgeon)

2. (3-4) The agony of unconfessed, hidden sin.

When I kept silent, my bones grew old
Through my groaning all the day long.
For day and night Your hand was heavy upon me;
My vitality was turned into the drought of summer. Selah

a. **When I kept silent, my bones grew old**: The now-forgiven David remembered his spiritual and mental state when he kept his sin hidden and was **silent** instead of confessing and repenting. The stress of a double life and unconfessed sin made him feel old, oppressed, and dry.

i. "*I kept silence,* not merely I was silent, I *kept* silence, resolutely, perseveringly; I kept it notwithstanding all the remembrance of my past mercies, notwithstanding my reproaches of conscience, and my anguish of heart." (Evans, cited in Spurgeon)

ii. "If David's symptoms are exception, his stubbornness is common enough." (Kidner)

b. **For day and night Your hand was heavy upon me**: No doubt David was slow to acknowledge this, yet in looking back he understood that his misery was directly connected to the oppression of unresolved sin and rebellion against God.

i. "God's hand is very helpful when it uplifts, but it is awful when it presses down: better a world on the shoulder, like Atlas, than God's hand on the heart, like David." (Spurgeon)

ii. David seemed to ache under the *result* of his sin (guilt and the lack of true fellowship with God) more than the sin itself. Ideally we are all terribly grieved by sin itself, but there is something to be said for confession and humility for the sake of the result of our sins.

c. **My vitality was turned into the drought of summer**: David's dryness and misery were actually a *good* thing. They demonstrated that he was in fact a son of God, and that the covenant God would not allow him to remain comfortable in habitual or unconfessed sin. One who feels no misery or dryness in such a state has far greater concerns for time and eternity.

i. "The pain of a blow upon an ulcerated part, however exquisite, is well compensated for, if, by promoting a discharge, it effect a cure." (Horne)

ii. This work of the Holy Spirit, convicting the man or woman of God of his or her sin and hardness of heart, is an essential mark of those who truly belong to God. The consideration of this work is so important that David gave the pause for meditative consideration, **Selah**. "The Selah indicates a swell or prolongation of the accompaniment, to emphasise this terrible picture of a soul gnawing itself." (Maclaren)

3. (5) The goodness of confession and forgiveness.

I acknowledged my sin to You,
And my iniquity I have not hidden.
I said, "I will confess my transgressions to the LORD,"
And You forgave the iniquity of my sin. Selah

a. **I acknowledged my sin to You, and my iniquity I have not hidden**: David's first problem was the sin he committed – in this context, probably the immorality with Bathsheba and the murder of her husband to cover the immorality. David's second problem was the double life he lived to hide those sins. It was only as David was ready to repent and end the second problem that God would graciously forgive the first problem.

b. **I will confess my transgressions to the LORD**: Forgiveness was ready and waiting for David as he agreed with God about the nature and guilt of his sin. Restoration was ready, but the confession of sin was the path to it.

i. Before the communion service in the English Prayer Book, the minister is instructed to give this invitation: "Come to me or to some other discreet and learned minister of God's Word, and open your grief; that by the ministry of God's holy Word you may receive the benefit of absolution." There can be great value to *opening one's grief.*

ii. Real, deep, genuine confession of sin has been a feature of every genuine awakening or revival in the past 250 years. But it isn't anything new, as demonstrated by the revival in Ephesus recorded in Acts 19:17-20: *many who believed came confessing and telling their deeds. Christians* were getting right with God, and open confession was part of it.

iii. "Ah! but there are too many who make confession, having no broken hearts, no streaming eyes, no flowing tears, no humbled spirits. Know ye this, that ten thousand confessions, if they are made by hardened hearts, if they do not spring from really contrite spirits, they shall be only additions to your guilt as they are mockeries before the Most High." (Spurgeon)

c. **And You forgave the iniquity of my sin**: David's confession of sin did not *earn* forgiveness of his sins, but he did *receive* it. Fellowship with God was restored. David confessed and experienced this forgiveness immediately, just as the prodigal son confessed and was immediately forgiven. There was no probation, no wait-and-see period.

i. "Were angels to descend from heaven, to comfort the dejected spirit of a sinner, they could say nothing more effectual for the purpose, than what is said in the verse of our Psalm." (Horne)

ii. Adam Clarke on the **Selah** in Psalm 32:5: "This is all true; I *know* it; I *felt* it; I *feel* it."

B. Blessings for the pardoned: protection and guidance.

1. (6-7) The blessing of God's protection.

For this cause everyone who is godly shall pray to You
In a time when You may be found;
Surely in a flood of great waters
They shall not come near him.
You *are* my hiding place;
You shall preserve me from trouble;
You shall surround me with songs of deliverance. Selah

a. **For this cause everyone who is godly shall pray to You**: Knowing that God is so great in forgiving mercy gives the **godly** a greater reason to seek God in the confidence that He **may be found**, and is therefore ready to connect with His servant.

i. "Coming where it does, its call for a teachable spirit drives home the lesson of verses 1-5 in a positive form. If forgiveness is good, fellowship is better." (Kidner)

b. **Surely in a flood of great waters they shall not come near him**: David knew what it was to be overwhelmed and mired in the guilt and misery of sin – and that God could deliver in that crisis and others.

c. **You are my hiding place; You shall preserve me from trouble; You shall surround me with songs of deliverance**: Setting one term upon another, David gloried in the protection he now felt as one in fellowship with God and under His care.

- God Himself was his **hiding place**, a secure shelter. A good hiding place has strength and height, is not easily seen, and is reliable. In more modern phrasing we might say that Jesus is our *safe-room* or *panic-room*.

- David found security surrounded by God's own **songs of deliverance**, sung in the joy and confidence of victory.

  i. The idea of God as our **hiding place** is also associated with the idea of finding shelter in the house of the Lord, in His own presence. This is indicated by the use of the same Hebrew phrasing in two earlier psalms.

  - *For in the time of trouble He shall hide me in His pavilion; in the secret place of His tabernacle...* (Psalm 27:5).
  - *You shall hide them in the secret place of Your presence* (Psalm 31:20).

  ii. "Observe that the same man who in the fourth verse was oppressed by the presence of God, here finds a shelter in him. See what honest confession and full forgiveness will do!" (Spurgeon)

2. (8-9) God appeals to His people to pay attention and gain understanding.

I will instruct you and teach you in the way you should go;
I will guide you with My eye.
Do not be like the horse *or* like the mule,
Which have no understanding,
Which must be harnessed with bit and bridle,
Else they will not come near you.

a. **I will instruct you and teach you in the way you should go; I will guide you with My eye**: Here David prophetically spoke in God's voice unto His people. Through this, God promised to **instruct**, **teach**, and **guide** His people.

b. **I will guide you with My eye**: The idea is of one who waits upon another so attentively that a mere look at the eye indicates the will. A butler waiting upon his master at dinner can illustrate this; the master need only *look* at the salt shaker and the butler understands that he wants it. God promised that for those who diligently seek and focus on God, He will also guide.

i. This is a great blessing that comes from being forgiven and having fellowship restored. In David's season of guilt and misery, he did not (so to speak) look upon God for the guidance of His eye, and therefore he could not receive it. When fellowship was restored, the blessing of such close relationship could be enjoyed again.

ii. Many modern translators put the sense as merely God watching over the believer, which is true. Yet since the context in the following lines regards guidance and responsiveness to the Lord, it's fair to render the lines as the King James and New King James versions do.

c. **Do not be like the horse or the mule, which have no understanding**: The **horse** and the **mule** are used as examples of animals that are not easily guided. They need the **bit and bridle**, and sometimes rigorous training, before they are useful to the master.

i. "The horse and the mule are turned with difficulty; they must be constrained with *bit* and *bridle*. Do not *be like them*; do not oblige your Maker to have continual recourse to afflictions, trials, and severe dispensations of providence, to keep you in the way, or to recover you after you have gone out of it." (Clarke)

d. **Else they will not come near you**: David understood this to describe *his* condition in his season of unconfessed sin – *he* was like a dumb animal that could only be guided through pain or severity. God allowed the Amalekites to devastate David and his men (1 Samuel 30). God sent Nathan to speak sharply to David in his sin (2 Samuel 12).

i. Like a dumb animal, David would not **come near** to God until he had these terrible experiences. God speaks to us through David's experience and says, "**Do not be like the horse or the mule, which have no understanding**."

3. (10-11) The blessings of mercy and joy.

Many sorrows *shall be* to the wicked;
But he who trusts in the LORD, mercy shall surround him.
Be glad in the LORD and rejoice, you righteous;
And shout for joy, all *you* upright in heart!

a. **Many sorrows shall be to the wicked; but he who trusts in the LORD, mercy shall surround him**: David understood what it was to live (at least for a season) as **the wicked**, and the **sorrows** that came with it. The repentant David then had a renewed experience of the **mercy** of God surrounding him.

b. **Be glad in the Lord and rejoice**: This psalm gives repeated and compelling reasons for the believer to **be glad**, to **rejoice**, to **shout for joy**. The psalm appropriately ends with a call for God's people to remember and respond to those reasons.

- Remember the blessedness of forgiveness.
- Remember the redemption from guilt.
- Remember the release from the hypocrisy and stress of double-living.
- Remember the protection God gives His people.
- Remember the guidance of the LORD.

Psalm 33 – The Great and Awesome God

"If the purest form of a hymn is praise to God for what He is and does, this is a fine example." (Derek Kidner)

A. Praising the great God.

1. (1-3) A call to praise with songs and joy.

Rejoice in the Lord, O you righteous!
***For* praise from the upright is beautiful.**
Praise the Lord with the harp;
Make melody to Him with an instrument of ten strings.
Sing to Him a new song;
Play skillfully with a shout of joy.

a. **Rejoice in the Lord, O you righteous**: This unattributed psalm begins with a call for God's **righteous** to **rejoice** and **praise**. The psalmist primarily referred to those among God's people who walked rightly.

i. "Psalm 32 ended by calling on the righteous to sing praises to God. This note is picked up on in Psalm 33, almost as if its first three verses were written as an elaboration of Psalm 32:11." (Boice)

ii. **Rejoice in the Lord**: "Calling upon the saints to be cheerful; and indeed there is hardly any duty more pressed in the Old and New Testament, or less practised." (Trapp)

iii. God's people are called to **rejoice in the Lord**, and in nothing else. "To rejoice in temporal comforts is dangerous, to rejoice in self is foolish, to rejoice in sin is fatal, but to rejoice in God is heavenly." (Spurgeon)

iv. Under the New Covenant we may extend this to those declared righteous through faith in Jesus (Romans 3:21-26). Those who are **righteous** by God's decree have an even greater responsibility to **rejoice** and **praise**.

b. **For praise from the upright is beautiful**: God regards worship from His people (both **upright** in a relative sense and declared to be **upright**) as **beautiful**. It pleases Him and creates the sense of appreciation for beauty. *God appreciates our praise.*

> i. "It is apparently meant for liturgical use.... The opening summons to praise takes us far away from the solitary wrestlings and communings in former psalms." (Maclaren)

> ii. "Take away the Christian's power of praising God, and you make him a poor earth-worm, bound here with doubts, and fears, and cares; but let him but kindle in his soul the flame that burns in heaven of seraphic love to God, and away he mounts." (Spurgeon)

> iii. "An upright person is one without deception (Psalm 32:2), full of integrity of heart, and the opposite of the perverse (Proverbs 8:8)." (VanGemeren)

> iv. "Praise in the mouth of a sinner is like an oracle in the mouth of a fool; how uncomely is it for him to praise God, whose whole life is a dishonouring of God? It is as indecent for a wicked man to praise God, who goes on in sinful practices, as it is for a usurer to talk of living by faith, or for the devil to quote Scripture." (Watson, cited in Spurgeon)

c. **Praise the LORD with the harp; make melody with an instrument of ten strings**: God also declared His satisfaction with worship through music and musical instruments. This can please God, the Creator of music and the Great Musician.

> i. "Experts tell us that the *kinnor* [**harp**]...and *nebel* [**instrument of ten strings**]...were both stringed instruments, differing in the position of the sounding board, which was below in the former and above in the latter, and also in the covering of the strings." (Maclaren)

> ii. The psalmist clearly exhorted God's people to praise Him with the accompaniment of musical instruments. Strangely, some have thought that such musical accompaniment belonged only to the Old Covenant and not to the New.

> iii. Spurgeon was one who preferred worship sung without musical instruments, but he would not command it. "We who do not believe these things to be expedient in worship, lest they should mar its simplicity, do not affirm them to be unlawful, and if any George Herbert or Martin Luther can worship God better by the aid of well-tuned instruments, who shall gainsay their right? We do not need them, they would hinder than help our praise but if others are otherwise minded, are they not living in gospel liberty?" (Spurgeon)

iv. Nevertheless, the most important instrument is the *heart*. "Music, both vocal and instrumental, is of eminent use in setting forth the praises of God; but there is no instrument like the rational soul, and no melody like that of well-tuned affections." (Horne)

d. **Sing to Him a new song**: God loves to receive the rejoicing and praise of His people expressed in **song**, especially the **new song**.

i. "'New song' simply means that every praise song should emerge from a fresh awareness of God's grace." (Boice)

ii. "As God gives you fresh occasions, so do not content yourselves with the old songs or psalms, made by the holy men of God, but make new ones suited to the occasions." (Poole)

iii. "Put off oldness ye know the new song. A new man, a New Testament, a new song. A new song belongeth not to men that are old; none learn that but new men, renewed through grace from oldness, and belonging now to the New Testament, which is the kingdom of heaven." (Augustine, cited in Spurgeon)

e. **Play skillfully with a shout of joy**: Skillful musicianship and enthusiasm fitting for the **joy** of God's people are other ways God is honored with praise.

i. **A shout of joy**: "Heartiness should be conspicuous in divine worship. Well-bred whispers are disreputable here. It is not that the Lord cannot hear us, but that it is natural for great exultation to express itself in the loudest manner. Men shout at the sight of their kings: shall we offer no loud hosannahs to the Son of David?" (Spurgeon)

ii. "Note the call in that verse for freshness and skill as well as fervour; three qualities rarely found together in religious music." (Kidner)

2. (4-5) The greatness of God expressed in His character, who He is.

For the word of the LORD is right,
And all His work *is done* in truth.
He loves righteousness and justice;
The earth is full of the goodness of the LORD.

a. **For the word of the LORD is right, and all His work is done in truth**: The **truth** of God's word is a further reason for praise. In addition, God does His work in truth – not with deceit or manipulation.

i. "His *word* and His *work* are inseparable, for His words are never empty." (Kidner)

ii. "In all this we find the true secret of our confidence, and so of our joy. The word and the work of God are ever one. His word never returns to Him empty – it accomplishes that which He pleases." (Morgan)

b. **He loves righteousness and justice**: The psalmist kept thinking of the greatness of God's character – His love for **righteousness and justice** and His **goodness** spread all over the **earth**. The psalmist rightly rejoiced that Yahweh, the God who is really there, is not amoral or without goodness. He is what we who are made in His image would understand as "good."

i. "The Psalmist means that there is no spot in [**the earth**] where the traces and footprints of God's love may not be discerned, if only the eyes and the heart are opened." (Meyer)

ii. "The Lord's love (*hesed*) is evident in his works on earth. With respect to the rest of creation, he shows the same loyalty, constancy, and love that has found particular expression in the covenant relationship with his people." (VanGemeren)

iii. "He might, if he had pleased, have made everything we tasted bitter, everything we saw loathsome, everything we touched a sting, every smell a stench, every sound a discord." (Paley, cited in Spurgeon)

iv. "Earth might have been as full of terror as of grace, but instead thereof it teems and overflows with kindness.... If earth be full of mercy, what must heaven be where goodness concentrates its beams?" (Spurgeon)

3. (6-7) The greatness of God expressed in His creation.

By the word of the LORD the heavens were made,
And all the host of them by the breath of His mouth.
He gathers the waters of the sea together as a heap;
He lays up the deep in storehouses.

a. **By the word of the LORD the heavens were made**: The greatness of God goes beyond His moral goodness; He is also the God of all power and authority. By His mere **word** the universe was created.

i. "It is noteworthy that the occasions of the new song are very old acts, stretching back to the first creation and continued down through the ages." (Maclaren)

ii. "The world was created by the 'word' or fiat of God, which may be here described, after the manner of men, as formed by 'the breath of his mouth.'" (Horne)

b. **He gathers the waters of the sea together as a heap**: The psalmist looked at the mighty oceans and understood that they reflected God's power and wisdom in creation.

i. "*In storehouses*; either in the clouds, or in the bowels of the earth, whence he can draw them forth when he sees fit." (Poole)

ii. "What is meant, however, here, is the separation of land and water at first, and possibly the continuance of the same power keeping them still apart, since the verbs in verse 7 are participles, which imply continued action." (Maclaren)

iii. "To speak of nature's obedient glory is to be reminded of man's blatant defiance." (Kidner)

4. (8-9) A call for all the earth to fear the LORD.

Let all the earth fear the LORD;
Let all the inhabitants of the world stand in awe of Him.
For He spoke, and it was *done;*
He commanded, and it stood fast.

a. **Let all the earth fear the LORD**: This is the logical response to recognizing a God who is perfect in both character and power. People should set themselves in a state of humble **awe** before Him.

i. "He who made all things, preserves all things, and can in a moment destroy all things, is the proper object of our 'fear'; and that we fear him so little, is a most convincing proof of the corruption and blindness of our hearts." (Horne)

b. **For He spoke, and it was done**: The psalmist again considered the *word* of God and its effective power. God never speaks empty words, they are full of active power to insure their fulfillment.

i. Luke 7:1-9 tells the story of a Roman centurion who so trusted Jesus that he believed, "**For He spoke, and it was done**." Jesus praised the faith of that centurion.

B. The greatness of God among the nations.

1. (10-12) The greatness of God among the nations and His nation.

The LORD brings the counsel of the nations to nothing;
He makes the plans of the peoples of no effect.
The counsel of the LORD stands forever,
The plans of His heart to all generations.
Blessed *is* the nation whose God *is* the LORD,
The people He has chosen as His own inheritance.

a. **The LORD brings the counsel of the nations to nothing**: The psalmist has already praised God for His moral character and His creative power. Now he praised God for His active, guiding hand through human history. God moves among the Gentile **nations** as He pleases to accomplish His **counsel** and the **plans of His heart**.

> i. "Their persecutions, slanders, falsehoods, are like puff-balls flung against a granite wall – they produce no result at all; for the Lord overrules the evil, and brings good out of it. The cause of God is never in danger: infernal craft is outwitted by infinite wisdom, and Satanic malice held in check by boundless power." (Spurgeon)

b. **Blessed is the nation whose God is the LORD**: In considering the perfections of God, it shows the blessedness of the **nation** that will consciously align itself with God and His purposes.

> i. "The nations feared many gods, each of whom ruled over the various heavenly bodies and over the sky, land, and sea…. Since the Lord made everything and rules sovereign over the whole universe, the nations should recognize that he alone is the Creator-Ruler." (VanGemeren)

> ii. "O how happy is that nation which has *Jehovah* for its *Elohim*; the self-existent and eternal Lord for its covenant God; one who should unite himself to it by connections and ties the most powerful and endearing!" (Clarke)

c. **The people He has chosen as His own inheritance**: In a national sense this is Israel, the people and nation chosen for a unique place in the plan of God. In a broader sense it speaks of the blessing that belongs to all those chosen by the LORD, regarded as **His own inheritance**.

> i. "So thrice happy is that people of Israel, who, though they be despised by the Gentiles, are chosen by this Almighty God, to be his peculiar portion, and friends, and servants." (Poole)

2. (13-15) The greatness of God over each individual.

The LORD looks from heaven;
He sees all the sons of men.
From the place of His dwelling He looks
On all the inhabitants of the earth;
He fashions their hearts individually;
He considers all their works.

a. **He sees all the sons of men**: God in all His perfections and plans for the nations and ages also has His eye on humanity as individuals. His greatness does not exclude His individual interest in **all the inhabitants of the earth**.

b. **He fashions their hearts individually**: God made us one by one, each with our own particular physical, mental, emotional makeup, including the allowance of our weaknesses and sinful inclinations. As our Maker He has the right of inspection, so **He considers all** our **works**.

3. (16-17) The weakness of even the mighty among men.

No king *is* saved by the multitude of an army;
A mighty man is not delivered by great strength.
A horse *is* a vain hope for safety;
Neither shall it deliver *any* by its great strength.

a. **No king is saved by the multitude of an army**: In considering the greatness of God and the extent of His reach, the psalmist understood that human effort *alone* does not determine events. God's work and plan in, and beyond, and sometimes instead of human effort, accomplish His purpose.

i. "All along the line of history this verse has been verified. The strongest battalions melt like snowflakes when God is against them." (Spurgeon)

b. **A horse is a vain hope for safety**: Horses were some of the most advanced military tools in that day. Because there is a God in heaven who governs the affairs and destiny of men, even the use of the most effective resources and technologies cannot in themselves determine the outcome.

i. "If the strength of horses be of God, or be his gift (Job 39:19), then trust not in the strength of horses: use the strength of horses, but do not trust the strength of horses." (Caryl, cited in Spurgeon)

4. (18-19) The care of God for the individual.

Behold, the eye of the LORD is on those who fear Him,
On those who hope in His mercy,
To deliver their soul from death,
And to keep them alive in famine.

a. **The eye of the LORD is on those who fear Him**: The psalmist continues to think both of God's hand in world-shaking events (such as the battles of kings), and His most minute care for the individual.

i. Jesus told us that God cares for the smallest of birds (Matthew 10:29); surely He will care for those who honor Him, who are made in His image.

ii. "They who fear God need not fear anything else; let them fix their eye of faith on him, and his eye of love will always rest upon them." (Spurgeon)

b. **On those who hope in His mercy**: Those who truly **fear** the LORD find their **hope in His mercy**, not in their own goodness or righteousness.

i. **To deliver their soul**: "Freedom from troubles he promiseth not; but deliverance in due time he assureth them." (Trapp)

5. (20-22) Resolution in light of God's greatness.

Our soul waits for the LORD;
He *is* our help and our shield.
For our heart shall rejoice in Him,
Because we have trusted in His holy name.
Let Your mercy, O LORD, be upon us,
Just as we hope in You.

a. **Our soul waits for the LORD**: Having praised Him and considered God's greatness from many angles, it was appropriate to simply *wait* for the LORD – for His guidance, His word, His deliverance – looking to Him as **our help and shield**.

b. **For our heart shall rejoice in Him, because we have trusted in His holy name**: Earlier the psalmist called God's people to rejoice because of God's character and might. Now he calls us to praise God because of our blessed experience of trusting in **His holy name**.

i. **Our heart shall rejoice in him**: "Here is the fruit of our confidence: our souls are always *happy*, because we have taken God for our *portion*." (Clarke)

ii. **Let Your mercy, O LORD, be upon us**: "The hymn concludes with a prayer, requesting that God will refresh his people with his love (*hesed*)." (VanGemeren)

Psalm 34 – Praise from the Cave

This psalm is titled **A Psalm of David when he pretended madness before Abimelech, who drove him away, and he departed.** *A fugitive from Saul, David went to the Philistine city of Gath but found no refuge there and narrowly escaped. Those events are recorded in 1 Samuel 21:10-22:1. Following that, David went to the cave at Adullam where many desperate men joined him. This joyful and wise psalm seems to have been written from that cave, and sung in the presence of those men.*

The structure of this psalm is an acrostic, or nearly so. Each verse begins with another letter of the Hebrew alphabet, except for the letter waw. *The purpose of the acrostic format in this psalm mainly seems to be as a device used to encourage learning and memorization.*

Abimelech *was probably a title given to rulers among the Philistines; the ruler's proper name was Achish (1 Samuel 21:10).*

A. Calling God's people to praise.

1. (1-2) A life overflowing with praise.

I will bless the Lord at all times;
His praise *shall* continually *be* in my mouth.
My soul shall make its boast in the Lord;
The humble shall hear *of it* and be glad.

> a. **I will bless the Lord at all times**: Given the title of this psalm and its historical setting, we see David triumphant and relieved at God's rescue when he was held by the Philistines (1 Samuel 21:10-22:1).

> > i. "He may have acted like a fool, but he was not so foolish as to neglect praise of him who was his only true wisdom. He may have been hiding in a dismal cave, but this psalm tells us that in his heart he was hiding in the Lord." (Boice)

ii. **Praise shall continually be in my mouth**: "Not in my heart merely, but in my mouth too. Our thankfulness is not to be a dumb thing; it should be one of the daughters of music." (Spurgeon)

b. **My soul shall make its boast in the LORD**: David might have boasted in himself. The 1 Samuel account describes how David cleverly won his freedom by pretending madness, but he knew that the working of the thing was due to God, not his own cleverness.

i. "What scope there is for holy boasting in Jehovah! His person, attributes, covenant, promises, works, and a thousand things besides, are all incomparable, unparalleled, matchless; we may cry them up as we please, but we shall never be convicted of vain and empty speech in so doing." (Spurgeon)

ii. Yet in a sense, David had little to **boast** of, from a human perspective. He had to humiliate himself like a madman to escape the Philistines, whom he had foolishly sought refuge among – even bringing Goliath's sword with him to Gath!

iii. Therefore this is a humble **boast** of David, boasting in the LORD and even a bit in his own humiliation. "Paul, in his great passage on boasting, may have remembered this saying and this episode, and so recalled his own ignominious escape from another foreign king (2 Corinthians 11:30-33), and the lessons learned in such straits." (Kidner)

iv. "The seeming idiot scribbling on the gate is now saint, poet, and preacher; and, looking back on the deliverance won by a trick, he thinks of it as an instance of Jehovah's answer to prayer!" (Maclaren)

c. **The humble shall hear of it and be glad**: David won his freedom by a radical display of humility. Other **humble** people would be **glad** to hear how God blessed and rewarded David's humility.

i. It's significant that he calls the people of God in general **the humble**. It is as if being *proud* were a denial of God Himself – and in a sense, it is.

2. (3-7) The testimony of the delivered one.

Oh, magnify the LORD with me,
And let us exalt His name together.
I sought the LORD, and He heard me,
And delivered me from all my fears.
They looked to Him and were radiant,
And their faces were not ashamed.
This poor man cried out, and the LORD heard *him*,

And saved him out of all his troubles.
The angel of the LORD encamps all around those who fear Him,
And delivers them.

a. **Oh, magnify the LORD with me**: David knew there was something *magnetic* about the true praise of God. When one genuinely praises God, he or she wants to draw others into the practice of praise. If it is good for one to **exalt His name**, then it is even better to do it **together** with His people.

> i. David thought praising God was to **magnify** Him – that is, to make Him larger in one's perception. Magnification does not actually make an object bigger, and we can't make God bigger. But to **magnify** something or someone is to *perceive* it as bigger, and we must do that regarding the LORD God.

> ii. "As not sufficient to do a great work himself, he calleth in the help of others." (Trapp)

> iii. "The Christian, not only himself magnifies God, but exhorts others to do likewise; and longs for that day to come, when all nations and languages, laying aside their contentions and animosities, their prejudices and their errors, their unbelief, their heresies, and their schisms, shall make their sound to be heard as one, in magnifying and exalting their great Redeemer's name." (Horne)

b. **I sought the LORD, and He heard me, and delivered me from all my fears**: David's simple testimony is still powerful thousands of years later. David **sought the LORD** – looked to Him in loving trust. God then **heard** His servant, with the implication that He heard him with love, sympathy, and action. God responded when He **delivered** David from all his **fears**.

> i. Commentators are divided regarding whether or not David sinned when he feigned madness among the Philistines, or if he was obedient and guided by God. Morgan observed, "There does seem to be incongruity between David feigning madness to save his life, and this exalted outpouring of praise to God as the Great Deliverer."

> ii. "Wherein, whether he sinned or not, is matter of dispute; but this is undoubted, that God's favour and his deliverance at that time was very remarkable, and deserved this solemn acknowledgment." (Poole)

> iii. "Even when I was in the enemies' hands, and playing my pranks as a mad-man amongst them, I prayed secretly and inwardly." (Trapp)

> iv. Even if David sinned in feigning madness, God **delivered** him and did not abandon him. "It is easy to understand how, in the quietness and solemnity of that cave of refuge, he recovered, and that with

new power, his sense of the Divine care and wisdom and might and sufficiency. So he sang." (Morgan)

c. **They looked to Him and were radiant, and their faces were not ashamed**: In moving from "**I**" to "**They**," David indicates that this experience was not his alone. Many others have known and will know what it is to set the focus of their loving trust upon God and receive His help.

 i. **They looked to Him**: "The more we can think upon our Lord, and the less upon ourselves, the better. Looking to him, as he is seated upon the right hand of the throne of God, will keep our heads, and especially our hearts, steady when going through the deep waters of affliction." (Smith, cited in Spurgeon)

 ii. **And were radiant**: The idea is that they draw radiance from God's own glory. Later, the Apostle Paul would explain much the same thought: *But we all, with unveiled face, beholding as in a mirror the glory of the Lord, are being transformed into the same image from glory to glory, just as by the Spirit of the Lord* (2 Corinthians 3:18). This radiance is evidence that one has truly **looked to Him**.

 iii. "*Radiant* is a word found again in Isaiah 60:5, where it describes a mother's face lighting up at the sight of her children, long given up for lost." (Kidner)

 iv. **And their faces were not ashamed**: David also knew that God would never forsake the one who trusts in Him. God would give him confidence in the moment and vindication in time.

d. **This poor man cried out, and the LORD heard him**: David again emphasized his *personal experience* of these truths. *He* was the one. *He* was the **poor man** who **cried out** to God, and God graciously answered.

- A cry is short, and not sweet.
- A cry is brief, and bitter.
- A cry is the language of pain.
- A cry is a natural production.
- A cry has much meaning and no music.

 i. Acting the madman among the Philistines, David certainly was the **poor man**. "To get the force of David's words one has only to recall his peril and his abject clowning to save his life." (Kidner)

e. **The angel of the LORD encamps all around those who fear Him**: David narrowly escaped death among the Philistines. He was still a hunted, wanted man with King Saul determined to kill him. A rag-tag group of desperate losers gathered to him at Adullam. David was at a genuine low point; yet he was still filled with praise and trust, even knowing that God had an angelic camp **all around** him.

i. The triumph and joy of this song is so clear that it is easy to forget the life context of the psalm. "It is for people who find themselves at the absolute low point in life, which is where David was. Or find themselves between a rock, which in this case was King Saul, and a hard place, which was King Achish. It is for you when everything seems against you." (Boice)

ii. David's protection was real, even if it was invisible. He could not see the angelic presence around him, but it was real. Many times in the Old Testament, the **angel of the LORD** was an actual material appearance of Yahweh Himself (as in Judges 13). We don't know if David meant an angelic being sent by God, or God Himself present with the believer. Both are true.

iii. "The fugitive, in his rude shelter in the cave of Adullam, thinks of Jacob, who, in his hour of defenceless need, was heartened by the vision of the angel encampment surrounding." (Maclaren)

iv. Psalm 34:7 is one passage that gives support to the thought of a *guardian angel* for everyone, or perhaps at least for believers. One can't say that this passage *proves* the idea, but it is consistent with it. "Let the consideration of these invisible guardians, who are also spectators of our actions, at once restrain us from evil, and incite us to good." (Horne)

3. (8-10) An invitation to share the joyful testimony.

Oh, taste and see that the LORD is good;
Blessed *is* the man *who* trusts in Him!
Oh, fear the LORD, you His saints!
***There is* no want to those who fear Him.**
The young lions lack and suffer hunger;
But those who seek the LORD shall not lack any good *thing*.

a. **Oh, taste and see that the LORD is good**: After telling of his own experience, David challenged the reader (or singer) of this psalm to experience God's goodness for himself or herself. It could only come through a personal encounter, in some ways similar to a **taste** or to **see**.

i. **Taste** and sight are physical senses, ways in which we interact with the material world. In some ways, faith is like a spiritual sense, and with it we interact with the spiritual world. In this sense to **taste** and to **see** are like trusting God, loving Him, seeking Him, looking unto Him.

ii. "*Taste*, i.e. consider it seriously, and thoroughly, and affectionately; make trial of it by your own and others' experiences. This is opposed by those slight and vanishing thoughts which men have of it." (Poole)

iii. "As he that feels the fire hot, or as he that tasteth honey sweet, ye need not use arguments to persuade him to believe it; so here, let a man but once taste that the Lord is good, and he will thenceforth, as a new-born babe, desire the sincere milk of the word." (Trapp)

iv. "Both Hebrews 6:5 and 1 Peter 2:3 use this verse to describe the first venture into faith, and to urge that the tasting should be more than a casual sampling." (Kidner)

v. "There are some things, especially in the depths of the religious life, which can only be understood by being experienced, and which even then are incapable of being adequately embodied in words. '*O taste and see that the Lord is good.*' The enjoyment must come before the illumination; or rather the enjoyment is the illumination." (Binney, cited in Spurgeon)

b. **Blessed is the man who trusts in Him**: David was sure that the one who did **taste and see** – or, who trusted in God – would not be forsaken. God would make him **blessed**.

c. **Oh, fear the L**ORD**, you His saints**: David thought that to **fear** the LORD was much like trusting Him and experiencing His goodness. This fear is the proper reverence and respect that man has for Deity. If you really experience God's goodness, if you really experience the blessedness of trusting Him, you will also have an appropriate fear of the LORD.

d. **Those who seek the L**ORD **shall not lack any good thing**: Even one as strong as the **young lions** may **lack and suffer hunger**; but David testified of God's greater provision.

i. "The word 'lions' may be a metaphor for those who are strong, oppressive, and evil." (VanGemeren)

ii. "Were there lions prowling around the camp at Adullam, and did the psalmist take their growls as typical of all vain attempts to satisfy the soul?" (Maclaren)

iii. David experienced a **good thing** from God in his deliverance among the Philistines. He knew that the good thing was not due to his own strength or might; it was the goodness of God extended to **those who seek the L**ORD.

iv. "Although God doth usually take a special care to supply the wants of good men, and hath oft done it by extraordinary ways, when ordinary have failed, yet sometimes he knows, and it is certainly true, that wants and crosses are more needful and useful to them than bread, and in such cases it is a greater mercy of God to deny them supplies than to grant them." (Poole)

v. "Paul had nothing, and yet possessed all things." (Trapp)

B. Teaching the people of God.

1. (11-14) Living in the fear of the LORD.

Come, you children, listen to me;
I will teach you the fear of the LORD.
Who *is* the man *who* desires life,
And loves *many* days, that he may see good?
Keep your tongue from evil,
And your lips from speaking deceit.
Depart from evil and do good;
Seek peace and pursue it.

a. **Come, you children, listen to me**: Following David's deliverance from feigned madness among the Philistines, many who were in distress, in debt, or in discontent gathered to him at the cave at Adullam (1 Samuel 22:1-2). It's reasonable to think that David taught these men his own recent lessons of faith, including **the fear of the LORD**.

i. As David describes the **fear of the LORD**, it is rooted in action, not religious feelings. "David is saying that the fear of the Lord is doing right, that is, that it involves obedience." (Boice)

b. **Who is the man who desires life**: David taught his unusual group of followers what one must do to see God's blessing on his life – to live in **the fear of the LORD**.

- **Keep your tongue from evil**: David taught his men – rough as they were – that they should not speak evil.

- **And your lips from speaking deceit**: David taught them that a particular form of evil to avoid is that of lying and **deceit**.

- **Depart from evil and do good**: David spoke to his men about simply directing the life away **from evil** and towards **good**.

- **Seek peace and pursue it**: David taught his men to think not only in terms of war and battles, but in terms of **peace**, and the pursuit of it. Peace with God and among men should be sought.

c. **And loves many days, that he may see good**: David's instruction of his men at the cave at Adullam was very much in light of the Old Covenant, by which he and the rest of Israel related to God. Under the New Covenant, God's blessing is in Jesus Christ and received by faith, not only by our own obedience.

> i. "To teach men how to live and how to die, is the aim of all useful religious instruction. The rewards of virtue are the baits with which the young are to be drawn to morality. While we teach piety to God we should also dwell much upon morality towards man." (Spurgeon)

2. (15-16) Living under the watchful eye of God.

The eyes of the LORD are on the righteous,
And His ears *are open* to their cry.
The face of the LORD is against those who do evil,
To cut off the remembrance of them from the earth.

a. **The eyes of the LORD are on the righteous**: David continued to instruct his men, teaching them about the watchful eye and attentive ear of God upon His people. This was another aspect of the reward for those who lived the obedience described in Psalm 34:13-14.

b. **The face of the LORD is against those who do evil**: It was important for David's men to also know that – particularly under the Old Covenant – there were not only blessings for obedience, but curses for disobedience. Those stuck in their **evil** and rebellion could find their **remembrance** gone **from the earth**.

3. (17-18) God, the helper of the humble.

The righteous cry out, and the LORD hears,
And delivers them out of all their troubles.
The LORD is near to those who have a broken heart,
And saves such as have a contrite spirit.

a. **The righteous cry out, and the LORD hears**: David reminded his men at the cave at Adullam that God's attentive care is upon the **righteous**. David's testimony was that God had delivered him out of all his **troubles**.

b. **The LORD is near to those who have a broken heart**: This teaching from David was wonderful for the men at the cave at Adullam to hear. They – being in debt, distressed, and discontent – were likely those with **a broken heart** and **a contrite spirit**. They were objects of God's favor and salvation, not His scorn.

i. "Those whose spirits are oppressed, and even broken, with the greatness of their calamities.... Those whose hearts or spirits are truly and deeply humbled under the hand of God." (Poole)

ii. "A bird with a broken wing, an animal with a broken leg, a woman with a broken heart, a man with a broken purpose in life – these seem to drop out of the main current of life into shadow. They go apart to suffer and droop. The busy rush of life goes on without them. But God draws nigh." (Meyer)

iii. "Broken hearts think God is far away, when he is really most near to them; their eyes are holden so that they see not their best friend. Indeed, he is with them, and in them, but they know it not." (Spurgeon)

iv. **A contrite spirit**: "'The beaten-out spirit'…the *hammer* is necessarily implied; in breaking to pieces the ore first, and then plating out the metal when it has been separated from the ore." (Clarke)

4. (19-22) God's care for His righteous ones.

Many *are* the afflictions of the righteous,
But the LORD delivers him out of them all.
He guards all his bones;
Not one of them is broken.
Evil shall slay the wicked,
And those who hate the righteous shall be condemned.
The LORD redeems the soul of His servants,
And none of those who trust in Him shall be condemned.

a. **Many are the afflictions of the righteous**: David spoke from his own experience to his men at the cave at Adullam. Though he was relatively young, he had still suffered many **afflictions**, even as a **righteous** man.

i. "'Many are the afflictions,' but more are the deliverances." (Maclaren)

b. **But the LORD delivers him out of them all**: This was the principle that answered the previous statement. Indeed, the righteous had many afflictions; yet God's deliverance was real in David's life and still is real in the experience of many of God's people.

c. **He guards all his bones; not one of them is broken**: David could look at his own body and see that though he had endured many battles, accidents, and hardships – yet not one bone was **broken**.

i. According to the Gospel of John, David spoke not only of his own experience. He also spoke prophetically of the Messiah to come, Jesus Christ. John explained that the Roman soldiers who supervised the crucifixion of Jesus came to His body on the cross, expecting to hasten and guarantee His death in the traditional way – breaking the legs of the crucified victim. When they looked carefully, they learned that Jesus was already dead and they pierced His side to confirm it. John wrote, *for these things were done that the Scripture should be fulfilled, "Not one of His bones shall be broken"* (John 19:36).

ii. "Christ's bones were in themselves breakable, but could not actually be broken by all the violence in the world, because God had foredecreed, *a bone of him shall not be broken.*" (Fuller, cited in Spurgeon)

d. **Evil shall slay the wicked, and those who hate the righteous shall be condemned**: David had confidence in more than the rescue of the righteous. He was also confident that the wicked and those who hate would be judged.

i. **Evil shall slay the wicked**: "Either, 1. The evil of sin. His own wickedness, though designed against others, shall destroy himself. Or, 2. The evil of misery. When the afflictions of good men shall have a happy issue, [the affliction of the wicked] shall end in their total and final destruction." (Poole)

e. **None of those who trust in Him shall be condemned**: David could proclaim that God would rescue **the soul of His servants**, and they would be found in a place outside God's condemnation.

i. Many centuries later the Apostle Paul would write, *There is therefore now no condemnation to those who are in Christ Jesus* (Romans 8:1). Even under the Old Covenant, David knew something of this freedom from condemnation.

Psalm 35 – "Awake to My Vindication"

This psalm is simply titled **A Psalm of David**. *This is one of what are commonly known as the Imprecatory Psalms, which in strong terms ask God to defeat and destroy the enemies of His people. As you read through the book of Psalms, the Imprecatory Psalms become more intense. Psalm 7 is perhaps the mildest, while some count at least 30 curses in Psalm 109.*

It is difficult to assign this psalm to any particular period of David's life. However, the phrasing of Psalm 35:1a is similar to what David said to Saul in 1 Samuel 24:15, so it may be linked to the period of David's life when Saul pursued him.

A. David and his adversaries.

1. (1-3) David pleads to God for defense.

Plead *my cause*, O LORD, with those who strive with me;
Fight against those who fight against me.
Take hold of shield and buckler,
And stand up for my help.
Also draw out the spear,
And stop those who pursue me.
Say to my soul,
"I *am* your salvation."

a. **Plead my cause, O LORD, with those who strive with me**: Many adversaries fought against David, and many were the times he prayed, **"Fight against those who fight against me."** He could rightly pray this prayer because he generally lived in God's will, and those who fought against him were opposed to God.

i. "The prayer in verse 1*a* uses the same word and metaphor as David does with his remonstrance with Saul (1 Samuel 24:15)." (Maclaren)

ii. "The verb 'contend' [**strive**] is a legal term, frequently used among the prophets." (VanGemeren)

275

iii. "More literally, *litigate, O Lord, with them* that litigate against me, contend against them that contend with me." (Cresswell, cited in Spurgeon)

iv. "Every saint of God shall have this privilege: the accuser of the brethren shall be met by the Advocate of the saints." (Spurgeon)

b. **Take hold of shield and buckler, and stand up for my help**: With vivid images David called upon God to put on His armor and fight on David's behalf.

i. We often don't think of God having armor, but He does. Isaiah 59:17 says of the LORD: *For He put on righteousness as a breastplate, and a helmet of salvation on His head; He put on the garments of vengeance for clothing, and was clad with zeal as a cloak.*

ii. "The Lord is likened to a warrior who contends on behalf of his own. He comes with a small shield (*magen*) and a 'buckler' (*sinnah*, a large, possibly rectangular shield often carried by a shield-bearer; cf. 1 Samuel 17:7, 41), together with a 'spear and javelin.'" (VanGemeren)

c. **Also draw out the spear**: A **shield** and a **buckler** are primarily defensive weapons, but David also called upon God to be on the offense for him. As David found protection behind God's **shield** and **buckler**, he also asked God to keep his enemies at a distance with a **spear**.

i. "This armed Jehovah, grasping shield and drawing spear, utters no battle shout, but whispers consolation to the trembling man crouching behind his shield. The outward side of Divine activity, turned to the foe, is martial and menacing; the inner side is full of tender, secret breathings of comfort and love." (Maclaren)

ii. "Before the enemy comes to close quarters the Lord can push them off as with a long spear." (Spurgeon)

d. **Say to my soul, "I am your salvation"**: David needed to hear it again and again in his **soul** – that God was his salvation, and no one else. David was not his own salvation; God reminded his soul, "**I am your salvation**."

i. "So trying were the circumstances, so poignant the pain, that he was at least in danger of losing his assurance in God. Hence the plea that God would give him the inward sense of certainty: 'Say unto my soul – I am thy salvation.' It was a request for the renewing or strengthening of the inner communion with God, which is ever the secret of strength in days of turmoil and sorrow." (Morgan)

ii. "Brethren, there is nothing that can make you strong to labor for God, bold to fight against your enemies, and mighty to resist your temptations, like a full assurance that God is your God, and your sure salvation." (Spurgeon)

iii. This statement suggests many aspects of David's assurance.

- David had his doubts.
- David was not content when he had his doubts.
- David knew where to obtain full assurance.
- David's assurance had a divine source.
- David's assurance was deep and personal.
- David's assurance was present, not future.

2. (4-8) David prays for the destruction of his enemies.

Let those be put to shame and brought to dishonor
Who seek after my life;
Let those be turned back and brought to confusion
Who plot my hurt.
Let them be like chaff before the wind,
And let the angel of the LORD chase *them.*
Let their way be dark and slippery,
And let the angel of the LORD pursue them.
For without cause they have hidden their net for me *in* **a pit,**
Which **they have dug without cause for my life.**
Let destruction come upon him unexpectedly,
And let his net that he has hidden catch himself;
Into that very destruction let him fall.

a. **Let those be put to shame and brought to dishonor who seek after my life**: David asked God to not only protect him, but also to vindicate him. He wanted it to be seen and known that he really did serve and obey God, and that those who opposed him were made **like chaff before the wind**.

i. "Viewing sinners as men, we love them and seek their good, but regarding them as enemies of God, we cannot think of them with anything but detestation, and a loyal desire for the confusion of their devices. No loyal subject can wish well to rebels. Squeamish sentimentality may object to the strong language here used, but in their hearts all good men wish confusion to mischief-makers." (Spurgeon)

b. **Let the angel of the LORD chase them**: For emphasis, David prayed twice for the intervention of God's special messenger, **the angel of the LORD**.

i. Knowingly or not, David called upon God the Son for His help. "In my judgment this figure was a preincarnate manifestation of the second person of the Trinity, the Lord Jesus Christ, which is why he is regularly called 'the Lord.'" (Boice)

ii. "*The angel of the Lord* is either our salvation or our doom; *cf.* Exodus 23:20-22." (Kidner)

iii. "Chaff driven before the wind may rest against a wall; but where shall they rest who are chased by an angel?" (Trapp)

c. **Without cause they have hidden their net for me in a pit**: For emphasis, twice David asked God to note that his enemies came against him **without cause**.

i. It's easy to be too confident in one's own blamelessness, and many have repeated the sense of David's prayer without being blameless. Nevertheless David could rightly pray that those who came against him did so **without cause**.

ii. "*Without cause*, twice here, and again in 19, touches the very nerve of David's pain…. The psalms make us specially sensitive to the hurt of injustice." (Kidner)

iii. "Net-making and pit-digging require time and labour, and both of these the wicked will expend cheerfully if they may but overthrow the people of God." (Spurgeon)

d. **Let his net that he has hidden catch himself**: David prayed that the guilty one would truly be caught in his own trap – and the guilty one was his adversary. David prayed that **destruction** would come upon his adversary **unexpectedly**.

i. We can pray on the same principle against our spiritual adversaries, the principalities and powers that battle against us in the spiritual realm. The devil has snares (1 Timothy 3:7, 2 Timothy 2:26) and he has strategies (2 Corinthians 2:11) set against us. We may rightly pray that the devil is caught in and by his own snares and strategies.

3. (9-10) Promised praise for anticipated deliverance.

And my soul shall be joyful in the Lord;
It shall rejoice in His salvation.
All my bones shall say,
"Lord, who *is* like You,
Delivering the poor from him who is too strong for him,
Yes, the poor and the needy from him who plunders him?"

a. **And my soul shall be joyful in the LORD**: After pleading to God for deliverance and protection, David promised that his **soul** would be appropriately happy in the LORD.

> i. "We do not triumph in the destruction of others, but in the salvation given to us of God." (Spurgeon)

b. **All my bones shall say, "LORD, who is like You"**: David promised that his entire being would be given in honor to God, who delivers **the poor from him who is too strong for him**.

4. (11-14) David's previous care for his adversaries.

Fierce witnesses rise up;
They ask me *things* **that I do not know.**
They reward me evil for good,
To **the sorrow of my soul.**
But as for me, when they were sick,
My clothing *was* **sackcloth;**
I humbled myself with fasting;
And my prayer would return to my own heart.
I paced about as though *he were* **my friend** *or* **brother;**
I bowed down heavily, as one who mourns *for his* **mother.**

a. **They reward me evil for good**: David remembered the dishonor of his enemies, who gave him **evil** when he gave them **good** – all **to the sorrow of** his **soul**.

> i. "Causeless hatred is the lot of the good in this evil world. Their goodness is cause enough; for men's likes and dislikes follow their moral character." (Maclaren)

> ii. **They reward me evil for good**: "This was never more literally true of David, than it was of the holy Jesus, when, standing before Pontius Pilate, he received no other return from the Jews, for all the gracious words which he had spoken, and all the merciful works which he had done among them, than that of being slandered, and put to death." (Horne)

> iii. **To the sorrow of my soul**: To be misunderstood or be made the deliberate target of false accusation is great sorrow. Smyth (cited in Spurgeon) suggested several reasons why God might allow such a sorrowful trial.

> - To humble His people.

> - To cause them to seek Him in urgent prayer.

> - To prevent them from pursuing the very thing falsely accused of.

- To test whether His people will rely upon Him in all things.
- To teach them how to behave towards others when they are falsely accused.
- To warn them against making false accusations against others.

b. **When they were sick, my clothing was sackcloth**: David described some of the good that he did for his enemies. He showed remarkable love and concern for them **when they were sick**, making their problems his own and caring for them **as though** they **were my friend or brother**.

5. (15-16) How David's adversaries betrayed him.

But in my adversity they rejoiced
And gathered together;
Attackers gathered against me,
And I did not know *it;*
They tore *at me* **and did not cease;**
With ungodly mockers at feasts
They gnashed at me with their teeth.

a. **But in my adversity they rejoiced**: David treated these enemies well in their adversity, but they were happy in David's time of crisis.

i. "This mobbing of one who has suddenly become vulnerable, whose goodness has put men to shame, was eagerly re-enacted at the trial of Jesus." (Kidner)

b. **Attackers gathered against me, and I did not know it**: The attacks from David's enemies were worse because they were hidden from David and came upon him as a surprise.

6. (17-18) Praise promised for prayed-for deliverance.

Lord, how long will You look on?
Rescue me from their destructions,
My precious *life* **from the lions.**
I will give You thanks in the great assembly;
I will praise You among many people.

a. **Lord, how long will You look on?** David spoke honestly before God, admitting that he felt God was passive and indifferent. He begged God for **rescue** in his distress – which was so bad he felt **lions** were after him.

b. **I will give You thanks in the great assembly**: David vowed that he would give God the glory for His deliverance and do so publically.

B. The prayer for vindication.

1. (19-22) Reasons for vindication before his enemies.

Let them not rejoice over me who are wrongfully my enemies;
Nor let them wink with the eye who hate me without a cause.
For they do not speak peace,
But they devise deceitful matters
Against *the* quiet ones in the land.
They also opened their mouth wide against me,
And said, "Aha, aha!
Our eyes have seen *it.*"
This You have seen, O LORD;
Do not keep silence.
O Lord, do not be far from me.

a. **Let them not rejoice over me who are wrongfully my enemies**: David continued his prayer, asking God to vindicate him before his **enemies**.

i. "*Wink with their eye,* i.e. mock me, or insult over me, as the phrase signifies, Proverbs 6:13; 10:10." (Poole)

ii. **Who hate me without a cause**: "Jesus identified with those who suffer without apparent cause, because he applies the words of v. 19 (cf. 69:4) to himself (John 15:25)." (VanGemeren)

b. **They devise deceitful matters against the quiet ones in the land**: David prayed for vindication against his enemies because they plotted against God's humble, simple people.

i. The German Lutheran Bible translated the phrase **the quiet ones in the land** as *die Stillen im Lande.* It later became a phrase to describe believers in Germany, especially those from the Pietistic tradition. They emphasized living a quiet, devoted life of peace before God and man, and trusting in God to defend them.

ii. "In every age God has had his quiet ones. Retired from its noise and strife, withdrawn from its ambitions and jealousies, unshaken by its alarms; because they had entered into the secret of a life hidden in God." (Meyer)

iii. "When men rage about thee, go and tell Jesus. When storms are high, hide thee in his secret place. When others compete for fame and applause, and their passion might infect thee, get into thy closet, and shut thy door, and quiet thyself as a weaned babe." (Meyer)

c. **This You have seen, O LORD.... O Lord, do not be far from me**: David continued his plea to God, using two different names for God in the Hebrew text – two different names that are often translated in English by one word.

- LORD, with small capital letters, translates the Hebrew word *Yahweh* – the covenant name of God.

- Lord, with regular letters, translates the Hebrew word *Adonai* – the ancient Hebrew word for *Lord*. Sometimes *adonai* has the sense of *Sir* and sometimes it has the sense of *God*.

    i. **This You have seen, O LORD**: "God has seen the facts of the case, and these include not only David's innocence, but also that he is being falsely accused and slandered." (Boice)

    ii. **This You have seen, O LORD**: "*Thou hast seen* is a perfect foil to the enemy's cry, 'our eyes have seen it!'" (Kidner)

2. (23-26) The plea for Divine vindication.

Stir up Yourself, and awake to my vindication,
To my cause, my God and my Lord.
Vindicate me, O LORD my God, according to Your righteousness;
And let them not rejoice over me.
Let them not say in their hearts, "Ah, so we would have it!"
Let them not say, "We have swallowed him up."
Let them be ashamed and brought to mutual confusion
Who rejoice at my hurt;
Let them be clothed with shame and dishonor
Who exalt themselves against me.

a. **Stir up Yourself, and awake to my vindication**: David was confident that he was on God's side in his contention with his enemies, yet he longed for God to actively vindicate him. It seemed that God was too passive, so David cried out for Him to **stir up Yourself** and to **awake** on David's behalf.

b. **My God and my Lord**: Here David used another word in the Hebrew vocabulary for God, the word *Elohim* – commonly translated as **God**. This is the plural for the generic word for God.

    i. **My God and my Lord**: "The cry of Thomas when he saw the wounds of Jesus. If he did not count our Lord to be divine, neither does David here ascribe Deity to Jehovah, for there is no difference except in the order of the words and the tongue in which they were spoken; the meaning is identical." (Spurgeon)

c. **Let them be ashamed and brought to mutual confusion who rejoice at my hurt**: David simply and powerfully asked God to be his defense before his enemies.

i. **Let them be clothed with shame and dishonor**: "He will shame them for shaming his people, bring them to confusion for making confusion, pull off their fine apparel and give them a beggarly suit of dishonour, and turn all their rejoicing into weeping and wailing, and gnashing of teeth. Truly, the saints can afford to wait." (Spurgeon)

3. (27-28) Asking that the people of God take joy in David's vindication.

Let them shout for joy and be glad,
Who favor my righteous cause;
And let them say continually,
"Let the LORD be magnified,
Who has pleasure in the prosperity of His servant."
And my tongue shall speak of Your righteousness
***And* of Your praise all the day long.**

a. **Let them shout for joy and be glad, who favor my righteous cause**: Through the psalms in general, we see that David did not think of himself as perfect in a sinless sense. Yet in many of the disputes with his enemies, he had no problem seeing that he was on God's side and they were not. In many of these conflicts, we don't sense that David was troubled by self-doubt.

i. "The enemy's fall is the occasion of glad praise, not because his intended victim yields to the temptation to take malicious delight in his calamity (*Schadenfreude*). His own deliverance, not the other's destruction, makes the singer joyful in Jehovah." (Maclaren)

b. **Let the LORD be magnified**: David spoke much of his own need and trouble in this psalm. Yet he ended with a strong focus on God and His praise. He thought of the people of God enlarging the LORD in their hearts and minds, and of his continual praise to God (**my tongue shall speak of Your righteousness and of Your praise all the day long**).

i. "Mine enemies' great design is *to magnify themselves*, verse 26, but my chief desire is that God may be magnified." (Poole)

Psalm 36 – Mercy to the Heavens

This psalm is titled **To the Chief Musician.** *A* **Psalm** *of* **David the servant of the** L*ORD*. *Only Psalm 18 also uses the phrase* **the servant of the** L*ORD in the title, and John Trapp observed that Psalm 18 comes from David's old age, and Psalm 36 comes from a younger David. From youth to old age, he was* **David the servant of the** L*ORD and "He took more pleasure in the names of duty than of dignity." (John Trapp)*

A. A contrast between the wicked man and the righteous God.

1. (1-4) The wicked man.

An oracle within my heart concerning the transgression of the wicked:
***There is* no fear of God before his eyes.**
For he flatters himself in his own eyes,
When he finds out his iniquity *and* when he hates.
The words of his mouth *are* wickedness and deceit;
He has ceased to be wise *and* to do good.
He devises wickedness on his bed;
He sets himself in a way *that is* not good;
He does not abhor evil.

> a. **An oracle within my heart concerning the transgression of the wicked:** The sense in the original is that this is literally *an oracle of transgression*, as if David were divinely taught by the sins of others.

> > i. The same Hebrew word (*neum*) is used in many places describing an utterance from God (such as in the phrase *says the* L*ORD in* Genesis 22:16 and Numbers 14:28). It is used to describe an oracle of David in 2 Samuel 23:11 (*thus says David the son of Jesse*). The use in Psalm 36:1 is interesting: it is "thus says transgression" or *an oracle of transgression*.

> > ii. "Men's sins have a voice to godly ears. They are the outer index of an inner evil." (Spurgeon)

iii. There is a secondary way to understand this: that the **oracle** of **transgression** is that which speaks in the heart of the sinner himself. "We have then a bold personification of 'Transgression' as speaking in the secret heart of the wicked, as in some dark cave, such as heathen oracle-mongers haunted…. This is the account of how men come to do evil: that there is a voice within whispering falsehood." (Maclaren)

b. **There is no fear of God before his eyes**: This may be obvious but is often forgotten. The foundation of the **wicked** man's character and deeds is a lack of the **fear of God**. He does not respect or reverence God as he should.

i. "It is likely that Paul had this psalm in mind as he composed the opening chapters of his great letter, since he quotes verse 1 in Romans 3:18." (Boice)

ii. "The description of the evil man is graphic. He has by some means persuaded himself that God does not interfere with men. Consequently he has no fear of God, enthrones himself at the centre of his own being, and goes in the way of wickedness in thought and in action." (Morgan)

c. **He flatters himself in his own eyes**: The wicked man lowers his estimation of God and raises his estimation of himself. He thinks of himself much more highly than he should both in regard to his sins (**his iniquity**) and his prejudices (**hates**).

i. The essence of flattery is found in *words that say one is better than he or she actually is*. We usually think of flattery as coming from others, but we are entirely able to tell ourselves that we are better than we actually are.

ii. Matthew Poole described several ways one may flatter oneself in regard to sin:

- That his sins "are not sins, which a mind bribed by passion and interest can easily believe."
- That his sins "are but small and venial sins."
- That his sins "will be excused, if not justified by honest intentions, or by outward professions and exercise of religion, or by some good actions, wherewith he thinks to make some compensation for them or some other way."

iii. "He had not God before his eyes in holy awe, therefore he puts himself there in unholy admiration. He who makes little of God makes much of himself. They who forget adoration fall into adulation. The eyes must see something, and if they admire not God they will flatter self." (Spurgeon)

iv. **When he finds out his iniquity**: "He vainly thinks his crimes may be concealed, or disguised, till a discovery breaks the charm, and disperses the delusion." (Horne)

v. "Until God by some dreadful judgment undeceive him." (Poole)

vi. **He flatters himself** when the sin is discovered. "To smooth over one's own conduct to one's conscience (which is the meaning of the Hebrew) is to smooth one's own path to hell." (Spurgeon)

d. **He has ceased to be wise and to do good**: The character of the wicked man is shown in his words (which are **wickedness and deceit**), in his plans (**he devises wickedness**), in his habits (**sets himself in a way that is not good**), and in his attractions (**he does not abhor evil**).

i. **Iniquity and deceit**: "This pair of hell dogs generally hunt together, and what one does not catch the other will; if iniquity cannot win by oppression, deceit will gain by chicanery." (Spurgeon)

ii. **He devises wickedness on his bed**: "Which notes that he doth it, 1. Constantly and unweariedly, preferring it before his own rest. 2. Earnestly and seriously, when his mind is freed from all outward distractions, and wholly at leisure to attend that business about which it is employed, compare Psalm 4:4. 3. Freely, from his own inclination, when none are present to provoke him to it." (Poole)

iii. "The evil person is not merely drifting into evil ways. He is inventing ways to do it, in contrast to the godly who spent the wakeful hours of the night meditating on God and his commandments [as in Psalm 1:2 and 63:6]." (Boice)

iv. **On his bed...in a way**: "The phrase 'on his bed' is parallel with 'on the way'. The ungodly considers evil both in his lying down and in his walking." (VanGemeren)

v. **He sets himself in a way that is not good**: "And there meaneth to keep him, as the word importeth; set he is, and he will not be removed, being every whit as good as ever he meaneth to be." (Trapp)

vi. **He does not abhor evil**: "So far from having a contempt and abhorrence for evil, he even rejoices in it, and patronises it. He never hates a wrong thing because it is wrong, but he meditates on it, defends it, and practises it." (Spurgeon)

vii. Sin is found in what we don't do as well as in what we do. "A striking note in this description is the prominence of negative sins among the positive ones: *viz. ceased...not good...spurns not.*" (Kidner)

2. (5-6) The good and righteous God.

Your mercy, O Lord, *is* in the heavens;
Your faithfulness *reaches* to the clouds.
Your righteousness *is* like the great mountains;
Your judgments *are* a great deep;
O Lord, You preserve man and beast.

a. **Your mercy, O Lord, is in the heavens**: We sense that David has thought long enough about the wicked man. Now he turns to the great **mercy** and **faithfulness** of Yahweh (the **Lord**), the covenant God of Israel.

i. The translation of **mercy** here is inconsistent, for the same Hebrew word *hesed* is translated as *lovingkindness* in both Psalm 36:7 and 36:10. This wonderful word speaks of God's love and mercy, especially to His covenant people.

ii. "The most important of the attributes from the perspective of this psalm is *hesed*, usually translated 'unfailing love' or 'lovingkindness.'" (Boice)

iii. "One can easily imagine that the psalm was written on some natural height from which the singer looked out on a far-stretching scene in which he saw symbols of truth concerning his God. Note the sweep of vision: the heavens, the skies or clouds, the mountains, the great deep, the river, and over all, the light." (Morgan)

iv. **Your mercy, O Lord, is in the heavens**: "Like the ethereal blue, it encompasses the whole earth, smiling upon universal nature, acting as a canopy for all the creatures of earth, surmounting the loftiest peaks of human provocations, and rising high above the mists of mortal transgression." (Spurgeon)

b. **Mercy...faithfulness...righteousness...judgments**: David can only describe these attributes of God with the biggest things he can think of – the **heavens**, the **clouds** that fill the sky, the **great mountains**, and the **great deep** of the sea.

i. **Reaches to the clouds**: Hebrew, "*ad shechakim*, to the eternal regions; above all visible space." (Clarke)

ii. **Great mountains**: In Hebrew, "mountains of God.... David, that is, after the manner of the Hebrew tongue, which, when it would magnify anything, addeth the name of God." (Trapp)

c. **O Lord, You preserve man and beast**: The goodness of God is shown in the way He cares for His creatures. The ecosystem of His creation has enough to provide for the needs of those He has created, both **man and beast**.

B. Looking to the God of mercy for help against wicked men.

1. (7-9) Thanks for the goodness of God toward His people.

How precious *is* Your lovingkindness, O God!
Therefore the children of men put their trust under the shadow of
Your wings.
They are abundantly satisfied with the fullness of Your house,
And You give them drink from the river of Your pleasures.
For with You *is* the fountain of life;
In Your light we see light.

a. **How precious is Your lovingkindness, O God**: Considering the care of God for His people and His creation, David felt the mercy of God to be a **precious** and personal thing.

i. "The word *precious* establishes at once the change of scale from the immense to the intimate and personal." (Kidner)

ii. The repeated use of the word **lovingkindness** is instructive. It "needs both emphases: that of verse 5 as too great to grasp, and of verse 7 as too good to let slip." (Kidner)

b. **Therefore the children of men put their trust under the shadow of Your wings**: The merciful God is a place of rest and protection for the people of God. God invites *all* among **the children of men** to find this refuge of trust in Him.

i. There are two main ways that commentators understand the figure **shadow of Your wings**. Some take it to mean the wings of the cherubim represented in His tabernacle and the later temple. Cherubim wings were depicted on the lid of the ark of the covenant, which was the representation of God's throne. Others take it in the sense that a hen covers her young chicks under her wings to protect, hide, and shelter them.

ii. "These...are the *two wings* of the Divine goodness, under which the children of men take refuge. The allusion may be to the *wings of the cherubim*, above the mercy-seat." (Clarke)

iii. "As chickens in a storm, or when the puttock threateneth, hover and cover under the hen." (Trapp)

iv. "The picture of taking *refuge in the shadow of thy wings* was used of Ruth by Boaz (Ruth 2:12), and of Jerusalem by Jesus (Matthew 23:37); it shows an aspect of salvation which is as humbling as it is reassuring." (Kidner)

c. **They are abundantly satisfied with the fullness of Your house**: God cares for and protects those who trust in Him as a gracious and honorable host would for anyone in his **house**. The **fullness** of God's house is enough to satisfy anyone, offering a virtual **river of...pleasures** in Him.

i. **They are abundantly satisfied with the fullness of Your house**: The word **fullness** here is literally *fatness*, and its use is suggestive. "The fattest is esteemed the fairest and the most excellent food; therefore the saint was enjoined to offer the fat in sacrifice under the law. As God expects the best from us, so he gives the best to us." (Swinnock, cited in Spurgeon)

ii. **The fullness of Your house**: Spurgeon cited a story by Arnot regarding a man who moved his family to a much larger and better equipped home. His young son kept running through the house yelling, "Is this ours, father? And is this ours?" Arnot observed: "The child did not say [Is this] 'yours;' and I observed that the father while he told the story was not offended with the freedom. You could read in his glistening eye that the infant's confidence in appropriating as his own all that his father had, was an important element in his satisfaction." This will be one of our great joys in heaven when we come to our Father's house. With unmeasured satisfaction we will have the right to roam heaven and say, "Is this ours? And is this ours?" and say it unto eternity.

iii. **The river of Your pleasures**: "Union with Him is the source of all delight, as of all true fruition of desires. Possibly a reference to Eden may be intended in the selection of the word for 'pleasures,' which is a cognate with that name." (Maclaren)

iv. **The river of Your pleasures**: "Some drops from the celestial cup are sufficient, for a time, to make us forget our sorrows, even while we are in the midst of them. What then may we not expect from full draughts of those pleasures which are at thy right hand, O Lord, for evermore?" (Horne)

v. "Augustine tells us that one day, when he was about to write something upon the eighth verse of the thirty-sixth Psalm, '*Thou shalt make them drink of the rivers of thy pleasures,*' and being almost swallowed up with the contemplation of heavenly joys." (Brooks, cited in Spurgeon)

vi. "The psalmist's conception of religion is essentially joyful. No doubt there are sources of sadness peculiar to a religious man, and he is necessarily shut out from much of the effervescent poison of earthly joys drugged with sin. Much in his life is inevitably grave, stern, and sad. But the sources of joy opened are far deeper than those that are closed." (Maclaren)

d. **With You is the fountain of life; in Your light we see light**: The satisfaction and **pleasures** found in God are connected to **life** and **light**. They heal and build, giving **life**; they are full of the **light** of truth and goodness.

i. A **fountain** speaks of "1. Causality. It is in God as in a fountain, and from him is derived to us. 2. Abundance. 3. Excellency. Water is sweetest in the fountain." (Poole)

ii. "Of all the abundant and varying life, He is the Source or Fountain, and the sunshine of His face is the light on everything." (Morgan)

iii. **In Your light we see light**: "'Tis but a kind of dim twilight comparatively, which we enjoy here in this world. While we are hid in this prison-house we can see but little; but our Father's house above is full of light." (Cruso, cited in Spurgeon)

iv. **In Your light we see light** is similar in thought to what John wrote in the opening words of his Gospel: Jesus *was the true Light which gives light to every man* (John 1:9). "It is hard to doubt that John was thinking of Psalm 36:9 as he composed the prelude." (Boice)

2. (10-12) Prayer for continued blessing and protection.

Oh, continue Your lovingkindness to those who know You,
And Your righteousness to the upright in heart.
Let not the foot of pride come against me,
And let not the hand of the wicked drive me away.
There the workers of iniquity have fallen;
They have been cast down and are not able to rise.

a. **Continue Your lovingkindness to those who know You**: Having *received* the good mercy and **righteousness** of God, David rightly prays that it would **continue** for himself and all those who know God in right relationship.

i. **Continue Your lovingkindness**: "The Hebrew is, *draw forth*, or draw out thy lovingkindness: a metaphor either taken from vessels of wine, which being set abroach once, yield not only one cup, but many cups; so when God setteth abroach the wine of his mercy, he will not fill your cup once, but twice and seven times." (Greenhill, cited in Spurgeon)

ii. "Learn from this verse, that although a continuance of mercy is guaranteed in the covenant, we are yet to make it a matter of prayer." (Spurgeon)

iii. We note the parallelism between **those who know You** and **the upright in heart**. David naturally thought that those who genuinely knew God would be **upright in heart**.

b. **Let not the foot of pride come against me**: David earlier praised God as the one who protects and blesses His people (Psalm 36:7). Now David prayed that God would fulfill this aspect of His character, protecting His servant against both the **foot** and the **hand of the wicked**.

c. **There the workers of iniquity have fallen**: David considered the end of the wicked men that he thought of at the beginning of this psalm. They are **fallen**, and so much so that they **are not able to rise**. Unlike the righteous who may fall seven times yet rise up again (Proverbs 24:16), the **workers of iniquity** remain in the dust as God protects His servants.

i. "From his serene shelter under the wing, the suppliant looks out on the rout of baffled foes, and sees the end which gives the lie to the oracle of transgression and its flatteries. 'They are struck down,' the same word as in the picture of the pursuing angel of the Lord in Psalm 35." (Maclaren)

ii. There is some emphasis on the word **there** in this phrase. Some think it refers to the **pride** mentioned in the previous verse, ans others to the place where the **workers of iniquity** practiced their sin.

iii. "THERE, has been applied by many of the fathers to the *pride* spoken of in the preceding verse. *There*, in or by pride, says *Augustine*, do all sinners perish." (Clarke)

iv. "*There*, where they come against me, and hope to ruin me. He seems as it were to point to the place with his finger." (Poole)

v. "There, where they plotted or practised the downfall of the righteous; as Henry III of France was stabbed in the same chamber where he and others had contrived the Parisian massacre." (Trapp)

Psalm 37 – Wisdom Over Worry

This psalm is simply titled A Psalm of David. Verse 25 tells us that it is David in his older years, giving wisdom in the pattern of a song. This psalm is roughly acrostic in arrangement, with the lines arranged with Hebrew sentences that begin with the successive letters of the Hebrew alphabet. In style this is a wisdom psalm, directed not to man but to God, teaching after the manner of the Book of Proverbs.

A. Counsel for the afflicted people of God.

1. (1-2) Don't worry about the ungodly.

Do not fret because of evildoers,
Nor be envious of the workers of iniquity.
For they shall soon be cut down like the grass,
And wither as the green herb.

    a. **Do not fret because of evildoers**: It is a common thing for the righteous to **fret** or **be envious** of the wicked. Asaph was bothered by this problem in Psalm 73, wondering why the wicked often experienced so much prosperity.

        i. "The words 'do not fret' literally mean 'do not get heated,' which is also how we might express it. Or we might say, 'Don't get all worked up.' Or even, 'Be cool.'" (Boice)

        ii. "To fret is to worry, to have the heart-burn, to fume, to become vexed. Nature is very apt to kindle a fire of jealousy when it sees law-breakers riding on horses, and obedient subjects walking in the mire." (Spurgeon)

        iii. Morgan wrote of this worry, this **fret**: "It is wrong; it is harmful; it is needless. Let the trusting wait. Events will justify the action."

        iv. "It is as foolish as it is wicked to repine or be envious at the prosperity of others. Whether they are godly or ungodly, it is God who is the dispenser of the *bounty* they enjoy; and, most assuredly, he has a right to do what he will with his own. To be envious in such a case, is to arraign the providence of God." (Clarke)

b. **They shall soon be cut down like the grass**: David gives the same answer Asaph came to in Psalm 73, understanding that any prosperity experienced by the **workers of iniquity** was only temporary. Grass is green for a season, and so is the **herb** – but they both **wither** quickly.

> i. "In the Middle East the lush spring vegetation may lose its beauty in a few days after a hot, dry desert wind (*hamsin*) has parched the land." (VanGemeren)

> ii. We think of a wicked man eating a magnificent dinner while a godly man goes hungry. The wicked man eats anything and everything he wants, and his table is loaded as he enjoys his meal. Then we see the bigger picture: he eats his last meal on death row and in a moment will face terrible judgment. *Now*, with larger perspective, the godly man doesn't envy or worry about the wicked man. "Evil men instead of being envied, are to be viewed with horror and aversion; yet their loaded tables, and gilded trappings, are too apt to fascinate our poor half-opened eyes." (Spurgeon)

> iii. "The test is found in Time. All the apparent prosperity of the wicked is transient; it passes and perishes, as do the wicked themselves." (Morgan)

2. (3-4) Put your trust and delight in the LORD.

Trust in the LORD, and do good;
Dwell in the land, and feed on His faithfulness.
Delight yourself also in the LORD,
And He shall give you the desires of your heart.

a. **Trust in the LORD, and do good**: Instead of worrying and envying, David counseled the man or woman of God to simply **trust** God and **do good** for His glory. It is remarkable how quickly we can get distracted from the simple work of trusting God and doing good. Looking at the seeming prosperity of the wicked is one way we are often distracted.

> i. "Faith cures fretting. Sight is cross-eyed, and views things only as they seem, hence her envy; faith has clearer optics to behold things as they really are, hence her peace." (Spurgeon)

b. **Dwell in the land, and feed on His faithfulness**: David also counseled the man or woman of God to leave aside worry and envy by simply enjoying the blessings God gives. He provided Israel a **land** to enjoy, and His **faithfulness** was like food for them every day.

c. **Delight yourself also in the Lord**: David advised the man or woman of God to replace worry and envy with a conscious **delight** in the Lord. This means to cheer one's heart and mind by considering and by faith receiving the multiple blessings of God.

i. **Delight yourself**: Several writers explain and apply this idea.

- "Expect all thy happiness *from* him, and seek it *in* him." (Clarke)
- "It includes a deliberate redirection of one's emotions...[such as] Paul and Silas in prison, singing as well as praying." (Kidner)
- "We cannot delight thus without effort. We must withdraw our eager desires from the things of earth, fastening and fixing them on Him." (Meyer)
- "In a certain sense imitate the wicked; they delight in their portion – take care to delight in yours, and so far from envying you will pity them." (Spurgeon)
- "The reason many apparent Christians do not delight in God is that they do not know him very well, and the reason they do not know him very well is that they do not spend time with him." (Boice)

ii. "Do not think first of the desires of thy heart, but think first of delighting thyself in thy God. If thou hast accepted him as thy Lord, he is thine; so delight in him, and then he will give thee the desires of thy heart." (Spurgeon)

iii. We notice that David wrote **delight yourself also in the Lord**. The word **also** is important, reminding us that there are legitimate joys and pleasures in life outside the life of the spirit. The believer who truly trusts God has the capability to **also** find true **delight** in **the Lord**.

iv. "Again, *he delights in you;* I speak to such of whom this may be supposed. And it is indefinitely said, 'His delights were with the sons of men,' Proverbs 8:31. Think what he is, and what you are; and at once, both wonder and yield." (Howe, cited in Spurgeon)

d. **And He shall give you the desires of your heart**: This is a wonderful and even safe promise. The one who truly **delights** in the Lord will find his heart and desires changed, steadily aligning with God's own good desires for his life. Thus we see that finding delight in God is *a key to a happy, satisfied life.*

i. This shows that God intends to fulfill the heart desires of the redeemed man or woman of God. To be sure, it is possible for such desires to be clouded by sin or selfishness; yet even when so clouded there is almost always a godly root to the desire that is entirely in the will of God. The man or woman of God should find his or her rest in this, and leave aside worry and envy.

ii. "They said of Martin Luther as he walked the streets, 'There comes a man that can have anything of God he likes.' You ask the reason of it. Because Luther delighted himself in his God." (Spurgeon)

iii. The principle of Psalm 37:4 is the foundation for a principle sometimes called *Christian Hedonism*. Normally, we think of hedonism as the idolatry of pleasure. The term *Christian Hedonism* has been used to describe a righteous pursuit of satisfaction and pleasure, one that is rooted in a delighted focus upon God.

iv. Most of all, it shows that when we **delight** ourselves **in the LORD**, He gives us our delight. If He is our delight, He gives us more of Himself. "Longings fixed on Him fulfill themselves." (Maclaren)

3. (5-6) Trust God to protect and promote you.

Commit your way to the LORD,
Trust also in Him,
And He shall bring *it* to pass.
He shall bring forth your righteousness as the light,
And your justice as the noonday.

a. **Commit your way to the LORD, trust also in Him**: Here David explained what it means to delight one's self in the LORD, as described in the previous verse. It means to **commit** one's way to Him and to truly **trust** in the LORD. It means to find peace, protection, and satisfaction in a surrendered focus upon God.

i. **Commit your way**: "The Hebrew for *commit* is literally 'roll', as though getting rid of a burden (*cf.* Joshua 5:9). But it comes to be used simply as a synonym for 'entrust' (Proverbs 16:3) or 'trust'; *cf.* Psalm 22:8." (Kidner)

b. **And He shall bring it to pass**: The one who has this delighted focus upon God will see Him **bring** these promises **to pass**. Fame and fortune are not promised, but the true and deep desires of the heart find their fulfillment.

i. "The more we fret in this case, the worse for us. Our strength is to sit still. The Lord will clear the slandered. If we look to his honour, he will see to ours." (Spurgeon)

c. **He shall bring forth your righteousness as the light**: As God fulfills these desires of heart, the **righteousness** of the man or woman of God is revealed, shining forth in **light** like the **noonday** sun.

> i. **He shall bring forth your righteousness**: "To the view of the world; from which it hath hitherto seemed to be hid or eclipsed by reproaches, and by grievous calamities." (Poole)

> ii. **As the light**: "It shall be as visible to men as the light of the sun, and that at noon-day." (Poole)

> iii. "As God said in the beginning, 'Let there be light, and there was light;' so he shall say, Let thy innocence appear, and it will appear as suddenly and as evident as the *light* was at the beginning." (Clarke)

4. (7-8) Find rest in the God who deals with the wicked.

Rest in the LORD, and wait patiently for Him;
Do not fret because of him who prospers in his way,
Because of the man who brings wicked schemes to pass.
Cease from anger, and forsake wrath;
Do not fret—*it* only *causes* harm.

a. **Rest in the LORD, and wait patiently for Him**: Because God has promised to faithfully take care of those who put their trust in Him, we can **rest in the LORD**. We can **wait patiently for Him** instead of fretting and fearing that God has forgotten us or intends evil for us.

> i. **Rest in the LORD** speaks of a particular kind of **rest** – the rest of *silence*, ceasing from words of self-defense. The idea is that we will not speak to vindicate ourselves; we will trust in God to protect us.

> ii. "Do not murmur or repine at his dealings, but silently and quietly submit to his will, and adore his judgments, and, as follows, *wait* for his help." (Poole)

> iii. "If the spotless Lamb of God was dumb, before those who were divesting him of his honours, and robbing him of his life, 'silent' resignation cannot but become one who suffers for his sins." (Horne)

b. **Cease from anger, and forsake wrath; do not fret – it only causes harm**: David wisely advised the man or woman of God to give up **anger**, **wrath**, and worry (**fret**). They accomplish nothing except **harm**. They are the opposite of delighting oneself in the LORD and patiently waiting upon Him.

> i. **Cease from anger**: "Especially anger against the arrangements of Providence, and jealousies of the temporary pleasures of those who are

so soon to be banished from all comfort. Anger anywhere is madness, here it is aggravated insanity." (Spurgeon)

5. (9-11) Trust that God will punish evildoers and reward the meek.

For evildoers shall be cut off;
But those who wait on the LORD,
They shall inherit the earth.
For yet a little while and the wicked *shall be* no *more;*
Indeed, you will look carefully for his place,
But it *shall be* no *more*.
But the meek shall inherit the earth,
And shall delight themselves in the abundance of peace.

a. **Those who wait on the LORD, they shall inherit the earth**: This is another reason for our delight in and rest upon the LORD. We can trust His promise that He will take care of His own not only in this world, but in the world to come. In contrast, **evildoers shall be cut off**.

i. "I have frequently remarked to you that, although the wolf is very strong and fierce, and the sheep is very weak and timid, yet there are more sheep in the world than there are wolves; and the day will come when the last wolf will be dead, and then the sheep shall cover the plains and feed upon the hills. Weak as the righteous often are, they 'shall inherit the land' when the wicked shall have been cut off from the earth." (Spurgeon)

b. **For yet a little while and the wicked shall be no more**: The evildoers have their day of prosperity, but it is short-lived. Soon the wicked who are the famous and praised in this world will be of no notice or standing at all (**you will look carefully for his place, but it shall be no more**).

i. "The shortness of life makes us see that the glitter of the wicked great [ones] is not true gold." (Spurgeon)

ii. "The whole duration of the world itself is but 'a little while' in the sight of him whose hope is full of immortality." (Horne)

c. **But the meek shall inherit the earth**: For emphasis, David repeated the idea of God's care for and reward to the **meek**. They, not the evildoers of this world, **shall delight themselves in the abundance of peace**.

i. "The 'meek' are they who bear their own adversities, and the prosperity of their enemies, without envy, anger, or complaint." (Horne)

ii. "The context gives the best possible definition of *the meek*: they are those who choose the way of patient faith instead of self-assertion." (Kidner)

iii. **The meek shall inherit the earth**: Jesus quoted this line in the Sermon on the Mount, in the third beatitude (Matthew 5:5). "It is right to say that Psalm 37 is an exposition of the third beatitude, even though it was written a thousand years before Jesus began his public ministry. It unfolds the character of the meek or trusting person in the face of the apparent prosperity of the wicked." (Boice)

B. The triumph of the godly and the passing of the wicked.

1. (12-15) With a laugh, God defeats the wicked.

The wicked plots against the just,
And gnashes at him with his teeth.
The Lord laughs at him,
For He sees that his day is coming.
The wicked have drawn the sword
And have bent their bow,
To cast down the poor and needy,
To slay those who are of upright conduct.
Their sword shall enter their own heart,
And their bows shall be broken.

a. **The wicked plots against the just, and gnashes at him with his teeth**: Earlier in this psalm, David contrasted the fate of the righteous with the fate of the wicked. Now he considered the inevitable conflict between the righteous and the **wicked** – how, without reason, **the wicked plots against the just**. Their gnashing of teeth shows the depth of their anger and hatred.

i. "The wicked show by their gestures what they would do if they could; if they cannot gnaw they will gnash: if they may not bite they will at least bark." (Spurgeon)

b. **The Lord laughs at him, for He sees that his day is coming**: For all the plotting and gnashing of teeth of the wicked, they accomplish nothing against the Lord and His people. God simply **laughs** at them, knowing their end.

i. "If God can laugh at the wicked, shouldn't we be able at least to refrain from being agitated by them?" (Boice)

ii. **For He sees that his day is coming**: "The evil man does not see how close his destruction is upon his heels; he boasts of crushing others when the foot of justice is already uplifted to trample him as the mire of the streets." (Spurgeon)

c. **The wicked have drawn the sword and have bent their bow**: The wicked plot and gnash their teeth, but they do not stop there. They work to carry out their plots and their fierce anger against God's people. Even so,

God shall protect His own and **their sword shall enter their own heart, and their bows shall be broken**.

i. "Like Haman they shall be hanged upon the gallows built by themselves for Mordecai. Hundreds of times has this been the case. Saul, who sought to slay David, fell on his own sword." (Spurgeon)

2. (16-17) God's blessing upon the humble righteous.

A little that a righteous man has
***Is* better than the riches of many wicked.**
For the arms of the wicked shall be broken,
But the LORD upholds the righteous.

a. **A little that a righteous man has is better than the riches of many wicked**: Since whatever the wicked has cannot last, the little that the **righteous man has is better** than all that the wicked possess. A God-trusting, righteous life is the best long-term investment strategy.

i. "His blessing can multiply a mite into a talent, but his curse will shrink a talent to a mite." (Horne)

ii. "A little blest is better than a great deal curst; a little blest is better than a world enjoyed; a pound blest is better than a thousand curst; a black crust blest is better than a feast curst; the gleanings blest are better than the whole harvest curst; a drop of mercy blest is better than a sea of mercy curst." (Brooks, cited in Spurgeon)

b. **For the arms of the wicked shall be broken, but the LORD upholds the righteous**: The reward of the wicked is to have their own arms **broken**. The reward of the righteous is to be upheld by God's own arms.

3. (18-20) The lasting good of the upright.

The LORD knows the days of the upright,
And their inheritance shall be forever.
They shall not be ashamed in the evil time,
And in the days of famine they shall be satisfied.
But the wicked shall perish;
And the enemies of the LORD,
Like the splendor of the meadows, shall vanish.
Into smoke they shall vanish away.

a. **The LORD knows the days of the upright, and their inheritance shall be forever**: The apparent reward of the wicked is temporary and fleeting. The **inheritance** of the upright is eternal. All this is more reason to avoid worry or envy of the wicked in their seeming (yet temporary) prosperity.

i. **For the LORD knows the days of the upright**: "He is acquainted with all his *circumstances, severings*, and *ability* to bear them; and he will either *shorten his trials* or *increase his power*." (Clarke)

b. **In the days of famine they shall be satisfied**: God can even find a way to provide for His own when others have nothing.

c. **Into smoke they shall vanish away**: The success, fame, and prosperity of the wicked is as temporary as **smoke**. It never has any real substance and soon vanishes completely.

i. **Into smoke they shall vanish away**: Adam Clarke noted that some ancient manuscripts render this line differently. "If we follow the *Hebrew*, it intimates that *they shall consume as the fat of lambs*. That is, as the *fat* is *wholly consumed* in sacrifices by the fire on the altar, so shall they consume away in the fire of God's wrath."

4. (21-22) Blessing and cursing.

The wicked borrows and does not repay,
But the righteous shows mercy and gives.
For *those* blessed by Him shall inherit the earth,
But *those* cursed by Him shall be cut off.

a. **The wicked borrows and does not repay, but the righteous shows mercy and gives**: David knew that the difference between the wicked and the righteous was not only found in what they believed and in whom they trusted. The difference was also often seen in their conduct. The **wicked** are takers, borrowing and not repaying. The **righteous** are givers, full of **mercy**.

i. **Does not repay**: "May *refuse* to do it, because he is a *wicked man*; or be *unable* to do it, because he is reduced to *beggary*." (Clarke)

b. **Those blessed by Him shall inherit the earth**: The promise of earth-inheritance is repeated a third time. This is a blessing for the righteous, while the wicked find themselves **cursed by** the LORD and **cut off**.

5. (23-24) God's guidance and support for the good man.

The steps of a *good* man are ordered by the LORD,
And He delights in his way.
Though he fall, he shall not be utterly cast down;
For the LORD upholds *him with* His hand.

a. **The steps of a good man are ordered by the LORD**: The reward for the righteous is not only in the age to come. In the present day, God guides **the steps of a good man**. As he seeks the LORD and delights in Him, he finds his life proves the good and acceptable and perfect will of God (Romans 12:1-2).

i. **The steps of a *good* man are ordered by the LORD**: "There is nothing for *good* in the text. *Geber* is the original word, and it properly signifies *a strong man*, a *conqueror* or *hero*; and it appears to be used here to show, that even the *most powerful* must be supported by the Lord, otherwise their strength and courage will be of little avail." (Clarke)

ii. "This was emphatically true of the man Christ, whose steps Jehovah established, and in whose way he delighted." (Horne)

b. **And He delights in his way**: Another great and present benefit for the righteous man or woman is the knowledge that God **delights** in him. This is especially clear for the believer under the New Covenant who knows and experiences a standing in grace, having been justified by faith (Romans 5:1-2).

c. **Though he fall, he shall not be utterly cast down; for the LORD upholds him with His hand**: David described a third great benefit for the righteous man or woman who trusts in the LORD. Though he may at times **fall** (in the sense of stumbling), he will not fall *away* – that is, **shall not be utterly cast down**. This is not because of his own internal strength or goodness, but because **the LORD upholds him**.

C. Wisdom from a man after God's heart.

1. (25-26) A testimony of God's blessing and care for the righteous.

I have been young, and *now* am old;
Yet I have not seen the righteous forsaken,
Nor his descendants begging bread.
***He is* ever merciful, and lends;**
And his descendants *are* blessed.

a. **I have not seen the righteous forsaken, nor his descendants begging bread**: David gave a testimony from his own experience. He noted that God cared for those who trusted in Him and walked in His righteousness. They were not **forsaken** and their **descendants** were also blessed.

i. This was David's testimony after many years (**I have been young, and now am old**). Seeing God's faithfulness to His people, David wanted a younger generation to also trust in Him, learning from his wisdom.

ii. David knew that among his ancestors were some who left Israel, fearful in a time of famine (Ruth 1). When they returned after several disastrous years in Moab, they found the people of Bethlehem had been provided for. God knew how to take care of those who trusted in Him in times of famine, and has done so since then.

iii. One way that God provides for the **righteous** and their **descendants** is through the ethic of hard work that belongs to the redeemed, who know that all things should be done heartily, as unto the LORD – including working for a living.

b. **I have not seen the righteous forsaken, nor his descendants begging bread**: This statement is troublesome to some, because they have seen or experienced instances where godly men or women – or their offspring – have been in famine, extreme poverty, or reduced to begging.

i. We first note that this psalm is a wisdom psalm, very much like Proverbs. In the Bible's wisdom literature, *general principles* are often presented in the absolute when they are intended to be understood as general or even overwhelming principles – understanding that there can be exceptions.

ii. We also note that David simply wrote of *his* experience. He did not write that this was an absolute principle, but his own observation.

iii. Some, like Adam Clarke, had the same experience and observation: "I believe this to be literally true in all cases. I am now grey-headed myself; I have travelled in different countries, and have had many opportunities of seeing and conversing with religious people in all situations in life; and I have not, to my knowledge, seen one instance to the contrary. I have seen no *righteous man forsaken*, nor any *children* of the righteous *begging their bread*. God puts this honour upon all that fear him; and thus careful is he of *them*, and of their *posterity*."

iv. Others, like Charles Spurgeon, did not have the same experience and observation: "It is not my observation just as it stands, for I have relieved the children of undoubtedly good men, who have appealed to me as common [beggars]. But this does not cast a doubt upon the observation of David."

v. "And it has been my unhappy lot, within these very walls, to have to minister relief to the unworthy and reprobate sons of Christian ministers, about whose piety I could entertain no doubt, and some of whom, are now in heaven. These good men's children have walked contrary to God, so God has walked contrary to them. I have often hoped that the poverty I saw might be the means of bringing them to seek the God of their fathers!" (Spurgeon)

vi. "With the more complex civilization in the midst of which we live, perhaps sometimes the righteous have been driven to beg, but even now such cases are surely rare, and after some varied experience I would want to subject him who begs to somewhat severe cross-examination before accepting his testimony against the psalmist." (Morgan)

c. **He is ever merciful, and lends**: In times of scarcity, the righteous one not only receives God's provision, but with a generous and **merciful** heart he **lends** to others in need.

i. "How stingy, covetous professors can hope for salvation is a marvel to those who read such verses as this in the Bible." (Spurgeon)

2. (27-29) The promised reward for obedience.

Depart from evil, and do good;
And dwell forevermore.
For the LORD loves justice,
And does not forsake His saints;
They are preserved forever,
But the descendants of the wicked shall be cut off.
The righteous shall inherit the land,
And dwell in it forever.

a. **Depart from evil, and do good**: The righteous man or woman trusts in God, but also receives and values moral instruction. God's care for him does not make him careless, but careful in pleasing Him.

i. This line also speaks to the righteous man or woman in the heat of difficulty. "A conflict with evil too often tempts one to fight the enemy with his own weapons." (Kidner)

ii. "Having therefore these glorious promises and privileges, let no man do any evil or unjust thing to enrich or secure himself, nor abstain from pious and charitable actions for fear of undoing himself by them." (Poole)

b. **For the LORD loves justice, and does not forsake His saints**: Since God loves justice, so should His people. He is faithful to them and does not **forsake** them, **but the descendants of the wicked shall be cut off.**

i. **The descendants of the wicked shall be cut off**: "The children who follow the wicked steps of wicked parents shall, like their parents, be cut off. God's *judgments descend to posterity*, as well as his *mercies*." (Clarke)

c. **The righteous shall inherit the land, and dwell in it forever**: Once again in this psalm, David described the blessing appointed to the righteous in the coming age. They would find a secure place and inheritance in the world to come.

i. The saints shall one day have power over all things; and meanwhile they are sure of a sufficiency, if not a superfluity." (Trapp)

3. (30-31) The character of God's righteous one.

The mouth of the righteous speaks wisdom,
And his tongue talks of justice.
The law of his God *is* in his heart;
None of his steps shall slide.

a. **The mouth of the righteous speaks wisdom**: David again turns to the conduct of God's righteous man or woman, noted for their wise and just words.

b. **The law of his God is in his heart**: The righteous man (or woman) is also noted by his possession of and love for the word of God. In a way that would be truly fulfilled by the New Covenant, he has the word of God in his heart (Jeremiah 31:33). Because of this knowledge of and reliance upon God's word, **none of his steps shall slide**.

i. "He hath a Bible in his head and another in his heart." (Trapp)

4. (32-33) The character and the response of the wicked.

The wicked watches the righteous,
And seeks to slay him.
The LORD will not leave him in his hand,
Nor condemn him when he is judged.

a. **The wicked watches the righteous, and seeks to slay him**: In considering the remarkable blessings God has appointed to the righteous, David did not think it meant life would be easy. One danger continually faced was from the wicked who hated the righteous without cause.

i. "There want not those still that carry about Cain's bloody club, hating to the death that goodness in another that they neglect in themselves." (Trapp)

b. **The LORD will not leave him in his hand**: Thankfully, the righteous man or woman is not at the mercy of the wicked. God will protect him, particularly in the ultimate judgment (**nor condemn him when he is judged**).

i. "And the day is coming, when he who hath stood tamely at the bar of men, and hath suffered for truth and righteousness, shall be advanced to a throne among the saints and martyrs, to assist at the trial of his once-insulting judges." (Horne)

5. (34-36) An exhortation to trust, based on testimony.

Wait on the LORD,
And keep His way,
And He shall exalt you to inherit the land;
When the wicked are cut off, you shall see *it.*
I have seen the wicked in great power,
And spreading himself like a native green tree.
Yet he passed away, and behold, he *was* no *more;*
Indeed I sought him, but he could not be found.

a. **Wait on the LORD, and keep His way, and He shall exalt you to inherit the land**: For the *fifth time* in this psalm, David promised the people of God that they would **inherit the land**. As king of Israel, David had a concern for their territory, but he could also extend that thought to the age to come. God's people have their place, even a **land** of some sort in the coming age.

I, **Wait on the LORD**: "Wait in obedience as a servant, in hope as an heir, in expectation as a believer." (Spurgeon)

ii. **Wait on the LORD, and keep His way**: "While we are waiting let us take heed of wavering." (Watson, cited in Spurgeon)

b. **When the wicked are cut off, you shall see it**: For the *fifth time* in this psalm, David promised that the wicked would be **cut off** or cut down in some sense. Their coming doom was just as certain as the coming blessing and security of the righteous.

i. David used a **green tree** as a picture of the wicked in their prosperity. Psalm 1 uses a flourishing tree as a picture of the righteous. "Here it is used in reverse, the wicked being compared to a green tree which flourishes for a time but soon passes away and is seen no more." (Boice)

c. **I have seen the wicked in great power**: David once again relied on his personal experience and testimony. He had seen wicked people rise to great security and success, only to have **passed away** and to have become **no more**.

i. **Behold, he was no more**: "What clean sweeps death makes! To the surprise of all men the great man was gone, his estates sold, his business bankrupt, his house alienated, his name forgotten, and all in a few months!" (Spurgeon)

6. (37-38) An invitation to gain the same testimony.

Mark the blameless *man,* and observe the upright;
For the future of *that* man *is* peace.
But the transgressors shall be destroyed together;
The future of the wicked shall be cut off.

a. **Mark the blameless man, and observe the upright**: The righteous men and women of this world get little attention. The culture is more interested in the godless and the wicked. Yet David counseled us to notice the **blameless** and the **upright** of this world, because **the future of that man is peace**.

b. **The future of the wicked shall be cut off**: For the sixth and final time in this psalm, David reminds us that the future of the wicked is no future to be desired.

i. "There is nothing unworthy in solemn thankfulness when God's judgments break the teeth of some devouring lion." (Maclaren)

7. (39-40) The reliable help and deliverance of the LORD.

But the salvation of the righteous *is* from the LORD;
***He is* their strength in the time of trouble.**
And the LORD shall help them and deliver them;
He shall deliver them from the wicked,
And save them,
Because they trust in Him.

a. **The salvation of the righteous is from the LORD**: This is a helpful thought at the end of this psalm. In David's praise and encouragement of righteous men or women, it is possible that one might think those ones are saved by their own righteousness. David reminds us that their salvation **is from the LORD**, and that **He is their strength in the time of trouble**.

i. **He is their strength in the time of trouble**: "While trouble overthrows the wicked, it only drives the righteous to their strong Helper, who rejoices to uphold them." (Spurgeon)

b. **He shall deliver them from the wicked, and save them, because they trust in Him**: David brings the thought back to the fundamental **trust** that the righteous have in God. Their place in Him is secured in their trusting love of the LORD.

Psalm 38 – The Sick Sinner's Only Hope

This psalm is titled **A Psalm of David. To bring to remembrance**. *"Since with God to remember is to act, this word speaks of laying before Him a situation that cries out for His help." (Derek Kidner)*

It is a song full of pain and dark with guilt, as David felt the sore effects (seemingly both physical and spiritual) of his sin. Commentators guess at the occasion of this in David's life, but there is no certain link to a specific time or event.

"The same title is given to Psalm 70, where in like manner the Psalmist pours out his complaint before the Lord." (Charles Spurgeon)

This is one of those noted as the penitential psalms, along with Psalms 6, 32, 51, 102, 130, and 143.

A. The depth of David's trouble.

1. (1-2) Pierced by God's displeasure.

O Lord, do not rebuke me in Your wrath,
Nor chasten me in Your hot displeasure!
For Your arrows pierce me deeply,
And Your hand presses me down.

    a. **Do not rebuke me in Your wrath**: Under a sense of God's deep displeasure, David cried out to God. He followed a wise path, drawing near to the Lord though he sensed both God's **wrath** and **displeasure**.

        i. "The anger of others I can bear, but not thine. As thy love is most sweet to my heart, so thy displeasure is most cutting to my conscience." (Spurgeon)

        ii. "The petition here preferred, as in the sixth Psalm, is, that Jehovah would not condemn as a judge, but chasten as a father, for the amendment and preservation of the offender." (Horne)

b. **Your arrows pierce me deeply, and Your hand presses me down**: David used poetic pictures to describe how deeply he sensed the displeasure of God.

> i. **Your arrows pierce me**: "This no doubt, refers to the *acute pains* which he endured; each appearing to his feeling as if an arrow were shot into his body." (Clarke)

c. **Your hand presses me down**: We read of the deep distress and agony of David in the psalm and recognize that it was because of his own sin (as will be described). We then understand that on the cross Jesus was made the target of the same agony, but *for our sins, not for His own*. This **hand** pressed **down** upon Jesus, and in a greater way than David ever knew.

> i. "The holy Jesus, at the time of his passion, received these arrows, and sustained this weight, for the sins of the whole world." (Horne)

> ii. Understanding the agony helps us to understand something of the greatness of the love that sent Him to the cross – *for us*.

2. (3-5) Overwhelmed by iniquity.

There is no soundness in my flesh
Because of Your anger,
Nor *any* health in my bones
Because of my sin.
For my iniquities have gone over my head;
Like a heavy burden they are too heavy for me.
My wounds are foul *and* festering
Because of my foolishness.

a. **There is no soundness in my flesh because of Your anger**: David not only sensed God's displeasure spiritually, but also physically. This may have been because the chastening hand of God was evident in some kind of illness or injury, or it may have been because of the physical toll of stress in a season of deep spiritual depression.

> i. "That David describes a *natural disease* here cannot reasonably be doubted; but what that disease was, who shall attempt to say? However, this is evident, that whatever it was, he most deeply deplored the cause of it; and as he worthily lamented it, so he found mercy at the hand of God." (Clarke)

b. **Nor any health in my bones because of my sin**: David recognized the hand of God in his misery, but he did not think it was without cause. He knew that it was **because of** his **sin**, his **iniquities**, and his **foolishness**. David was miserable, but not a victim in the commonly understood sense – because his sins were the cause of the crisis.

i. "'*Thine anger...my sin.*' I, alas! am as an anvil under two hammers; one of thine anger, another of my sin; both of them beating incessantly upon me." (Baker, cited in Spurgeon)

ii. **Because of my sin**: "For although David confesses that he is being judged for his sin – God has made this clear to him – he is nevertheless glorifying God in the way he deals with it. Primarily, he is not faulting God." (Boice)

c. **Like a heavy burden they are too heavy for me**: David felt oppressed under the weight of his sins. He hoped that an honest and heartfelt telling of his misery would move God's compassion.

i. **My wounds are foul and festering**: "Sin is the wound of the soul, which must be washed with the tears of repentance, cleansed by the blood of Christ, and healed by the Spirit of the Holy One." (Horne)

ii. "Am I addressing any, who think they are not saved because they have not known such terrors as some others have experienced? Let me remind you, dear friends, that there are many of the true children of God who have never known these horrors…. *These horrors and terrors are not essential to salvation, or else they would have been commanded.*" (Spurgeon)

3. (6-8) David's trouble and turmoil.

I am troubled, I am bowed down greatly;
I go mourning all the day long.
For my loins are full of inflammation,
And *there is* no soundness in my flesh.
I am feeble and severely broken;
I groan because of the turmoil of my heart.

a. **I am troubled, I am bowed down greatly**: The pain of David's sin affected him in almost every way. He described a severe depression and melancholy as well as specific bodily afflictions (**full of inflammation…no soundness in my fles**). He was weak and **severely broken**.

i. "No fastidiousness keeps the psalmist from describing offensive details." (Maclaren)

ii. **Loins are full of inflammation**: Barnes suggested that this might refer to a problem with the kidneys, such as painful kidney stones. "The word here used, according to Gesenius, properly denotes the internal muscles of the loins near the kidneys." (Barnes, cited in Spurgeon)

iii. **Bowed down greatly**: "As the body by pain, so the soul by guilt, is 'distorted' from its original uprightness; it is 'bowed down' to the earth, through shame and fear." (Horne)

b. **I groan because of the turmoil of my heart**: David was known as the sweet psalmist of Israel (2 Samuel 23:1). Yet with great honesty, he could also **groan** before God and man, composing a bitter psalm describing his misery in the strongest of terms.

i. **I groan**: The King James Version may follow the Hebrew more accurately by translating, *I have roared.* "When our prayers appear to be rather animal than spiritual, they are none the less prevalent with the…Father of mercy." (Spurgeon)

5. (9-10) Hiding nothing in his misery.

Lord, all my desire *is* before You;
And my sighing is not hidden from You.
My heart pants, my strength fails me;
As for the light of my eyes, it also has gone from me.

a. **Lord, all my desire is before You**: Speaking to God as his master (**Lord**, *Adonai*), David appealed to God with complete transparency. His misery was not **hidden from** God or from any who would hear this psalm.

i. Our instinct is to follow the pattern of Adam and Eve and hide our sin and hide from God. David here is an example of the kind of unconcealed communication that is important for the one who truly desires God.

ii. **All my desire**: "Intense groaning desires towards God are in themselves works of grace." (Spurgeon)

b. **As for the light of my eyes, it also has gone from me**: David felt so low that life and **light** were leaving him.

i. **My heart pants**: "The heart's action is described by a rare word, which in its root means to go round and round, and is here in an intensive form expressive of violent motion." (Maclaren)

6. (11-14) Forsaken by friends, hunted by enemies.

My loved ones and my friends stand aloof from my plague,
And my relatives stand afar off.
Those also who seek my life lay snares *for me;*
Those who seek my hurt speak of destruction,
And plan deception all the day long.
But I, like a deaf *man,* do not hear;
And *I am* like a mute *who* does not open his mouth.

Thus I am like a man who does not hear,
And in whose mouth *is* no response.

a. **My loved ones and my friends stand aloof from my plague**: David's misery was unrelieved by either **friends** or **relatives**. His **loved ones** either did not care or could not help David.

i. "Relief may come in the form of the little pleasures of life and in the moments of shared experiences with friends, but the psalmist had none of these." (VanGemeren)

ii. "The word *plague* is perhaps chosen for its associations with leprosy (*e.g.*, four times in Leviticus 13:3, Hebrew), for this is how his friends were treating David." (Kidner)

b. **Those also who seek my life lay snares for me**: David endured worse than the lack of support from friends and relatives. He also faced determined enemies who constantly plotted his **destruction**.

c. **I am like a man who does not hear**: David was so depressed and afflicted that he felt powerless to respond to these attacks. His inability to defend himself meant that he needed God more than ever.

i. **In whose mouth is no response**: "Like David, when he let Shimei shriek his curses at him from the hillside and answered not, the psalmist is deaf and dumb to malicious tongues. He will speak to God, but to man he is silent, in utter submission of will." (Maclaren)

ii. "David was bravely silent, and herein was eminently typical of our Lord Jesus, whose marvellous silence before Pilate was far more eloquent than words." (Spurgeon)

B. The glimmer of hope in the LORD.

1. (15-16) Hope in the God who will hear.

For in You, O LORD, I hope;
You will hear, O Lord my God.
For I said, *"Hear me,* lest they rejoice over me,
Lest, when my foot slips, they exalt *themselves* against me."

a. **For in You, O LORD, I hope**: Despite his spiritual depression, David clung to **hope** in the LORD. Though he did not feel it, in faith he said, **You will hear**. David chose to allow his affliction to press him towards God instead of away from the God who was his only hope.

b. **LORD...Lord...God**: Psalm 38:15 is an example of the use of the three Hebrew words most commonly used to refer to God in one verse.

• **LORD**, translated *Yahweh*, referring to the covenant God of Israel.

- **Lord**, translated *Adonai*, referring to God as Master or person of respect.

- **God**, translated *Elohim*, the plural of the word for God in the generic sense.

c. **Hear me, lest they rejoice over me**: David appealed to God not only because he was miserable, but also because he did not want his adversaries to rejoice over him.

2. (17-20) Ready to fall before strong enemies.

For I *am* ready to fall,
And my sorrow *is* continually before me.
For I will declare my iniquity;
I will be in anguish over my sin.
But my enemies *are* vigorous, *and* they are strong;
And those who hate me wrongfully have multiplied.
Those also who render evil for good,
They are my adversaries, because I follow *what is* good.

a. **For I will declare my iniquity**: David again thought about his own sin that was the cause of his misery. In many other psalms David declared his innocence, especially in comparison to his enemies – but not in this psalm. This psalm came out of David's **anguish over** his **sin**.

i. "To be sorry for sin is no atonement for it, but it is the right spirit in which to [turn] to Jesus, who is the reconciliation and the Saviour." (Spurgeon)

b. **My enemies are vigorous, and they are strong**: David appealed to God for help in light of the energy and strength of his enemies, and because they were against him for no good reason (**I follow what is good**).

i. **They are my adversaries**: The Hebrew word translated **adversaries** is the root for the title *Satan*. "They Satanically hate me, as if they were transformed into so many breathing devils." (Trapp)

3. (21-22) The urgent plea unto God.

Do not forsake me, O LORD;
O my God, be not far from me!
Make haste to help me,
O Lord, my salvation!

a. **Do not forsake me, O LORD**: The psalm closes without eloquence, only with a heartfelt cry. More than anything, David wanted the sense of God's presence (**be not far from me**). It is likely that the absence of that sense was David's greatest trial in this dark season.

i. "Whoever carefully reads over this psalm will see what a grievous and bitter thing it is to sin against the Lord, and especially to sin after having known his mercy, and after having escaped from the corruption that is in the world. Reader, be on thy guard; a life of righteousness may be lost by giving way to a moment's temptation, and a fair character sullied for ever!" (Clarke)

b. **Make haste to help me, O Lord, my salvation**: David pressed his need before God with urgency and looked to the LORD as his only **salvation**. The psalm ends without a change in circumstances but with continued faith in God.

i. In these last two verses, David again used the three most common Hebrew references to Deity. "The God he knew by name (Yahweh, 21a) and by covenant (*my God*), and as Master and Saviour (22b)." (Kidner)

Psalm 39 – Wisdom to Speak Under God's Correction

This psalm is titled **To the Chief Musician. To Jeduthun. A Psalm of David.**

The Chief Musician *is thought by some to be the Lord* G OD *Himself, and others suppose him to be a leader of choirs or musicians in David's time, such as Heman the singer or Asaph (1 Chronicles 6:33, 16:5-7, and 25:6).*

Jeduthun *(mentioned also in the titles of Psalm 62 and 77) was one of the musicians appointed by David to lead Israel's public worship (1 Chronicles 16:41; 25:1-3).*

This is a **Psalm of David***, though it cannot be connected to any specific point in his life. It is possible that it was from his last few years of life.*

A. David finds the words to pray a prayer of wisdom.

1. (1-3) David's silent agony.

I said, "I will guard my ways,
Lest I sin with my tongue;
I will restrain my mouth with a muzzle,
While the wicked are before me."
I was mute with silence,
I held my peace *even* from good;
And my sorrow was stirred up.
My heart was hot within me;
While I was musing, the fire burned.
Then I spoke with my tongue:

a. **I will guard my ways, lest I sin with my tongue**: David began this psalm by recounting his prayer – asking God's help in not speaking foolishly or sinfully when **the wicked are before me**.

i. "David's feelings were running high enough to be taken for disloyalty if he had vented them in the wrong company." (Kidner)

314

ii. "He knew how his words would be misunderstood and misused by such persons. To them his words would seem to be a criticism of God and his ways." (Boice)

iii. "The firmest believers are exercised with unbelief, and it would be doing the devil's work with a vengeance if they were to publish abroad all their questionings and suspicions." (Spurgeon)

b. **I was mute with silence, I held my peace even from good**: David found it easier to speak *nothing* than to speak *wisely*. He soon felt the pressure that one feels when intense feelings are kept silent.

i. In the previous psalm David showed his godliness by his silence before his accusers (*I am like a mute who does not open his mouth*, Psalm 38:13). In Psalm 38 the idea was that David did well to not defend himself. Here he did well to not speak his doubts and fears **while the wicked are before me**.

ii. "Perhaps he feared that if he began to talk at all, he would be sure to speak amiss, and, therefore, he totally abstained. It was an easy, safe, and effectual way of avoiding sin, if it did not involve a neglect of the duty which he owed to God to speak well of his name." (Spurgeon)

c. **My heart was hot within me**: In this instance silence was not golden for David. It brought him sorrow and inner turmoil (**the fire burned**).

i. "The metaphors 'my heart grew hot' and 'the fire burned' express anger (cf. Deuteronomy 19:6; Jeremiah 51:39; Ezekiel 36:5). The more he reflected on his situation, the more he became exasperated." (VanGemeren)

2. (4-6) David's wise words.

"LORD, make me to know my end,
And what *is* the measure of my days,
That I may know how frail I *am.*
Indeed, You have made my days *as* handbreadths,
And my age *is* as nothing before You;
Certainly every man at his best state *is* but vapor." Selah

"Surely every man walks about like a shadow;
Surely they busy themselves in vain;
He heaps up *riches*,
And does not know who will gather them."

a. **LORD, make me to know my end**: David's silence was broken in the best way – by humble prayer to God. He would not speak his fears and doubts before the wicked, but he would pour them out before His God.

Here David asked God for wisdom – specifically, the wisdom to know the shortness and the frailty of his life (**that I may know how frail I am**).

i. We might have expected David to break his silence by telling off his enemies or by defending his own righteousness. He did neither; he sought God for wisdom. "It is well that the vent of his soul was Godward and not towards man. Oh! if my swelling heart must speak, Lord let it speak with thee." (Spurgeon)

ii. **Make me to know my end**: "This was not a prayer inspired by a desire to know when life would end; it was not a request to be told the date of death. It was a prayer for an accurate apprehension of the fact that life quantitatively – that is, as to the number of its days – is as nothing." (Morgan)

iii. **You have made my days as handbreadths**: "He compares it to a 'handbreadth,' one of the smallest units of measurement in ancient Israel. It is equivalent to 'a couple of inches.'" (VanGemeren)

iv. "Life is very short, but *a great deal may be done.* Our Lord Jesus Christ, in three years, saved the world. Some of his followers in three years have been the means of saving many and many a soul." (Spurgeon)

b. **Certainly every man at his best state is but a vapor**: David was a champion, an accomplished Special Forces warrior, a leader, a celebrity, a skilled poet, a musical genius, a survivor, and a king. If anyone might have thought more highly of himself, David had the right to. Yet he understood that he, like **every man** is – **at his best state** – merely **a vapor**, a puff of steam or smoke.

i. "He learns that, since life is short, the only real meaning of a man or woman's existence must be in his relationship to God, for God is eternal." (Boice)

c. **Selah**: The idea in the Hebrew for this word (occurring 74 times in the Old Testament) is for a *pause*. Most people think it speaks of a reflective pause, a pause to meditate on the words just spoken. It may also be a musical instruction, for a musical interlude of some kind.

i. This **Selah** is an appropriate call for each one to *pause* and think of the shortness and frailty of his life. It should drive us to great dependence upon God and great earnestness about life and doing good in the short time we do have.

d. **Surely they busy themselves in vain**: Sounding very much like the later Book of Ecclesiastes, David thought about the mass of humanity who lived ignoring the shortness and frailty of life.

- Each of them **walks about**, but like a **shadow**, living a life with no substance.

- They are **busy**, but in **vain**, being blind to eternal things.

- Each of them works hard and **heaps up riches**, yet does not think beyond his own short and frail life.

   i. *This* is the land of shadows. Heaven is the land of reality, of true high definition.

   ii. "Every man that *exists*, is vanity. All his projects, plans, schemes, etc., soon come to nothing. His body also moulders with the dust, and shortly passes both from the *sight* and *remembrance* of men." (Clarke)

B. The cause revealed, the cure requested.

1. (7-11) Trusting God in a season of correction for sin.

"And now, Lord, what do I wait for?
My hope *is* in You.
Deliver me from all my transgressions;
Do not make me the reproach of the foolish.
I was mute, I did not open my mouth,
Because it was You who did *it*.
Remove Your plague from me;
I am consumed by the blow of Your hand.
When with rebukes You correct man for iniquity,
You make his beauty melt away like a moth;
Surely every man *is* vapor." Selah

a. **And now, Lord, what do I wait for? My hope is in You**: Perceiving the shortness and frailty of life made David put his expectation and hope upon God and not upon himself. In right standing and friendship with the Living God, David could understand and prepare for life beyond this life.

   i. "Here the psalmist steps off the sand, and puts his foot on the rock. Happy is the man who can say to the Lord, 'My hope is in thee.'" (Spurgeon)

   ii. **My hope is in You**: "That is life, in which desire and expectation are centered in God. Such life is of an entirely different quality from that in which desire and expectation are centered in self, in circumstances, or in men." (Morgan)

b. **Deliver me from all my transgressions**: David looked to God and not to himself for deliverance from sin. He knew – as the Apostle Paul would later declare – that the focus should be on God and not self (Romans 7:24-8:4).

i. **Deliver me from all my transgressions:** "That I may not be disappointed of my hopes of enjoying thee and thy favour, which is the only thing that I desire, pardon all my sins, which stand like a thick cloud between thee and me, and fill me with fears about my condition both here and hereafter." (Poole)

c. **Remove Your plague from me; I am consumed by the blow of Your hand:** We learn that David prayed this prayer from a season of great weakness and the sense that he was under the painful correction of God. He successfully avoided speaking words of self-justification; as he poured out his heart to God, he also prayed for relief from his affliction.

i. "It is bold for a sufferer to say to God, 'Hold! enough!' but all depends on the tone in which it is said. It may be presumption, or it may be a child's free speech, not in the least trenching on a Father's authority." (Maclaren)

ii. **Because it was You who did it:** "He does not understand everything; but at least he knows that a personal God, instead of an impersonal force, is in charge over his life." (VanGemeren)

d. **When with rebukes You correct man for iniquity, You make his beauty melt away like a moth:** We learn that David's great sense of the shortness and frailty of life came under a deep and painful sense of the correction of God. We can suppose that this was one of the reasons God sent His correction to David: to give him the hunger for, the prayer for, and the blessing of this wisdom.

i. "The metaphor of a moth suggests the brevity of man's life or the destructive power of a moth." (VanGemeren)

2. (12-13) A humble prayer for restored favor and regained strength.

"Hear my prayer, O LORD,
And give ear to my cry;
Do not be silent at my tears;
For I *am* a stranger with You,
A sojourner, as all my fathers *were*.
Remove Your gaze from me, that I may regain strength,
Before I go away and am no more."

a. **Do not be silent at my tears; for I am a stranger with You:** David appealed to Yahweh, the covenant God of Israel, asking that He answer with mercy upon him in his sense of separation from God.

i. **My tears:** "His prayer swells into crying, and that again melts into tears, which go straight to the great Father's heart. Weeping eyes are never turned to heaven in vain; the gates of mercy open wide when the hot drops touch them." (Maclaren)

b. **I am a stranger with You, a sojourner, as all my fathers were**: David was not only a native Israeli, but *the king of Israel*. If anyone had a claim to citizenship it was he; yet he understood that his real home was in heaven and not upon this earth.

i. Significantly, David did not say that he was a *stranger from God*, but a **stranger with** God. He was a **stranger**, but not alone. They were strangers together in a hostile world. "Here is a man still undergoing trial and acutely conscious of it, but he has found the secret place of communion and this conditions his attitudes." (Morgan)

ii. "Abraham first described himself as a stranger and a sojourner.... All his children, those who inherit a like faith, must say the same. Faith cannot find a home on this side of the stars. It has caught a glimpse of the Infinite, and it can never be content with anything else." (Meyer)

iii. "If an Englishman goes to the Continent, and tries to pass himself off as a German or a Frenchman he is soon detected; and, in a similar fashion, a true Christian reveals the, fact that he is an alien in this world, his ways and manners and customs are not those of the men of the world, who have their portion in this life." (Spurgeon)

iv. If we are indeed strangers and sojourners, then it follows that:

- It is sure we have a home somewhere.
- It is not surprising that we sometimes long to get home.
- If we are strangers, then we should treat each other well.
- It sould be a comfort to the Christian in death.

c. **Remove Your gaze from me, that I may regain strength**: Knowing that his weakness was due to the heavy hand of God upon him, David humbly asked God to look at him no longer with the eyes of correction. The psalm ends without resolution, but David appeals to and shows trust in the LORD.

i. "Yet for the moment, like Job or Jeremiah, he can see no more than death, and ask no more than respite.... The very presence of such prayers in Scripture is a witness to His understanding. He knows how men speak when they are desperate." (Kidner)

ii. **Before I go away and am no more**: "Hebrew *before I go*, to wit, unto the grave, as this phrase is used, Genesis 15:2, 25:32; or *the way* *of all the earth*, as the phrase is completed, Joshua 23:14; or *whence I shall not return*, as it is Job 10:21." (Poole)

iii. "This Psalm is, with the utmost propriety, appointed by the church to be used at the burial of the dead, as a funeral is indeed the best comment upon it." (Horne)

Psalm 40 – The Servant Comes to Do God's Will

This psalm is simply titled **To the Chief Musician. A Psalm of David.**

To the Chief Musician: *"Well might so exceedingly precious a Psalm be specially committed to the most skilled of the sacred musicians." (Charles Spurgeon)*

A Psalm of David: *G. Campbell Morgan speculated, "In this case the reason for the song in all probability was that of the deliverance of David from all the long experience of outlawry and suffering; and the fact that he had been brought to his coronation."*

A. Proclaiming a joyful deliverance.

1. (1-3) The blessed results of patient waiting for the LORD.

> **I waited patiently for the LORD;**
> **And He inclined to me,**
> **And heard my cry.**
> **He also brought me up out of a horrible pit,**
> **Out of the miry clay,**
> **And set my feet upon a rock,**
> ***And* established my steps.**
> **He has put a new song in my mouth—**
> **Praise to our God;**
> **Many will see *it* and fear,**
> **And will trust in the LORD.**

a. **I waited patiently for the LORD; and He inclined to me**: The idea of David waiting on or for the LORD has been common, especially in the last few psalms (Psalm 25:5, 25:21, 27:14, 37:7, 37:9). In the previous psalm (39:7) David waited upon the LORD without immediate answer. Here, the answer is stated: **He inclined to me, and heard my cry.**

i. "*I waited patiently*, Heb. *in waiting I waited*; which doubling of the word notes that he waited diligently and earnestly, patiently and perseveringly, until God should please to help him." (Poole)

ii. "The theme of waiting, expounded in Psalm 37, has had its painful application in Psalms 38 and 39, but now its triumphant outcome." (Kidner)

iii. "Think ye, brethren, might it not read – 'I waited impatiently for the Lord,' in the case of most of us?" (Spurgeon)

b. **He inclined to me, and heard my cry**: The word **inclined** has the sense of God bending down to David in his affliction, removing any perceived distance between the LORD and His servant. When David knew God **heard** his cry, he was confident of a favorable answer.

i. "The patient waiting resulted in the singer's feeling that Jehovah was bending over him and listening to his cry." (Morgan)

ii. "As when someone's attention is arrested and riveted." (Kidner)

c. **He also brought me up out of a horrible pit...and set my feet upon a rock**: These were further benefits to David as he **waited patiently for the LORD**. God delivered him from his present crisis (which was like **miry clay**), and set him in a much better and more secure place (**established my steps**). David's prayer for deliverance was answered.

d. **He has put a new song in my mouth – praise to our God**: This is another benefit to David in waiting on the Lord. His deliverance brought forth spontaneous praise, a **new song** that came from God Himself.

i. God will inspire songs and words of praise. This almost sounds selfish or self-serving, but when we understand how good and right it is for the creature to praise the Creator, the redeemed to praise the Redeemer, the delivered to praise the Deliverer, then it makes sense. We are grateful that God gives us the ability to praise Him.

ii. It is possible that this psalm was the **new song** God put into David's mouth. "The suffering servant of God always becomes the singing one. For as the secret of song is ever that of waiting for God, doing the will of God, in and through suffering, the result is always deliverance, and the issue a song." (Morgan)

e. **Many will see it and fear, and will trust in the LORD**: This is one more benefit from David's patient waiting for the LORD. The deliverance and the praise that came from it were an effective testimony to others. They were inspired to **fear** the LORD and to **trust** in Him.

i. **Trust in the LORD**: "Trusting in the Lord is the evidence nay the essence of salvation. He who is a true believer is evidently redeemed from the dominion of sin and Satan." (Spurgeon)

2. (4-5) Trusting the God who thinks about His people.

Blessed *is* that man who makes the LORD his trust,
And does not respect the proud, nor such as turn aside to lies.
Many, O LORD my God, *are* Your wonderful works
***Which* You have done;**
And Your thoughts toward us
Cannot be recounted to You in order;
***If* I would declare and speak *of them*,**
They are more than can be numbered.

a. **Blessed is that man who makes the LORD his trust**: This is a natural and appropriate thought flowing from what David had just experienced. He knew by experience that **trust** – as shown by waiting patiently for the LORD – is **blessed**.

i. "A man may be as poor as Lazarus, as hated as Mordecai, as sick as Hezekiah, as lonely as Elijah, but while his hand of faith can keep its hold on God, none of his outward afflictions can prevent his being numbered among the blessed, but the wealthiest and most prosperous man who has no faith is accursed, be he who he may." (Spurgeon)

b. **And does not respect the proud, nor such as turn aside to lies**: David connected trusting God with moral conduct – in this case, the ability to discern and judge the character of others and act appropriately toward them. Perhaps David's crisis came from refusing to **respect the proud** or those who **turn aside to lies**.

i. **Does not respect the proud**: "For the *proud* he uses the term that became the nickname for Egypt, the empty blusterer, Isaiah 30:7." (Kidner)

c. **Many, O LORD my God, are Your wonderful works...and Your thoughts toward us cannot be recounted**: David praised God as the worker of many wonderful works *and* for His **thoughts** toward His people. David knew that God thought about him (and His people), and thought about them favorably – otherwise there would be no blessing in those thoughts.

i. "Creation, providence, and redemption, teem with wonders as the sea with life." (Spurgeon)

ii. "The past is full of His miracles (*wondrous deeds*), the future full of his plans – this is the force of the word *thoughts*." (Kidner)

iii. In Psalm 8:4 David wondered, *What is man that You are mindful of him?* He considered the greatness of the universe and was amazed that God would think about man at all. Here he took that idea much further and is amazed at *how much* God thinks about His people. By implication he is also amazed that God thinks such loving, gracious thoughts toward His people, and so many that **they are more than can be numbered**.

iv. God's **thoughts toward us** are wonderful because they are *God's* thoughts. "When *I* think, it is a poor, little, weak, empty head that is thinking; but when God thinks, the gigantic mind which framed the universe is thinking upon me." (Spurgeon)

v. God's **thoughts toward us** are wonderful because they are *so many*; they **cannot be recounted**. "You cannot count God's thoughts of you.... One gracious thought is followed by another, swiftly as the beams of light flash from the sun, so that it is impossible for us to number them." (Spurgeon)

B. The willing servant proclaims God's praise.

"Here we enter upon one of the most wonderful passages in the whole of the Old Testament, a passage in which the incarnate Son of God is seen not through a glass darkly, but as it were face to face." (Spurgeon)

1. (6-8) The coming of the Bond Servant.

Sacrifice and offering You did not desire;
My ears You have opened.
Burnt offering and sin offering You did not require.
Then I said, "Behold, I come;
In the scroll of the book *it is* **written of me.**
I delight to do Your will, O my God,
And Your law *is* **within my heart."**

a. **Sacrifice and offering You did not desire; My ears You have opened**: David understood that in a relative sense, God didn't want animal sacrifices. God wanted surrendered, willing servants.

i. In Psalm 40:6 four kinds of offering are mentioned:

- **Sacrifice** (offerings made with blood).
- **Offering** (offerings made without blood).
- **Burnt offering** (offerings of total consecration).
- **Sin offering** (offerings to atone for sin).

ii. What did God **desire** instead of sacrifice? *Obedience.* This was true for David's predecessor Saul. King Saul offered sacrifices just fine; what he didn't do was obey God (1 Samuel 15:22-23). Ultimately this was fulfilled by the Son of David. Jesus came and was perfectly obedient, and His obedience is credited unto us.

b. **My ears You have opened**: Instead of animal sacrifices, God wants servants who will *listen* to Him and surrender to Him as a willing slave surrenders to his master.

i. David likely referred to the custom of marking a bond-servant according to Exodus 21:5-6, where a slave who *wanted* to remain in his master's house and in his master's service would be marked with an **opened** ear – that is, *his master shall pierce his ear with an awl; and he shall serve him forever* (Exodus 21:6).

ii. It's a remarkable thing to think of this ceremony being carried out in ancient Israel. A servant said, "I know I have fulfilled my *obligations* to my master, and I have served what I have owed. Yet I love my master and am so grateful for what he has given that I will gladly obligate myself for life, not out of debt or shame or defeat, but out of love." *This was David's heart towards God*, and this heart and life were greater than any animal sacrifice.

iii. The ceremony in Exodus 21:5-6 described only *one* ear being pierced through or opened. The text of Psalm 40 describes *two* **ears You have opened**. Some regard this as evidence that the psalmist had something else in mind other than the bond-slave ceremony, such as simply opening the ear to hear and obey. It is better to regard it as David's expression of total surrender – beyond what the law itself demanded, as if he said "Lord, take *both* my **ears!**"

iv. Horne gives an explanation apart from the Exodus 21:5-6 ceremony: "For the expression, 'Mine ears hast thou opened,' seems equivalent to, 'Thou hast made me obedient.' Thus, Isaiah 50:5, 'The Lord God hath opened mine ears, and I was not rebellious, neither turned away back.'" (Horne)

c. **Sacrifice and offering You did not desire; My ears You have opened**: David's surrender to God was wonderful and an impressive example. Yet he only foreshadowed the ultimate submission to God carried out by the Messiah, Jesus Christ. Hebrews 10:5-10 quotes the Septuagint (ancient Greek) translation of Psalm 40:6-8. This is a wonderful and remarkable prophecy of the work of Jesus.

- It shows God's ultimate dissatisfaction in animal sacrifices, looking forward to a Perfect Sacrifice (**Sacrifice and offering You did not desire**).

- It shows that God the Son came in a prepared body (the Septuagint reads, *But a body You have prepared for Me*, Hebrews 10:5).

- It shows the public, open coming of the Messiah. It was as if Jesus said, "**Behold**, here I am – I am the One." (**Behold, I come**).

- It shows the Messiah as the great theme of the Hebrew Scriptures (**In the scroll of the book it is written of Me**).

- It shows the dedication of the Messiah to the will of God (**I delight to do Your will**).

- It shows the Messiah's love for and obedience to the word of God (**Your law is within My heart**).

   i. **Sacrifice and offering You did not desire**: "It is remarkable, that all the offerings and sacrifices which were considered to be of an atoning or cleansing nature, offered under the law, are here enumerated by the psalmist and the apostle, to show that *none* of them, nor *all* of them, could take away sin; and that the grand sacrifice of Christ was that alone which could do it." (Clarke)

   ii. "The Septuagint, from which Paul quoted, has translated this passage, 'A body hast thou prepared me:' how this reading arose it is not easy to imagine, but since apostolical authority has sanctioned the variation, we accept it as no mistake, but as an instance of various readings equally inspired." (Spurgeon)

d. **In the scroll of the book it is written of me**: In a far lesser sense David could say this of himself, because his ascension to the throne of Israel was prophesied long before it took place. Yet any fulfillment of this in David is a pale shadow to its amazing and perfect fulfillment in David's greater Son, Jesus the Messiah.

e. **I delight to do Your will, O my God**: Again, in a far lesser sense this was true of David, the man after God's heart. Yet any fulfillment of this in David is a pale shadow of its amazing and perfect fulfillment in David's greater Son, Jesus the Messiah. Jesus said that doing God's will was to Him as necessary and delightful as food (John 4:34).

   i. **I delight to do Your will**: "Jesus not only did the Father's will, but found a delight therein; from old eternity he had desired the work set before him; in his human life he was straitened till he reached the baptism of agony in which he magnified the law, and even in

Gethsemane itself he chose the Father's will, and set aside his own."
(Spurgeon)

ii. **To do**: "It was Jesus who was the doer of the work. The Father
willed it; but he did not do it. It was Jesus who did it, who wrought
it out; who brought it in; who carried it within the veil, and laid it as
an acceptable and meritorious offering at the feet of his well-pleased
Father. The work then is done; it is finished. We need not attempt
to do it. We cannot do it. We cannot do that which is already done;
and we could not do it, though it were yet undone." (Frame, cited in
Spurgeon)

iii. **Your law is within my heart**: Open "up most men's hearts, and
there you shall find written, The god of this present world. But God's
law is in good men's hearts, to live and die with it." (Trapp)

2. (9-12) Public proclamation of the good news and God's praise.

I have proclaimed the good news of righteousness
In the great assembly;
Indeed, I do not restrain my lips,
O LORD, You Yourself know.
I have not hidden Your righteousness within my heart;
I have declared Your faithfulness and Your salvation;
I have not concealed Your lovingkindness and Your truth
From the great assembly.
Do not withhold Your tender mercies from me, O LORD;
Let Your lovingkindness and Your truth continually preserve me.
For innumerable evils have surrounded me;
My iniquities have overtaken me, so that I am not able to look up;
They are more than the hairs of my head;
Therefore my heart fails me.

a. **I have proclaimed the good news of righteousness in the great
assembly**: David said this to assure God (and himself) that he had glorified
God among His people. This was part of the new song and praise that
came from his deliverance. David would **not restrain** his **lips** in offering
this praise.

i. Yet, as in the previous verses, this has a far greater and perfect
fulfillment in Jesus, the Son of David. It was true of Jesus in His
earthly ministry. "This is what Jesus can say. He was the Prince of
open-air preachers, the Great Itinerant, the President of the College of
all preachers of the gospel." (Spurgeon)

ii. It is also true of Jesus in eternity come. Of Jesus it is true, *in the midst of the assembly I will sing praise to You* (Hebrews 2:12 as a fulfillment of Psalm 22:22). It's a remarkable thing to think of Jesus leading the assembly of God's people in praise to God the Father!

b. **I have not hidden Your righteousness within my heart**: The righteousness of God was evident in both David's words and actions. It wasn't set in a secret place that had no connection with how he actually lived his life.

i. **I have not hidden**: "This intimates, that whoever undertook to preach the gospel of Christ would be in great temptation to hide it, and conceal it, because it must be preached with great contention, and in the face of great opposition." (Henry, cited in Spurgeon)

c. **Do not withhold Your tender mercies from me**: Though David praised God for past and present deliverance, he would not presume upon the future. He kept himself in humble prayer before God, asking for a constant supply of His **tender mercies**.

i. It is not difficult to see this as a prayer of Jesus, the Son of David. As He lived upon this earth, He did so as a man in constant reliance upon His fellowship and perfect communion with God the Father. We see this as a prayer of Jesus, perhaps especially in His sufferings on the cross: **Do not withhold Your tender mercies from Me, O LORD; let Your lovingkindness and Your truth continually preserve Me**.

ii. Truly it was on the cross that Jesus could say, **innumerable evils have surrounded Me**.

d. **My iniquities have overtaken me**: David needed this constant supply of the mercy, lovingkindness, and truth of God because he knew his own sins. He asked God to not leave him to his many sins (**more than the hairs of my head**), but to deliver him in mercy.

i. There is a sense in which Jesus could never say, "**My iniquities have overtaken Me**." He was and is the spotless Lamb of God, without any sin or defect. Yet in another sense those words are perfect in their description of Jesus, because in His life and especially His sufferings He consciously and perfectly identified with His people, taking on their sins as His own. For Jesus, they were **My iniquities** – but not because he committed the sins, but because out of love He chose to bear them and all the wrath they deserved.

ii. "If this be taken of Christ, he is Maximus peccatorum, the greatest of sinners by imputation, 2 Corinthians 5:21." (Trapp)

C. Proclaiming a heartfelt plea for help.

1. (13-15) The plea for deliverance.

Be pleased, O Lord, to deliver me;
O Lord, make haste to help me!
Let them be ashamed and brought to mutual confusion
Who seek to destroy my life;
Let them be driven backward and brought to dishonor
Who wish me evil.
Let them be confounded because of their shame,
Who say to me, "Aha, aha!"

a. **Be pleased, O Lord, to deliver me**: Despite his many iniquities, David could and did rely upon the Lord for deliverance. He skillfully phrased the request, not only asking God to deliver him, but asking God to take pleasure in his deliverance. He could ask boldly because he believed it to be consistent with God's pleasure.

i. We might take this principle and apply it to many of our requests.

* *Be pleased, O Lord, to forgive me.*
* *Be pleased, O Lord, to correct me.*
* *Be pleased, O Lord, to provide for me.*
* *Be pleased, O Lord, to heal me.*
* *Be pleased, O Lord, to guide me.*
* *Be pleased, O Lord, to bless me.*

ii. It should not surprise us that the psalm begins with triumphant praise and then desperately asks for help. "Are there any deliverances in this perilous and incomplete life so entire and permanent that they leave no room for future perils? Must not prevision of coming dangers accompany thankfulness for past escapes?" (Maclaren)

b. **O Lord, make haste to help me**: Though David made his request with skill, it was also made with urgency. David understood that help too long delayed was the same as help denied.

c. **Let them be ashamed and brought to mutual confusion who seek to destroy my life**: This was the help that David sought. God had graciously delivered him (Psalm 40:1-3), but the threat remained. David prayed that God would **dishonor** his enemies and cause them to be **confounded**.

i. As in many of his psalms, David is in trouble. Yet one would not know this from the first part of the psalm. Yes, David needed God's protection and help and would ask for it – but he could not forget or neglect the wonderful deliverance God had given up to that point, and make an appropriately surrendered response.

ii. "The psalmist prays for his enemies' fall and shame in accordance with the principles of justice and with the promise of God to curse those who cursed his own." (VanGemeren)

iii. **Who say to me, "Aha! Aha!"**: "O ungodly reader, if such a person glance over this page, beware of persecuting Christ and his people, for God will surely avenge his own elect. Your 'ahas' will cost you dear. It is hard for you to kick against the pricks." (Clarke)

2. (16-17) Praise with another plea.

Let all those who seek You rejoice and be glad in You;
Let such as love Your salvation say continually,
"The Lord be magnified!"
But I *am* poor and needy;
***Yet* the Lord thinks upon me.**
You *are* my help and my deliverer;
Do not delay, O my God.

a. **Let all those who seek You rejoice and be glad in You**: David called the people of God – at least those who **seek** Him – to be happy in Him, and to **say continually, "The Lord be magnified!"**

i. David thought praising God was to *magnify* Him – that is, to make Him larger in one's perception. Magnification does not actually make an object bigger, and we can't make God bigger. But to magnify something or someone is to *perceive* it as bigger, and we must do that regarding the Lord God.

ii. **Let such as love Your salvation say continually**: "One would think that self-love alone should make us love salvation. Ay, but they love it because it is his, 'that love *thy* salvation.' It is the character of a holy saint to love salvation itself; not as his own only, but as God's, as God's that saves him." (Goodwin, cited in Spurgeon)

b. **But I am poor and needy; yet the Lord thinks upon me**: David could combine his sense of great joy in God with a realistic appraisal of his present need. Secure in the truth that God cared for and thought about him, David again appealed to God to be his **help** and **deliverer**, and he needed God to do this without **delay**.

i. "He cries, 'I am poor and needy.' His joy is found in Another. He looks away from self, to the consolations which the eternal purpose has prepared for him." (Spurgeon)

ii. **Poor and needy**: "With such a Father and such a Friend, poverty becometh rich, and weakness itself is strong." (Horne)

iii. **Yet the LORD thinks upon me**: "He thought upon thee, and he thinks upon thee still. When the Father thinks of his children, he thinks of thee. When the great Judge of all thinks of the justified ones, he thinks of thee. O Christian, can you grasp the thought? The Eternal Father thinks of *you!*" (Spurgeon)

Psalms 1-40 – Bibliography

Adams, Reverend John *The Lenten Psalms* (New York: Charles Scribner's Sons, 1912)

Boice, James Montgomery *Psalms, Volume 1* (Grand Rapids, Michigan: Baker Books, 1994)

Chappell, Clovis G. *Sermons from the Psalms* (Nashville, Tennessee: Cokesbury Press, 1931)

Clarke, Adam *The Holy Bible, Containing the Old and New Testaments, with A Commentary and Critical Notes, Volume III – Job to Song of Solomon* (New York: Eaton and Mains, 1827?)

Harris, Arthur Emerson *The Psalms Outlined* (Philadelphia: The Judson Press, 1925)

Horne, George *Commentary on the Psalms* (Audubon, New Jersey: Old Paths Publications, 1997 of a 1771 edition)

Keller, Phillip *A Shepherd Looks at Psalm 23* (Grand Rapids, Michigan: Zondervan, 1970)

Kidner, Derek *Psalms 1-72, A Commentary* (Leicester, England: Inter-Varsity Press, 1973)

Maclaren, Alexander *The Psalms, Volume 1* (London: Hodder and Stoughton, 1892)

Meyer, F.B. *Our Daily Homily* (Westwood, New Jersey: Revell, 1966)

Morgan, G. Campbell *Searchlights from the Word* (New York: Revell, 1926)

Morgan, G. Campbell *An Exposition of the Whole Bible* (Old Tappan, New Jersey: Revell, 1959)

Poole, Matthew *A Commentary on the Holy Bible, Volume 2* (London: The Banner of Truth Trust, 1968)

Spurgeon, Charles Haddon *The Treasury of David, Volume 1* (Peabody, Massachusetts: Hendrickson)

Spurgeon, Charles Haddon *The New Park Street Pulpit, Volumes 1-6* and *The Metropolitan Tabernacle Pulpit, Volumes 7-63* (Pasadena, Texas: Pilgrim Publications, 1990)

Trapp, John *A Commentary on the Old and New Testaments, Volume 3 – Proverbs to Daniel* (Eureka, California: Tanski Publications, 1997)

VanGemeren, Willem A. "Psalms," *The Expositor's Bible Commentary, Volume 5: Psalms-Song of Songs* (Grand Rapids, Michigan: Zondervan, 1991)

As the years pass I love the work of studying, learning, and teaching the Bible more than ever. I'm so grateful that God is faithful to meet me in His Word.

I'm grateful for the help of Mary Osgood in proofreading and editorial suggestions. Mary, thanks for helping me write clearer and better!

Thanks to Brian Procedo for the cover design and the graphics work.

Most especially, thanks to my wife Inga-Lill. She is my loved and valued partner in life and in service to God and His people.

David Guzik

David Guzik's Bible commentary is regularly used and trusted by many thousands who want to know the Bible better. Pastors, teachers, class leaders, and everyday Christians find his commentary helpful for their own understanding and explanation of the Bible. David and his wife Inga-Lill live in Santa Barbara, California.

You can email David at
david@enduringword.com

For more resources by David Guzik,
go to www.enduringword.com

CPSIA information can be obtained
at www.ICGtesting.com
Printed in the USA
FFHW021126081019
55435851-61211FF